VULNERABILITY AND THE
ART OF PROTECTION

Carolina Academic Press
Ethnographic Studies in Medical Anthropology Series
Pamela J. Stewart *and* Andrew Strathern
Series Editors

Curing and Healing
Medical Anthropology in Global Perspective
Second Edition
Andrew Strathern and Pamela J. Stewart

Physicians at Work, Patients in Pain
Biomedical Practice and Patient Response in Mexico
Second Edition
Kaja Finkler

Healing the Modern in a Central Javanese City
Second Edition
Steve Ferzacca

Elusive Fragments
Making Power, Propriety and Health in Samoa
Douglass D. Drozdow-St. Christian

Endangered Species
Health, Illness, and Death Among Madagascar's People of the Forest
Janice Harper

The Practice of Concern
Ritual, Well-Being, and Aging in Rural Japan
John W. Traphagan

❧

Vulnerability and the Art of Protection

Embodiment and Health Care in Moroccan Households

Marybeth J. MacPhee
ASSOCIATE PROFESSOR
DEPARTMENT OF ANTHROPOLOGY+SOCIOLOGY
ROGER WILLIAMS UNIVERSITY

CAROLINA ACADEMIC PRESS
Durham, North Carolina

Library of Congress Cataloging-in-Publication Data

MacPhee, Marybeth Jeanette.
Vulnerability and the art of protection : embodiment and health care in Moroccan households / Marybeth J. MacPhee.
    p. cm. -- (Ethnographic studies in medical anthropology)
Includes bibliographical references and index.
ISBN 978-1-61163-160-9 (alk. paper)
1. Health--Social aspects--Morocco--Rachidia (Province) 2. Health--Social aspects--Sahara. 3. Health behavior--Morocco--Rachidia (Province) 4. Health behavior--Sahara. 5. Risk perception--Health aspects--Morocco--Rachidia (Province) 6. Risk perception--Health aspects--Sahara. 7. Women--Health and hygiene--Social aspects--Morocco--Rachidia (Province) 8. Women--Health and hygiene--Social aspects--Sahara. 9. Medical anthropology--Morocco--Rachidia (Province) 10. Medical anthropology--Sahara. I. Title. II. Series: Carolina Academic Press ethnographic studies in medical anthropology series.

RA418.3.M77M34 2012
362.10964--dc23   2012023667

CAROLINA ACADEMIC PRESS
700 Kent Street
Durham, North Carolina 27701
Telephone (919) 489-7486
Fax (919) 493-5668
www.cap-press.com

CONTENTS

FIGURES

WIVES, RESTLESS SPIRITS, AND PROTECTIVE DEVICES

Andrew Strathern & Pamela J. Stewart[*]

Most medical anthropology books begin with the phenomenon of illness and go on to discuss at length how it is treated, and how such treatment relates to ideas of the body and morality, politics, identity and the like. In this book Marybeth MacPhee takes a different tack. She concentrates on "the art of protection": how the people she studied in Morocco seek to protect themselves against illness conditions, seeing these as often caused by unruly spirits

* Prof. Pamela J. Stewart (Strathern) and Prof. Andrew Strathern are a husband and wife research team in the Department of Anthropology, University of Pittsburgh, and are the 2012 De Carle Distinguished Lecturers at the University of Otago, Dunedin, New Zealand. They are also Research Associates in the Research Institute of Irish and Scottish Studies, University of Aberdeen, Scotland, and have been Visiting Research Fellows at the Institute of Ethnology, Academia Sinica, Taipei, Taiwan, during parts of every year from 2002–2012. Their long-term, diverse, and creative research work has been published in over 45 books and over 200 influential articles on their research throughout the Pacific, Asia (mainly Taiwan), and Europe (primarily Scotland and Ireland, also on the European Union). Their most recent co-authored books include *Witchcraft, Sorcery, Rumors, and Gossip* (Cambridge University Press, 2004); and *Self and Group: Kinship in Action* (Prentice Hall, 2011). Their recent co-edited books include *Contesting Rituals: Islam and Practices of Identity-Making* (2005, Carolina Academic Press), *Exchange and Sacrifice* (Carolina Academic Press, 2008), *Religious and Ritual Change: Cosmologies and Histories* (Carolina Academic Press, 2009) and *Ritual* (London: Ashgate Publishing, 2010). They have broad interests which embrace and engage with global issues, utilizing their cross-cultural linguistic skills, a powerful comparative and interdisciplinary approach, and a uniquely engaged scholarly gaze. Their current research and writing is on the topics of Political Peace-making and the new arena that they are developing on Global Disaster Anthropology Studies. Their webpages are: (http://www.pitt.edu/~strather/sandspublicat.htm) (http://www.pitt.edu/~strather/) and (http://www.StewartStrathern.pitt.edu/).

(*jnun*) or the envious and malicious dispositions of neighbors. The focus of the study is on the agency of women, in their role as wives/housewives, who exert their efforts to protect themselves and their children. Men's agency appears in the background of the study, either designed to protect themselves or to ward off bad effects that threaten their wives and children. A hierarchy of spiritual forces is called upon. At the apex of the hierarchy is Allah himself, and Allah may be invoked as the ultimate protector or guardian in both minor and major circumstances of perceived danger.

Based on her ethnographic fieldwork and her personal experiences in the field, Dr. MacPhee identifies a major cultural theme around which she integrates her analysis. This is the theme of vulnerability, the continuous perception that people need to protect themselves against the possibility of misfortune through illness. Gender issues certainly enter in here, centered on sexual relations and reproduction, starting with engagements to marry, marriage itself, pregnancy, birth of children, and the health of young children exposed to the danger of diseases such as diarrhea. MacPhee devotes a whole chapter in this book to mothers' breastmilk, how it can become "bad" or insufficient, and what mothers do to optimize its virtues.

It emerges from the account that in sociological terms there is a great sense of distrust and edginess between women regarding child-bearing and marriage arrangements. Although MacPhee does not discuss this in great detail, the theme appears clearly. Perhaps there is an emphasis on reciprocity surrounding marriages via a pattern of marrying kin. Or perhaps there are tensions over polygyny in this Muslim society. In any case, people try to set up marriages for purposes of alliance. Yet divorce is apparently frequent, and men seem to be frequently away on work elsewhere. Married women are expected to be modest and not seek to be conspicuous in public; yet at marriage celebrations young women may openly display themselves in dancing for the wedding.

Neighbors are expected to be jealous. Compliments to a woman or her baby are considered dangerous as possible invocations of the "evil eye", which MacPhee refers to simply as "the Eye": like a transcendent force of ill-wishing, compounded out of individual dispositions. These observations fit well with the widespread Mediterranean theme of the evil eye, and on a much broader front with comparable data from New Guinea (explored in our book, Stewart and Strathern 2004). MacPhee explains that unbalanced humors in the body, envious neighbors, *jinn* spirits, sorcery, and microbes are all matters of potential fear and danger for people. The prevalence of humoral ideas of the body, correlated with careful attention given to the foods that new-born babies are fed, underlines the point that such foods (like herbs in other cultural contexts) function as kinds of medicines.

Cultural reasons for action are expressed often in striking images, such as the notion that excessive worrying leads to a pounding in the heart like spice pounded by a pestle in a mortar. Images of this sort correspond, in local usage, to the theoretical approach that MacPhee deploys in her study: cultural phenomenology. Steering a careful pathway between an emphasis on culture as collectively shared and implemented and a stress on culture as a framework within which individual make negotiations and compromises and balance complex issues and concerns, MacPhee decides that these two approaches can be seen a complementary. As we have noted, "culture" is abundantly evident in her data, but in a pluralistic form resulting from the historical admixture of diverse influences in the area.

The fact of pluralism also lends itself to the prevalence of choice-making and eclectic ways of dealing with contingencies in life patterns. The availability of biomedical options such as contraception or hospital birth simply adds to the plurality of choices women have. MacPhee's stress on the contextual constraints of decisions-making corresponds to what we in our work on conflict and peace-making have called "actionscapes". The frameworks of these actionscapes lend themselves to useful generalizations, of which the most notable in the study is the tension between closure and open-ness or interiority and exteriority. Protective devices safeguard interiority. They come into play particularly, as we might expect and MacPhee points out, at liminal moment of transition in the life cycle, pregnancy, birth, marriage—and surely, we might suggest, death, although this phase of the life cycle does not enter much into the account we are given. In some ways, a sense of liminality, and therefore vulnerability, pervades the whole life-cycle, because of the ever-present consciousness of the evil eye. People are cautious about letting neighbors know the good news of the birth of a son. Words of the Q'ran are written on slips of paper and dissolved into liquid for infants to drink. Women try to treat minor ailments with herbal remedies at home rather than taking children to hospital. Mothers try to conserve and maintain the quality of their breastmilk to feed their babies, and they are afraid that other women in the neighborhood may steal their milk. To prevent this happening, they have an interesting strategy: they try to behave well towards the women they suspect by offering them food, expecting that this positive act of generalized reciprocity will neutralize the specific negative reciprocity of the alleged theft: a neat extension of exteriority in order to protect interiority.

At several points we were reminded of emotive themes from an area of the world where we have done long-term fieldwork—that is, the Pacific. For example, pregnant women who develop cravings for a particular food should be listened to and satisfied, for otherwise the child they bear is said to develop a blemish like the food denied to its mother. This notion is like the notion in Mount Hagen, Papua New Guinea, that a woman who is *popokl*, resentful about some refusal to satisfy her needs, must have those needs attended to, because otherwise she will fall sick and pigs have to be sacrificed to make her well. The idea that breastmilk may be stolen by an envious neighboring woman is similar to the idea among the Wiru people of Pangia in Papua New Guinea that one woman may use magic to steal the sweet potato tubers from a garden strip of a rival within a polygynous household. While the Berber Moroccan women whose lives MacPhee portrays exert magic to protect their milk, in one Pangia village studied in the 1970s–1980s people secretly adopted a range of magical means to stop the envious ghosts of dead marital partners from coming back and claiming them to join them in the land of the dead (see Stewart and Strathern 2003): each culture to its own heart-pounding anxieties. Finally, MacPhee notes a practice whereby children at weddings were protected against the evil eye by dressing them in rags rather than fine clothes. In a village among the Duna people of Papua New Guinea in the 1990s we found that both adults and children intentionally wore poor, patched and torn clothing in order to avoid inciting the jealousy of local "witches" (see Stewart and Strathern 2004). The shared sociological context in all of these examples is the fear of competitive envy and the necessity to counteract this in one way or another.

In summary here, Dr. MacPhee's study contributes to the advancement of medical anthropology in a number ways. Ethnographically, her focus on women and their sense of vulnerability gives a convincing note to her discussions. Theoretically, her adoption of cultural phenomenology and with it the recognition of individual variability and choice among complex alternatives fits with the current recensions of theories of culture. And in comparative terms, parallels with other ethnographic contexts show that concrete circumstances of competition and jealousy, often exacerbated by rumor and gossip, lead to both suspicions of "witchcraft" and ritualized efforts to counteract it by protective devices.

Cromie Burn Research Unit
Department of Anthropology
University of Pittsburgh
2 May 2012
PJS and AJS

References

Stewart, Pamela J. and Andrew Strathern 2003. Dreaming and Ghosts among the Hagen and Duna of the Southern Highlands, Papua New Guinea. In, *Dream Travelers: Sleep Experiences and Culture in the Western Pacific*, Roger Ivar Lohmann (ed.), pp. 42–59. New York: Palgrave Macmillan.

Stewart, Pamela J. and Andrew J. Strathern 2004. *Witchcraft, Sorcery, Rumors, and Gossip*. No. 1 in the New Departures in Anthropology Series, Cambridge: Cambridge University Press.

ACKNOWLEDGMENTS

This book is the outcome of several years spent studying household health in Morocco and many people have contributed to my understanding of the topic. The foundations of this understanding formed during my field trips to Morocco. I am indebted to my research assistant, Mama, for her devotion to the project and for serving as my tutor, advisor, and confidant. Other members of our household also were instrumental in helping me to recruit participants, collect data, and interpret results. Their insights made this a far richer project than I could ever have accomplished on my own. Additionally, I thank the generous women of Errachidia and Zaouia who participated in the study. They introduced me to new perspectives on health and healing and catalyzed a transformation in my approach to anthropology.

The maturation of that transformation took place gradually with contributions from valued mentors. Foremost among these contributors was Mark Nichter. He recognized the theme of vulnerability in my data before I could articulate the essence of what I had learned in Morocco and he encouraged me to persevere in developing a phenomenological interpretation of vulnerability. I am also indebted to Robert Desjarlais. Our sporadic conversations over the years deepened my understanding of cultural phenomenology in the study of embodiment, vulnerability, and security. Lastly, Suzanne Heurtin-Roberts was instrumental in fostering my thinking about culture and health behavior.

Additionally, multiple colleagues and friends offered feedback, advice, and support during the process of creating this book. In particular, I am grateful to Jessica Skolnikoff and Christine Holmberg for reading drafts of the manuscript, and Liz Cartwright for reviewing the manuscript proposal. The support of Jeremy Campbell, Jason Patch, Joseph Roberts, Teal Rothschild, and Jim Tackach eased the final stages of the project while I was teaching full-time at Roger Williams University. Several other colleagues and mentors from the University of Arizona, MIT, Amherst College, and beyond offered ideas, critiques, and encouragement during the research and analysis phases of the project. This group of contributors includes: Anne Bennett, Anne Betteridge, Julia

Clancy-Smith, Laura Coughlin, Brian Edwards, Steve Ferzacca, Jane Hill, Oren Kosansky, Patrick McCray, Manju Mehta, Uday Mehta, Susan Miller, Mimi Nichter, Moore Quinn, Michelle Rein, Helen Robbins, Nancy Vuckovic, and Chris Walley. Special thanks goes to Elke Zuern for countless conversations about writing and for accompanying me on an emotionally charged return to Morocco after my divorce. Also, I am grateful to the series editors, Pamela Stewart and Andrew Strathern, and the editorial staff at Carolina Academic Press for helping me to transform the manuscript into a book. Finally, I want to thank my family for their unending support, patience, and assistance. More than anyone else, they made it possible for me to take the time I needed to make sense of the convoluted terrain of Saharan culture.

Several funding agencies provided grants to support the research described in the book. These include: the Foreign Language Area Studies fund (1994), the Fulbright Foundation (1996), the American Institute of Maghrebi Studies (1997), and Roger Williams University (2005). A portion of the data analysis was conducted while I was an Andrew Mellon Post-Doctoral Fellow at Amherst College (2000–2002). Research on integrative perspectives on health behavior was conducted partly during my post-doctoral fellowship in applied medical anthropology at National Cancer Institute (2002–2004). The Roger Williams University Foundation for Scholarship and Teaching supported the initial writing phase of the project through course release awards in 2006 and 2007.

SYSTEM OF TRANSLITERATION

This manuscript includes terms from the Colloquial Moroccan Arabic and Tamazight Berber languages. The system of transliteration that I use to represent these words for readers of English derives from two sources: *Historical Dictionary of Morocco* (Park 1996) and *A Dictionary of Moroccan Arabic* (Harrell and Sobelman 1966). The aim of this combination is to minimize the use of diacritical marks.

With a few exceptions, the chart below outlines the symbols I use to represent Arabic letters. The sound of words in the Moroccan dialect, which is primarily a spoken language, diverges from Modern Standard Arabic. As such, the representations I use have different spellings from similar words in dictionaries of MSA. For Moroccan place names and personal names, I use the French transliteration (without diacritical marks) that is used in Morocco. These nouns appear with standard capitalization to avoid confusion with the transcription code. A notable exception, however, is the term *ksar* (qSaar), which I write as it is written in Moroccan place-names.

ب	b	ع	e
ث ,ت	t	غ	gh
ج	j	ف	f
ح	H	ق	q
خ	kh	ك	k
د	d	ل	l
ذ	dh	م	m
ر	r	ن	n
ز	z	ه	h
س	s	و	w
ش	sh	ى	y
ص	S	اء	ʻ
ض	D	a, i, u	short vowels
ط ,ظ	T	aa, ii, uu	long vowels

PART I

Medical Pluralism and Embodied Knowledge

CHAPTER 1

INTRODUCTION

This book examines the way culture shapes the experience of vulnerability and the strategies people use to protect themselves. I became interested in the topic inadvertently, through my own sense of vulnerability while conducting ethnographic research on health development, medical pluralism, and household health care in rural Morocco in 1996 and 1997. In particular, I was interested in the local response to national initiatives that promoted family planning, female education, immunizations, and hospital births. At the same time that I was interviewing housewives about the way they addressed health problems, I fell in love and married into a local Berber family.

In the rural Saharan province of Errachidia where I lived, popular constructions of danger viewed brides-to-be as susceptible to the same kinds of illness agents I was learning about in my interviews on maternal and child health. My background in cultural anthropology had led me to think about folk etiologies, such as evil eye, magical curses, and invisible spirits as symbolic constructs that non-Western cultures used to explain illness and psychosocial distress. As explanatory models (Kleinman 1988), they provided culturally meaningful accounts of illness problems. The etiologies also challenged the power of the biomedical explanations offered at the provincial hospital and in health education campaigns. In the process of interpreting how Moroccan housewives constructed illness, I gave little thought to the dangers their constructs presented to me personally. I understood them as abstract ideas rather than *real* threats. My perspective changed dramatically, however, when local women started using traditional medical knowledge in attempt to cause me harm.

Although I had benefited from Saharan generosity and hospitality in the first months of my fieldwork, my marital engagement interfered with some women's hopes to match my fiancé, Yussef, with young women in their own families. His education, professional employment, and respected family background made him a highly desired bachelor among the struggling households of the southeastern Sahara. I was an easy target in their schemes to undermine our engagement and, later, our marriage. As an outsider living in a community where social ties were vital, I fit the local definition of vulnerable.

3

The first person to use a symbolic attack against me was Fulanah,[1] a woman from the remote agrarian village where Yussef spent his childhood. She was a formidable middle-aged woman, whose solid build matched a strong personality. The tattooed lines on her chin, the remnants of preventive health strategies in past generations, seemed to accentuate her powerful presence (although I did not have this impression of other women with similar facial markings). On a quiet afternoon in late spring when we were visiting her home, Fulanah greeted me by saying, "*endik SiHa daba, Maria*" (you have health now, Maria). I assumed she meant that I had gained some weight since I saw her last; according to Saharan cultural standards, a thin physique was a sign of illness for women of childbearing age. My recent interviews had revealed that this kind of compliment was dangerous, a way of activating the power of envy through the mechanism of *l-ein* (the Eye). To prevent the magical power of contrasts from making me ill, Fulanah should have added "*tabarak Allah*" (may God bless you). Instead, she only smirked.

I gasped as the force of her antagonism struck my chest while Yussef muttered "*khamza fi 'einik*" (five in your eye) sharply under his breath to block its effect on me. At that moment my interpretation of the Eye switched from a symbolic construct to a real threat to my well-being. Neither of us considered confronting her more directly at the time; she had higher status than we did, both in terms of age and local residence. We decided, however, that it would be the last time Fulanah would catch us off-guard. Even though Yussef viewed himself as a man of faith both in God and in science, the next day he took me to a Berber jewelry *suq* (market) to buy me an amulet. We chose an ornate brass pendant in the shape of an open hand with a blue bead at its center for added protection.

This new visceral appreciation of the uglier side of Saharan social relations stuck with me and shattered the illusion that I was purely an outside observer of Moroccan culture. My status as a bride-to-be intensified my investment in learning local customs and etiquette to avoid drawing attention to myself, for reasons of both safety and family honor. I started imitating the ways Saharan women protected themselves in the hope that these gestures would quell my nagging sense of vulnerability. Before long, I was using a wide range of local protective strategies habitually, including uttering religious invocations for the first time in my life. The more challenging tasks involved learning how to guard my emotions and to monitor what I said or ate when in the company of people outside our circle of trust. The trouble was that the boundaries of that circle were changing constantly.

Although this change in my subjectivity was disturbing at the time, I later came to see it as an asset to my research. The cultural dimensions of my experience in Morocco became even more apparent after Yussef and I divorced and I gained emotional distance from the social dynamics that I found to be so threatening when we lived in Morocco. The process through which I came to embody, at least partially, Saharan sensibilities for detecting danger and to employ their strategies of protection shifted my attention to dimensions of health seeking behavior that medical anthropologists have overlooked in the past. My original focus on discourse, meaning, and power provided the foundation for my transition in the field, but it was this unexpected exploration of embodied experience and practical logic that helped me to understand how culture structures the lived meaning of vulnerability and well-being.

Health Promotion Reconsidered

The motivation for revisiting this research now comes from a connection I see between my insights on the cultural forms of vulnerability in Saharan Morocco and broader research in public health. While working as an applied anthropologist at the U.S. National Cancer Institute (NCI) in 2002 and 2003, I observed that health researchers from a diversity of academic fields were interested in the relationship between culture and behavior. The driving force of this interest at NCI was the political mandate to address health disparities in the U.S. population, which was the main focus of my fellowship (MacPhee, et al. 2005). The applications of anthropology in public health, however, extend beyond this issue.

The distinct particulars of my ethnographic research in rural Morocco and my applied work in suburban Washington, D.C. converged on a common conundrum for health promotion: why do individuals at risk for health problems resist following scientific recommendations for health promotion and disease prevention? Whether the recommendations pertain to the benefits of trained birth attendants in a North African village or smoking cessation in an American city, public health researchers and practitioners have struggled to understand why so many interventions fall short of their goals to change behavior. In the literature on national health disparities and on global health, cultural difference often appears as a possible explanation for why programs fail. The argument juxtaposes cultural beliefs against scientific knowledge. Yet, even culturally tailored interventions (e.g., the use of the local language and terminology) have had limited success.

The insights I gained though my participation on the cancer disparities task force and my research on household health care in Morocco have led me to view the persistence of the conundrum as rooted in the narrow, static way that scholars have conceptualized the determinants of health behavior. In the past, rational actor theory permeated public health models for explaining health behavior and behavior change. The idea was that once people learned epidemiological facts about the cause of an illness, they would follow scientific recommendations about how to prevent or treat the illness. Unfortunately, the relationship between risk knowledge, risk perception, and behavior is complicated (Nichter 2003). Repeated evidence shows that risky practices such as unprotected sex, smoking, high calorie diets, and many others persist despite the efforts of health education campaigns to disseminate information about risk and prevention.

Although public health researchers and practitioners now criticize past assumptions about the straight-forward, linear relationship between knowledge and behavior (Glanz, et al. 2002), the new models, which focus on mediating factors have their own limitations. For example, the emphasis on cognitive variables such as beliefs, attitudes, and perceptions of risk in psychological and social marketing theories of behavior has downplayed the influence of external mediating factors. These theories assume that individual will is either free from external constraints (e.g., Health Belief Model) or geared toward adherence to social norms and positive reinforcement (e.g., Theory of Reasoned Action) (see Douglas 1983, Lupton 1999, and Yoder 1997 for more extensive critiques). The more recent ecological models (e.g., Berman, et al. 1994, Coreil 2010, Stokols 1996) do consider the influence of external social, cultural and political-economic factors on health behavior, but the uncritical use of this new multi-variable perspective has the potential to perpetuate old obstacles. The insights gained through the analysis of multiple variables are limited by cross-sectional, survey-driven methods, which continue to obscure the dynamic way those variables—in diverse forms—interact in the context of everyday life. Behavior is not the product of a person's cultural identity and socioeconomic status, but rather a process of negotiating particular problems and situations in everyday social life.

Health Behavior in Context

One of the challenges I faced in my work on the NCI health disparities task force was conveying the anthropological conceptualization of culture, and its dynamic relationship to behavior, to other members of the team. Even though the ecological models we discussed in our meetings were similar to the multidimensional model of household health behavior I used in Morocco, I realized that my understanding of culture was quite different from that of my colleagues.

To the psychologists, economists, and epidemiologists I worked with, "culture" was a variable that represented the ethnicity, language, or health beliefs of minority or non-Western populations. As Carla Obermeyer has pointed out in her research in Morocco (1993, 2000), conceptualizations such as these tend to frame culture as an obstacle to health and health care by emphasizing beliefs or habits that contradict public health recommendations. To the anthropologists on the NCI health disparities team, this view of culture was oversimplified and even ideological. On one hand, it glossed over the cultural underpinnings of biomedicine and undermined the practical logic of popular and non-Western knowledge about health, danger, and healing. On the other hand, it perpetuated the out-dated assumption that beliefs (or ethnicity and language) determine behavior. In contrast, we insisted, like so many of our colleagues in medical anthropology, that culture is a context in which behavior occurs. Our minds conjured images of social actors engaging in Geertzian webs of symbolic meaning, or Bourdieu's playing fields of intersecting rules, customs, and embodied dispositions.

Unfortunately, this complex, dynamic view of culture is vague and confusing to non-specialists. Anthropologists have struggled, as Stanley Yoder (1997:139–140) has pointed out, to convey the relevance of our holistic data on local knowledge, experience, and expectations to public health researchers and practitioners. Part of the difficulty lies in the gap between the tacit appreciation of cultural complexity that we gain from conducting qualitative field research and the concrete representations of culture we develop through writing ethnographic texts (c.f. Abu Lughod 1993). This gap has fueled an ongoing debate in anthropology about the definition of culture; some scholars, for example, argue that the concept encompasses only thought, while others include patterns of behavior. Some view culture as external to the individual and others view it as internalized in individual thought and experience. I fall into the group that defines culture as a concept that refers to the knowledge (including internalized knowledge) and practices a social group holds in common and teaches to new members, including children.

As an abstract definition, the meaning of culture seems straightforward, but the concept is far more complex when applied to real life. The complexity lies in the relationship between culture and the individual, or to frame it in terms relevant to health research, the relationship between culture and behavior.

Culture and the Individual

Anthropologists have long conveyed the difference between culture and individual behavior through the argument that people don't always do what they say they do. This insight is one of the reasons why our field methods often tri-angulate interviews with participant-observation. While the argument rejects a deterministic relationship between cultural beliefs or values and individual behavior, it is a mistake to conclude that anthropologists view individual behavior as unpredictable. Individuals learn how to anticipate the actions of other people by interpreting how cultural rules and regulations apply in particular social contexts. The prediction is not always accurate but social sanctions tend to maintain the boundaries of acceptable behavior for a given context.

This contextual appreciation of culture is missing from current models of health behavior, including more recent ecological models. To incorporate the dynamic aspects of culture into health research (and practices), there is a need for what Yoder calls a theory of knowledge-in-action. This perspective avoids essentializing culture as a definitive belief or normative stance about health and recognizes the diversity of behavior in a population (Yoder 1997:141). Through illuminating the dynamic relationship between culture and behav-ior, an anthropological theory of knowledge-in-action can offer new insights for understanding the gap between objective knowledge about health risks and the actual behavior of individuals (cf. Nichter 2003). While Yoder advocates for theories that situate cognitive components of culture—beliefs, norms, values, and meanings—in specific contexts of sociopolitical interaction, I argue that health researchers must also consider cultural structures of practice and em-bodied experience.

My perspective derives from the subfield of cultural anthropology that fo-cuses on the study of practice and experience. Scholarship in phenomenolog-ical anthropology has applied the ideas of 20th century phenomenology (e.g., Heiddeger (1962,1975), Merleau-Ponty (1962), and Schutz (1970)) to ethno-graphic research on a wide variety of topics that examine the relationship be-tween culture and the individual. One of the most influential theorists in the development of this subfield was French ethnologist Pierre Bourdieu. His the-ory of practice (Bourdieu 1977, 1990; Swartz 1997) provides the foundation for my understanding of knowledge-in-action as it applies to health behavior.

Bourdieu's theory centers on the concept of *habitus*, which is a heuristic for describing the principle or force that unites the multiple cultural structures that make up a social context. These structures of thought and practice, de-scribed in terms of binary oppositions (e.g., self-other, wet-dry, inside-out-side, etc.), compose an overall system of norms, rules, and values that organize everyday social and economic life. Using ethnographic examples from his re-search on the domestic and economic life of Algerian peasants, Bourdieu il-lustrates how the characteristics of a group's habitus appear redundantly in its rituals and proverbs, in the design of the houses and villages, in the rhythm of conversation and reciprocity, and in the style cooking and eating (Bourdieu 1990:200–270).

The concept of habitus is particularly useful for the study of health behavior because it provides a framework for linking cultural knowledge about health and illness with embodied experience. The corporeal dimension of habitus, which Bourdieu calls *bodily hexis* (Bourdieu 1977:82) describes how cultural constructions specific to the body organize the individual's practical sense of the world. Medical knowledge and practice represent one category of such cultural constructions, but they coexist with multiple other explicit and implicit dimensions of culture that shape the subjective experience *of* the body and *through* the body. Beginning in childhood, the habitual practices of everyday living provide a concrete foundation for understanding a vast array of abstract cultural knowledge that distinguishes normal from abnormal, right from wrong, and good from bad. In Bourdieu's words, "one could endlessly enumerate the values given body, *made* body, by the hidden persuasion of an implicit pedagogy which can instill a whole cosmology, through injunctions as insignificant as 'sit up straight' or 'don't hold your knife in your left hand'…," (Bourdieu 1990:69). He notes that "every society provides structural exercises which tend to transmit a particular form of practical mastery" (1990:75).

Although Bourdieu contends that individuals internalize the system tacitly as an embodied disposition or common sense, practice is not a straightforward enactment of cultural knowledge. The abstract classifications, rules, and codes that compose cultural knowledge encounter contradictions and ambiguities when applied to the practical, dynamic contexts of the social world (1990:10–12). For example, in Muslim North Africa the ideal wife for a young man is his first cousin, the daughter of his father's brother. If the prospective groom has no uncle or his uncle has only sons, the family is faced with a cultural dilemma. Bourdieu argues that the Algerians he observed were able to cope with these kinds of contingencies by adjusting their decisions about whom to marry, when to plough and plant, when to reciprocate a gift, and where to eat and sleep according to an internalized sense of habitus (Bourdieu 1990:200–270). Hence, Bourdieu frames the logic of practice as a matter of learning how to apply a small set of principles in particular contexts rather than the result of either mechanical obedience to a set of rules or pure innovative thinking. Habitus equips individuals with a tacit sense of how "to cope with unforeseen and ever-changing situations" (Bourdieu 1977:72). This perspective modifies the cognitive orientation of rational actor theory by emphasizing the implicit, taken-for-granted nature of practical logic. He views the strategies people use not as logical decisions of the mind but as non-reflexive gut-feelings about how to proceed. Past experience in a variety of contexts rather than exposure to abstract, objective knowledge sets up expectations—one might say educated guesses—about what should happen next.

The dispositions and practices that habitus generates are socially and historically specific, and as such, they may change over time or from one group to the next. Within a social group, however, conformity to its particular mode of practical mastery has both symbolic and economic rewards (Bourdieu 1990:16). In previous articles on Moroccan health behavior, for example, I have argued that the practical mastery of Islamic ritual prayer (MacPhee 2003) and the daily rhythm of domestic life (MacPhee 2004) generated dispositions that structured the lived meaning of health. Cultural expectations that required housewives to knead 10 loaves of bread each morning and perform prayer recitations despite the noise of the bickering children and satellite television in the background made physical strength and mental concentration important aspects of the local evaluation of health. Because these and other cultural expectations also contributed to a woman's social status, housewives sought out a variety of medicines and therapies to help them to attain context-specific health goals. This is not to say that biomedical definitions of health were irrelevant in Moroccan households, but rather that Western medical techniques for measuring the body (blood pressure, temperature, weight, etc.) interacted with multiple other cultural indices and injunctions. The concepts of habitus and bodily hexis provide a framework for examining the implicit connections among these multiple dimensions of knowledge related to the body and shed light on the cultural logic of health behavior.

The Household Production of Health

The applications of Bourdieu's theory of practice to the study of health behavior seem obvious to me now, but that insight emerged slowly, after years of struggling to make sense of the diverse mix of interviews, observations, and personal experiences I recorded during my fieldwork in Morocco. The principal framework that organized the design of my research methods in Morocco was a multi-dimensional perspective called the household production of health (Berman, et al. 1994, Schuman and Mosley 1994). The framework derives from the field of New Household Economics (NHE), which views certain aspects of domestic life such as health, education, and relaxation as commodities. Unlike other market commodities (e.g., food, technology, services) that households consume to increase their satisfaction, households *produce* health by purchasing goods and services and by utilizing the time and capacities of household members. Although the NHE model suggests that minimal health care inputs at the household level—where the majority of health care takes place—will improve the overall health status of the household members, the economic emphasis on rational decision-making and assumption of group consensus overlooks a number of social and cultural factors that affect household health behavior.

The Household Production of Health (HPH) framework employs an ecological perspective to incorporate those factors into the analysis and advance research on health behavior. In particular, it challenges the tendency to explain poor health outcomes as the result of irrational behavior attributed to lack of education or adherence to cultural beliefs that contradict biomedical advice. Past research in the fields of anthropology and social psychology has argued that households are embedded in contexts consisting of complex cultural, social and economic conditions that may interfere with medical compliance (Nichter & Kendall 1991, Schumann & Mosley 1994). For example, Ruthbeth Finnerman's (1989) ethnographic research on medical pluralism in southern Ecuador found that mothers accepted some aspects of biomedicine, such as pharmaceuticals and laboratory tests, but they resisted hospital care because it undermined the social status they gained as experts in traditional medical knowledge.

To take full advantage of the insights socio-cultural research can offer public health, Berman and colleagues (1994:206) define HPH broadly as "a dynamic behavioral process through which households combine their (internal) knowledge, resources, and behavioral norms and information, and skills to restore, maintain, and promote the health of their members." This integrative conceptual framework was well-suited for the exploratory nature of my research on health promotion and medical pluralism in Morocco because it incorporates multiple dimensions of behavior and decision-making simultaneously. It acknowledges that health seeking behavior entails multiple factors rather than simple cost-benefit decision-making and it recognizes that households are composed of multiple actors, who may disagree with each other in the health seeking process. Furthermore, the framework shifts the analysis from an emphasis on the behavioral changes needed to address a specific disease problem to a consideration of the overall household effort to maintain health on a day-to-day basis.

My goals in employing the HPH framework were more descriptive in nature than epidemiological or clinical. As such, evaluation of the household's health status was not part of the research. Instead I explored the various competing and complementary forms of medical knowledge and practice Saharan caregivers employed in their efforts to promote health in the household. I conceptualized "the household" as a culturally patterned set of social relations and as a place where members interact to carry out various functions of daily life, including health care. By focusing the investigation in households rather than a clinical setting, I hoped to elicit women's candid evaluations of recent public health initiatives and observe the extent to which they complied with them. As it turned out, my decision to focus the research on households was fortuitous because Saharans preferred to exhaust home treatments, sometimes for months, before consulting outside practitioners.

The breadth and flexibility of the HPH model was both an asset and a source of confusion and frustration in my research. First of all, the home treatments that Saharan housewives used in their attempts to produce health were pluralistic. In addition to state-supported biomedicine, Saharan health care also included Arab-Galenic (humoral) and Islamic spiritual medical knowledge. A less formal oral tradition of symbolic healing constituted a fourth resource available to household caregivers. The extent to which Saharan housewives used all of these approaches to health care was not apparent in my first interviews. Even though the open-ended design of my interviews invited the participants to respond in whatever way made sense to them, the public health terms I used in the questions I asked framed my identity as *barani* (an outsider) — the same social category Saharan women used to describe the staff in the provincial hospital and health dispensaries. My research assistant suspected that some claims of compliance with public health recommendations were deliberately misleading out of fear that I would criticize their use of folk remedies. Once they realized my respect for their traditional explanations of illness, however, the participants began to trust me as an unpretentious *bint-l-famila* (daughter of the family) and became more open about their vast knowledge of humoral, spiritual, and symbolic medicine.

The stories mothers and grandmothers told about their experiences with pregnancy, birth, and child care revealed an eclectic approach to household health care. Each of these informal healers and midwives was eager to convince her relatives, neighbors, and me that her slight variation on how to diagnose or treat an illness was better than the others. Resistance to doctors and hospitals was a recurring theme in the stories as women gained social status from their expertise in healing. Yet, pharmacy medicines — especially ones that migrant workers brought from Europe — were valued household resources as well. The diversity of knowledge recorded in my field notes was overwhelming, especially as I tried to learn how to distinguish the dozens of leaves, twigs, and powders — all wrapped in unmarked scraps of newspaper and plastic shopping bags — that housewives kept on hand for treating pains, colds, and fevers. Aside from knowing that housewives learned about healing from talking with other women and observing their techniques for diagnosis and treatment, I had little sense of why or when a healer would choose one particular health care strategy over another.

A second source of confusion in my data was variation in a single household. Despite the officially reported success of maternal-child health initiatives in southeastern Morocco (Direction de la Statistique 1994), health behavior varied among household members and over time. Housewives' use of amulets, herbal infusions, or even soap (e.g. for washing hands or tea glasses) varied according to the contextual configuration of factors such as the household's relationship to other people present, the time of day and year, and recent events affecting household members. Some women such as Khaira, an out-spoken Berber grandmother from Errachidia, were critical of biomedicine. During our first interview she explained bluntly that "doctors only treat symptoms and the sickness comes back. With *l-eshuub* (herbal medicine), you take out the sickness and you are fine." Khaira's confident tone suggested that she was an authority on health issues. She boasted that she had never been to a hospital because she was able to treat all of her illnesses with herbal medicines from a spice dealer located further south in the valley. Although Khaira's family respected her knowledge of traditional healing, they were also open to using modern biomedicine. On subsequent visits to the household I learned that both of her daughters-in-law had given birth at the provincial hospital. One liked the pain medication and delivered her youngest three children there; the other thought the episiotomy was painful and decided to deliver her second child at home.

The ease with which the household fluctuated between biomedicine and other local traditions seemed more flexible than the binary form of medical pluralism that Finnerman described in Ecuador. Although the Moroccan government promoted biomedicine through health education and outreach, the services were too limited in Errachidia to discredit the Arab, Islamic and symbolic medical traditions housewife healers employed. As such, biomedicine was one component in a bricolage of oral tradition, religious texts and healers, and symbolic practices that composed Saharan health knowledge. Even Chinese Traditional Medicine was making its way into the culture through the Chinese mission doctors who worked at the provincial hospital.

When faced with the task of analyzing the data I collected, I cursed the Household Production of Health framework for generating so much complexity. At first glance, the variety of practices housewives described in the interviews supported a post-modern interpretation of the research. The participants seemed to have considerable agency in choosing whatever strategy they wanted to treat or prevent illness. At the same time, however, I suspected that the collection of strategies I recorded and observed was more than a haphazard stream of trial and error. The senior housewives in particular were adept in describing a range of ways to prevent problems with childbirth or to treat common childhood illnesses. This is not to suggest that these households were free from illness, but rather that household healers knew which potential treatments made sense for a given set of symptoms or circumstances. Even if one of these strategies failed, the diverse repertoire of knowledge in the family and neighborhood allowed housewives to avoid the expense and uncertainty of consulting a professional healer outside their own social circle.

The dominant discursive theories in medical anthropology, which emphasized the construction of meaning (e.g., Good 1994, Kleinman 1988) and the negotiation of local power dynamics (e.g., Nichter 1981, Finnerman 1989) offered little help in organizing the interview data I collected because there was too much variation. My notes included information on the whole spectrum of health seeking behavior—from prevention to treatment—in a complex setting of medical pluralism and social diversity. But, my personal experience as a bride-to-be provided another angle for making sense of Saharan health culture.

In the process of learning how to protect myself and interpret local social dynamics, I noticed that housewives were enacting strategies of protection during my interactions with them. For example, they responded to my questions cautiously by interjecting expressions such as "God forbid" or "God protect" whenever they described the treatments for a hypothetical health problem. Similarly, both women and men said "*bismillah*" (in the name of God) before taking the first mouthful of a meal or boarding a taxi for a trip to *l-blad* (village, homeland). In addition to using religious phrases, Saharans also protected themselves by sharing food or henna with me, restricting my interactions with their daughters-in-law, and burning incense after an interview.

These observations, which I recorded toward the end of my fieldwork in 1996 and when I returned to Morocco in the summer of 1997, expanded my appreciation of the realm of knowledge, resources, and norms that affected the household production of health. I noticed that housewives spoke about the importance of charity, *Salat* (the daily prayer ritual), and dressing modestly in between narratives about surviving difficult births and treating childhood coughs or diarrhea. Alternatively, conversations about health encompassed the kinds of foods and spices one should use at different times of year and the customs for sharing food with guests and the neighbors. I would have dismissed many of these topics as tangential to my research had I not reacted so strongly to Fulanah's attempt to hit me with the Eye. Grasping a sense of these connections at practical level, however, was a far cry from explaining them in an anthropological analysis.

Grasping the Elusive

Bourdieu's theory of practice and concept of habitus provided a starting point for thinking about the cultural structures that linked ritual prayer and hospitality with health practices, but the task of analyzing the structures of Saharan habitus and bodily hexis was far less concrete than analyzing discursive data. On one hand, the implicit details of embodied knowledge are embedded in the invisible texture of social interaction and the silent assumptions in everyday conversation. Narrators leave those details out of their stories because habitus encompasses the taken-for-granted norms and expectations of common sense. On the other hand, my own embodied modes of practice and experience biased the kinds of data I collected, particularly at the beginning of the fieldwork. Bourdieu cautioned that habitus was an imperfect heuristic for organizing observations for this reason (1990:11). The ethnographer's own cultural and academic background has a strong conditioning influence on the way she interprets practice and experience in another culture.

More recent scholarship in phenomenological anthropology, however, has challenged Bourdieu's doubts and has offered new ethnographic strategies for the cross-cultural examination of embodiment and experience. In the past twenty years, the subfield of phenomenological anthropology has produced a variety of ethnographic and theoretical explorations on the interaction of body and culture in experiences of selfhood (Mahmood 2005, Simon 2009), livelihood (Ingold 2000), illness (Good 1994, Ferzacca 2001, Seligman 2010), suffering (Biehl, Good and Kleinman 2007; Luhrman 2006), and healing (Desjarlais 1992; Csordas 1994a, 1994b). (See Desjarlais and Throop 2011 for a comprehensive review of the subfield). Through attention to sensory experience and subjectivity in ritual and everyday life this new generation of anthropologists has expanded on Bourdieu's concepts in a way that renders them more applicable to research in medical anthropology and public health.

The conceptualization of the body in this literature diverges from the biomedical assumption of a universal human body. Instead, the anthropological concept builds on phenomenological notions of being-in-the-world to illuminate the cultural, historical and environmental forces that condition embodied experience. Bourdieu's concept of habitus integrated that perspective into the anthropological study of embodied subjectivity, but the more recent literature has placed a greater emphasis on the body as the site of sentient experience as well as conditioned practice. The focus on non-discursive aspects of awareness frames the concept of embodiment as a dialectic relationship between the individual body/self and the objectifying structures of culture (Jackson 1996, 1998; Throop and Murphy 2002). This subtle but important shift critiques Bourdieu's assertion that habitus operates automatically and unconsciously in the process of generating culturally appropriate practices, and argues instead that individual body/selves interpret experience and compose practices in relation to a set of cultural norms, values, skills, and meanings. Hence, the analysis moves beyond deconstructing how habitual and ritual practices reflect a unified framework of symbolic oppositions to examining how individual actors use cultural structures to create coherent experience.

The difference between the cultural phenomenological perspective and rational actor theory in public health is the idea that the volition to act emerges at least in part from embodied knowledge, which may contradict or modify cognitive knowledge about the same topic or situation. For example, in Chapter 6 I describe the case of a divorced Berber mother who avoided the immunization campaign in her village even though her pregnancy warranted a tetanus vaccine. Although she viewed immunizations as beneficial, this very public event posed other social and emotional risks because of her status as recently divorced and a newcomer in the village. Rational calculation and professed belief formed only one portion of the knowledge she enacted in the attempt to promote health. While psychologists have described mediating forces in terms of idiosyncratic attitudes and emotions, cultural phenomenology argues that culture shapes the way we experience and interpret the world through the process of embodiment. The internalization of a particular way of life through participation in structured, everyday practices over time generates similar sensibilities, preferences, and points of reference among members of a social group. It is this kind of awareness, rooted in the body that informs and mediates the meanings of health, illness, risk, and safety as individuals decide how to act.

By framing the individual as an agent who *uses* culture rather than as a constructed product of culture, this perspective also raises the possibility of cross-cultural intersubjectivity. Past scholarship in the anthropology of the senses has argued that some of the ambiguity inherent in cross-cultural investigations of illness and healing stems from biases in the ethnographer's embodied sense of the world. Paul Stoller, for example, described how his initial dependence on visual and linguistic aspects of knowledge caused him to gloss over the pivotal "realm of sensual sentiment"—sound, smell, and touch—in the study of Songhay spirit possession and ritual healing (Stoller 1989). Rather than viewing this difference as an obstacle to cross-cultural understanding, Stoller took on the challenge to learn Songhay modes of experience by becoming an apprentice to a local healer.

Robert Desjarlais (1992) took the apprentice approach to embodied ethnography a step further by comparing experience in everyday life to a more fo-

cused study of soul loss and ritual healing among the Yolmo in Nepal. Desjarlais learned the underlying principles of Yolmo experience through observation and mimesis of cultural styles in everyday life—drinking tea, greeting
a friend, or walking down a mountain road (1992:13–18). He argues that attention to local images, idioms, and poetics helps ethnographers to grasp the
aesthetic structures that shape the subjective experience of the body, the household, and the community.

The use of "aesthetics" in this approach to studying experience refers to cultural modes of being, feeling, and knowing rather than the philosophy of
beauty and taste. Individuals internalize the aesthetic structures of their culture through participating in a particular style of living—a way of organizing
activities such as work and leisure, or eating and sleeping in the temporal and
spatial contexts of everyday life. In turn, this level of embodied awareness influences the decisions they make and the lifestyles they reproduce at home, at
work, and in society. Even though aesthetics engage the body in ways that is
often difficult to convey in words, it is possible to discern the aesthetic structures of experience through systematic attention to cultural patterns of practice. For example, the way Saharans pose for photographs using props of silver
tea pots or hand drums reveals something about how they want to compose
themselves in the world.

Desjarlais' aesthetic approach to the study of embodied experience in Yolmo
illness and healing expands Bourdieu's theory in two ways that are useful for
the study of how culture influences health behavior. First, it conceptualizes
the implicit cultural qualities that shape subjectivity (what Bourdieu calls habitus) in terms of the way they affect individual experience, both positively and
negatively. In other words, the embodiment of particular cultural modes of
interpreting qualities such as harmony, balance, and wholeness provide an implicit index for measuring how one feels at a given moment. Second, Desjarlais' approach incorporates the possibility for individual agency by arguing that
individuals use that same embodied index to create desired aesthetic qualities
in their bodies, households, and communities. By the same token, embodied
knowledge also generates awareness of disruptions to the internalized sense of
order in everyday life that may arise in situations of illness and misfortune.

Vulnerability and Protection

My goal in this book is to convey anthropological insights about the cultural context of experience and practice in a way that is useful for students,
researchers, and practitioners interested in health behavior and health pro-

motion. Through the application of cultural phenomenology to my research on the household production of health in Saharan Morocco, I show how embodied knowledge and practical norms serve as key mediating factors in the relationship between objective medical knowledge and actual health behavior. This anthropological view of health behavior does not dismiss the importance of other mediating factors (e.g., economic barriers), but rather links together cultural factors at the intrapersonal level with factors at the interpersonal level (household, community, and society). The connection emerges from the conceptualization of human experience, including health-related experience as an inherently social and cultural process that is also rooted in physical bodies and environments. In particular, the concepts of embodiment and everyday aesthetics synthesize constructivist perspectives on the body, subjectivity, environment, and practice. I see cultural phenomenology as offering a way to expand ecological models, such as the Household Production of Health, by providing the conceptual tools to examine knowledge in action.

My exploration of embodied aesthetics and the art of protection in Morocco also adds to past scholarship in cultural phenomenology in that I examine its applications to the study of prevention and health promotion rather than illness and healing. My decision to focus on this aspect of the household production of health emerged from the constraints in my data rather than a conscious effort to expand the theory. I did not set out to investigate habitus, cultural aesthetics, or subjective experience, but these concepts provided a productive way to explain the connections between health behavior and other kinds of domestic activities I observed in Morocco. Although I collected information on the whole spectrum of health seeking behavior in Saharan households, the richest portion of these data pertains to prevention, the aspect of the household production of health that captivated my attention both personally and academically.

The study of health promotion and disease prevention in household health care entails considerable ambiguity, particularly in a setting of medical pluralism such as Saharan Morocco. Instead of examining patterns in the cultural construction of illness and healing, my analysis focused on cultural constructions of threats to health and local strategies for preventing illness. I framed these constructions in terms of vulnerability and the art of protection rather than the scientific concepts of risk and prevention to emphasize the influence of culture and the perspective of knowledge-in-action. The conceptualization of vulnerability here emphasizes subjective feelings of weakness, exposure, and susceptibility to harm (cf. Jackson 1998, Nichter 2003). Other scholars in public health, psychology, and other fields sometimes use the term vulnerability to refer to an objective condition of high exposure to harm or stress such as that found among individuals living in contexts of poverty or violence (c.f. Leatherman 2005; Ribera and Haussman-Muela 2011). Although the two communities I studied in Saharan Morocco may fit an objective definition of vulnerability to maternal-child health problems, my focus in this book is how culture shapes the subjective sense of vulnerability.

Following the framework of cultural phenomenology, I contend that feelings of vulnerability and strategies of protection arise in response to embodied experience in particular situations. The way an individual evaluates the relevance of abstract, generalized knowledge about risk and danger in a given context depends on his or her sense of strength or protection relative to the threat. That evaluation fluctuates according to the configuration of cultural principles that structure individual experience in terms of body-mind-environment interactions. By conducting observations over the course of 14 months between 1994 and 1997, I was able to see how health practices fluctuate over time, from one context to the next. The close analysis of the practical strategies Saharan housewives enacted (out of multiple choices) in relation to local aesthetic structures of the body, self, household, and society, illuminates the dynamic relationship between embodied experience and cultural practice.

In this way, the lens of cultural phenomenology extends previous insights about how local health discourses identify particular kinds of behavior as safe or dangerous. For example, Douglas and Widavsky (1983:6–9) have argued that risk perception is a social process, which conforms to structural patterns that organize a social group's overall way of life. Cultural phenomenology, in contrast, provides a more nuanced way of understanding the link between broader cultural patterns and individual subjectivity. I draw on Giddens' (1990, 1991) concept of ontological security to discuss the link I see between the experience of vulnerability and the structures of everyday life, but refer to the perspectives of Bourdieu and Desjarlais to show that the relationship is less deterministic than Douglas and Widavsky's theory suggests. Nonetheless, one needs to understand the cultural patterns that constitute the subjective experience of normal, healthy, and secure to be able to recognize the implicit cues that signal a state of vulnerability and the cultural strategies that restore a sense of security.

For this reason, my approach to interpreting health behavior wanders outside the usual boundaries of medical anthropology to include an examination of aesthetic structures in everyday life. The chapters in Part I provide an orientation to the cultural context of health care and domestic life in Saharan Morocco. In Chapter 3, I draw on interviews conducted with Saharan housewives to outline the nature of medical pluralism in the region with respect to maternal-child health. In particular, I focus on Saharan constructions of danger during pregnancy, childbirth, and the post-partum period. Chapter 4 broadens the discussion of Saharan culture to explain the implicit structures of daily practice. To comprehend how housewives interpreted and applied the multiple forms of health knowledge available to them, I followed Desjarlais' lead and organized my participant-observation data in terms of the cultural knowledge and practices that construct the body, self, household, and community in Saharan Morocco. The chapter incorporates explanations of Saharan social dynamics, religious practices, the structures of space and time, and the minute details of etiquette, ritual enactment, and everyday domestic life.

Part II integrates the description of Saharan health knowledge with the analysis of Saharan aesthetics of experience and practice and explores the role of vulnerability in Saharan health behavior. Chapter 5 develops a cultural phenomenological theory of vulnerability to illuminate the distinct ways that culture shapes embodied experience in relationship to local knowledge about what causes illness and the actions that are likely to prevent it. Chapters 6–8 present case studies related to maternal-child health to illustrate how the aesthetics of everyday life structure health experience and strategies of protection. Although the cultural descriptions and case studies I include in my discussion are particular to the cultural and historical context of my fieldwork in rural Morocco, the embodied, knowledge-in-action perspective I use offers insight into the cultural determinants of behavior that are missing in the dominant paradigms on health behavior. The concepts of embodiment and cultural practice are important contributions to the field of health promotion because the embodied dimensions of awareness—our tastes, intuition, and gut-feelings—often supersede rational thought both in the stress of a crisis and in the habitual routines of everyday life.

CHAPTER 2

Errachidia

In recent years vulnerability has emerged as a way for medical anthropologists to explore local interpretations of health risks (Chapman 2006, Nichter 2003, Ribera and Haussman-Muela 2011), but few anthropologists wrote about the concept explicitly prior to the past decade. Nonetheless, the theme of vulnerability has a long history in reflexive descriptions of anthropological fieldwork. The demands of the ethnographic method require researchers to maintain direct contact with the study participants for a prolonged period of time — typically ranging from several months to over a year. When an ethnographer conducts the research alone, which is often the case in cultural anthropology, the adjustment to living in an unfamiliar culture can be intimidating. Some of the most vivid accounts of the confusion, loneliness, and frustration that accompany ethnographic research are based on anthropologists' experiences in Morocco (Crapanzano 1980, Dwyer 1982, Rabinow 1977).

These descriptions struck me initially as being self-indulgent and tangential to Moroccan culture. My perspective changed, however, when I traveled to Morocco for the first time as a student in the summer of 1994. While studying Arabic in Fes and scouting potential locations for my research on household health practices, I encountered what seemed to be an endless stream of harassment whenever I ventured out in public. Although I did not set out to study vulnerability, my experience that summer pushed the issue of safety to the forefront of the challenges I faced as a female anthropologist in Morocco. I realized quickly that it was easier to identify a Moroccan community that was a target for health development than it was to find a place where I felt comfortable living as a single woman.

One of the reasons I was interested studying the cultural context of maternal-child health in Morocco was the social norm of sex segregation. This spatial and temporal pattern of organizing social, religious and economic activities restricted female mobility outside the home. Although the feminist movement created new opportunities for Moroccan women in the early 1990s, few women interacted socially with men outside their own family. I imagined that the custom, at least in socially conservative parts of the population would conflict with the promotion of hospital births and female education. I wanted to observe how that conflict affected the household production of health.

What I neglected to consider when I conceptualized the project was the difficulty I would have adjusting to the local customs of sex segregation. My American habit of smiling at strangers conveyed far more than the polite regard I intended and I encountered a persistent stream of solicitations from young men walking on the streets of cities and towns alike. Even after I adapted my behavior to match the local norms of public etiquette, my fair complexion and unveiled blonde hair made me a conspicuous curiosity. This attention was more an annoyance than a threat, but nonetheless it added unexpected stress to my search for a fieldsite.

The suggestion that I consider the southeastern Sahara as a possible fieldsite came from the family of a Berber graduate student who had been conducting field research in Morocco when I was a student in Fes. The family was from a village outside Errachidia but had moved in the 1980s to a small town in the agricultural belt of Western Morocco where there were better economic opportunities. The head of the household was Yussef, a 35-year-old senior manager in Morocco's industrial sector. His income and housing benefit supported his 4 sisters, 3 of whom were divorced with young children, and supplemented the meager salaries of his two brothers (one of whom was the graduate student). Over the course of the summer, this household became my refuge from the hassles of city life and helped me to improve my language skills. The family's accommodation of my vegetarianism when preparing the many meals we shared and their willingness to adjust their conversation to my elementary understanding of Arabic made me feel like a valued guest and, eventually, an honorary member of their household.

One of the recurring topics of conversation during my visits was the siblings' memories of their childhood. Their animated stories about the traditions and values of *l-blad* (homeland) piqued my curiosity about Saharan culture and society. They described the people of the region as morally *niishan* (literally, straight), modest, and trustworthy, and for those reasons they thought it would make a good location for my research. One of the sisters, known by the nickname Mama[1] had past experience as a traditional midwife and she was eager to introduce me to her Saharan friends and family who knew about traditional health practices. Their enthusiasm was contagious and they convinced me to travel to the region later that summer.

My trip to the southeast in August 1994 changed my view of Moroccan culture and society dramatically. The slow pace and modest demeanor of the Saharan people were a welcome contrast to the intrusive noise and crowded commotion I endured in Fes. The lack of attention I received in Errachidia was surprising given the religiously conservative culture and the dearth of tourists. In some respects, I was more conspicuous in the southeast as few Saharan women wore Western-styled clothing. Saharan customs of sex-segregation and gender ideology were more conservative than those of Western Morocco and, hence, few women worked outside the home. Nevertheless, I had more freedom to explore the central markets and main streets unsolicited than I had experienced anywhere else in the country. Without the help of Yussef and his family, I would not have predicted that the remote, socially conservative Province of Errachidia would be the safe and comfortable fieldsite I desired.

Town and Province

Errachidia is the capital of a vast desert province of the same name. The province stretches east from the junction of the Middle and High Atlas mountains to the encroaching dunes of the Sahara desert along the Algerian border. The population of the province (511,000) in 1994 was predominantly rural (Maroc Banque Central Populaire 1995:13). The rural portion of the population consisted of peasant villages in the river valleys and small oasis settlements and nomadic tent communities in the desert. The remaining 25% of the population lived in the provincial capital or smaller towns located along the national highway. Although the climate was semi-arid and the geography was technically pre-Saharan, the residents referred to themselves as *Saharawi* (Saharan). This southeastern region of Morocco, however, was culturally and politically distinct from the contested identity of the Western Sahara bordering Mauritania.

At the time of my fieldwork, the capital of the province was a large town that served as an administrative and market center for dozens of rural *ksour* (sing. *ksar*). These walled adobe villages clustered in the shade of date palms and olive trees in the lush Ziz River valley that runs from the Middle Atlas mountains toward the Tafilalt oasis at the edge of the Sahara desert. In contrast, the town of Errachidia sat on a barren plateau exposed to the unrelenting desert sun. The colonial history of Errachidia—formerly called *ksar as-souk*—was evident in the grand architecture of the government buildings and the grid layout of streets next to the river. This part of town, known as *l-village* included the central market, a small bus station, the police station, and provincial court as well as several banks and a few small hotels. Layers of densely built residential neighborhoods, composed of pink and beige cement buildings, encircled the central market and then extended north and east hugging the national road.

Although the capital had urban characteristics in the mid-1990s, it fell short of meeting the criteria of a city, even by Moroccan standards. The abundance of dirt roads and donkey carts gave Errachidia a rural feel, despite the dominance of the large military base near the center and the new engineering university on the northern perimeter of town. The mix of those elements with the vast barren landscape outside the town limits created the sense that Errachidia was on the fringe of economic development. There was evidence of modernization in the form of electricity, indoor plumbing, and gas stations, but Errachidia lacked the population density, rapid pace, and commotion I had observed in Fes and Rabat. Outside the capital there were fewer signs of modernization. The outlying villages relied on generators to supply electricity in the evenings and shared community taps for potable water. Despite promises from local politicians, access to the modern conveniences found in Western Morocco seemed far on the horizon.

Politics of Economic Development

Economic disparities between western and eastern Morocco trace back to the colonial era (1912–1956). French colonists characterized the southeastern part of Morocco as useless, and neglected to develop the rocky, arid region as anything more than a military outpost, even after they overcame a lengthy Berber resistance to French rule. Instead, the protectorate government focused its effort to develop industry, transportation, health care, and education in the fertile cities and towns west of the Atlas Mountains. The same trend continued in the decades following Independence in as much as the new national government had few resources to expand on the colonial infrastructure. The result was a country with two different economic identities. The economic status of the western portion of the country compared with middle-income countries in the developing world, while the predominantly rural, eastern portion struggled with issues related to poverty, health, education, and depopulation.

One of the results of unequal colonial and national development was that economic opportunities in the southeastern region as a whole were limited in the mid-1990s. The flow of labor migration to Europe, which helped some Saharan families to prosper in the 1960s and 1970s, had diminished to a trickle by the time I arrived 1994. Small-scale date and olive production in the villages was possible with irrigation from the Ziz River, but increasing aridity from the spread of Saharan sand constrained agricultural prospects overall. Few of the young men from the villages had an interest in farming anyway. The education system provided training in languages, science, and mechanics, but the jobs that required these skills were outside the region in Western Morocco or abroad. Errachidia offered some income alternatives through wage employment in the military and civil service as well as commercial opportunities in the French-influenced marché or the small *suq* (traditional market). Otherwise, households relied on informal, intermittent work to survive and often one worker's income supported an extended family.

Access to public services was also limited at the time. While there was no shortage of police, the waiting list to install a telephone was years long. Because few households in the capital or the outlying villages could afford a car, there was a high demand for public transportation. The supply, however, was uneven. Inexpensive buses and taxis that ran between towns along the national highway were regular enough to allow frequent visiting among extended family members, a custom that obscured the boundary between urban and rural. In the capital, however, public transportation consisted of a single, unpredictable bus line and the expensive "petit taxi" service. Walking and bicycling were far more common ways of getting around town.

The province had an extensive system of schools and health dispensaries thanks to the colonial infrastructure, but the limited national budget struggled just to maintain these services when there was a need to expand them. The schools were run-down and overcrowded both in the capital and the outlying villages. For example, the elementary school in the neighborhood where I lived had to schedule its classes in two shifts to accommodate all the students. Enrollment demands were less pressing at the secondary level, however, because few girls continued past primary school despite the national campaign to promote female education. One of the main obstacles to increasing female education rates was the hidden costs of secondary education. Primary schools were local, even for village communities, but education beyond the 6th grade required either daily travel to or boarding at one of the regional secondary schools. Few families could afford these costs for all of their children and the poorest families relied on their daughters to help with the considerable demands of household labor. While their brothers went to school and played soccer in the afternoons, the village girls would sweep the floors, wash the clothes, gather food for the animals, fetch water for cooking, and watch over their youngest siblings.

Health Care

Similarly, the health care system in Errachidia was run-down and involved hidden costs. With the exception of one pediatrician with a private practice, all other biomedical services and staff in the province were part of the public sector. This infrastructure included the small, poorly equipped provincial hospital in the capital and several smaller primary care dispensaries (staffed mostly by nurses) located in the outlying neighborhoods of Errachidia and market towns throughout the province. A small corps of traveling nurses and periodic outreach caravans extended the reach of biomedical services to more remote villages in the mountains and desert oases.

Public health efforts in the province focused on family planning, prenatal care, and immunizations with remarkable success. According to national health statistics (Direction de la Statistique 1994), the central-south economic region, which includes Errachidia, boasted some of the highest compliance rates in the country despite competition from midwives and traditional healers. For example, the immunization rate for children in the region in 1992 was over 90% (Direction de la Statistique 1994:228).[2]

The emphasis on prevention and health promotion conveyed the constraints on the provincial budget and infrastructure more than the health status of the community. The Ministry of Health relied on Chinese and American volunteers to fill personnel gaps at the hospital and health dispensaries, as few educated Moroccans were willing to work in such a remote location. Although the public health sector offered free medical care, participants in my study reported that they paid for bandages and medicine separately. In the past the Ministry of Health was able to provide free medicines and medical testing, but budget cuts forced hospitals to pass these costs to the patient. The patient's family would have to go to one of the few dozen privately owned pharmacies in town to buy medicines for the hospital staff to administer. Families also brought bedding and food for hospital patients because they viewed the quality of care at the hospital to be poor. For many Saharans, this negative evaluation extended to the health services as well. They mentioned practitioner inexperience and the lack of diagnostic tests as reasons for avoiding the hospital except in emergencies.

For health problems that were not life threatening, Saharans relied on a variety of other well-established healing traditions that have a longer history in the region. The dominant influences on Moroccan medicine outside the biomedical system were the Arab-Galenic (humoral) and Islamic-Prophetic text-based traditions. A less formal oral tradition of symbolic healing constituted an eclectic fourth resource for health knowledge. This knowledge incorporated elements of healing practices that came to Morocco through migration and the trans-Saharan and Mediterranean trade economies (Bellakhdar 1989:29). The types of local practitioners who employed these traditions in various configurations included *l-fqih* (Islamic scholar), *l-qabla* (midwife), *l-eshab* (herbalist), and *tbiib at-taqliidi* (traditional doctor). Some of the local healers identified by these titles gained reputations as experts in therapeutic technique or in treating particular kinds of illness, but with the exception of a dozen herbalist shop-keepers, these practitioners worked informally on an as-needed basis.

As I mentioned in the previous chapter, Saharans preferred to address health issues privately at home rather than consulting an unknown practitioner. A few housewives in the study acted as informal midwives or traditional doctors to friends and neighbors, but most of the participants limited themselves to pro-viding health care within their own households and families. The tendency to-ward self-care added complexity to the local practice of medical pluralism as housewives incorporated their ethnic and regional perspectives into the inter-pretation of the health knowledge available to them.

Social Diversity

The social composition of the neighborhoods of Errachidia was a micro-cosm of the social diversity in the province as a whole. The primary way Sa-harans distinguished social identity emphasized ethnic and residential differences. Economic instability in the region made class distinctions a less significant form social classification because wealth and income fluctuated over time and flowed between migrant, urban, and rural households. Instead, four princi-pal ethnic categories divided Saharan society with respect to language, cus-tom, and racial identity. Two of the ethnic groups—Arab and Haratine or *Hurtani* (descendents of subSaharan sharecroppers and slaves)—spoke Moroccan Arabic as a first language. The remaining two social groups—Berber and Rgaiga (people whose ancestors worked for Berbers)—spoke Tamazight as a first lan-guage. This contemporary pattern of classifying social identity was a conflation of historically contentious divisions in the kin-based social structure of the Sahara. In the centuries preceding the French occupation, the southeastern Sahara was the site of considerable conflict among Berber nomadic pastoral-ists and between those groups and Arab peasant farmers. The historic threat of the aggressive, nomadic *qabilat* (kin-based decent groups) influenced the region's distinct architectural style in which village households clustered to-gether in one walled ksar community, built from mud bricks.

As more Berber nomads began to settle in villages in the twentieth century, village membership transcended qabil affiliations as a primary marker of so-cial identity. A household's association with a kin-based identity continued to hold importance in marital arrangements and lifecycle customs, but the com-munal ksar structure of Saharan village life fostered strong social ties with neighbors as well. Home village was also an important social marker in the capital because so many of the residents were immigrants from other parts of the province or part-time dwellers in a house shared by extended family members. Aside from the few blocks surrounding the suq, Errachidia lacked an identifiable cultural history of its own. The other neighborhoods in town were newer developments that housed a diverse mix of migrant families from smaller villages throughout the province, and more rarely other parts of Morocco.

Local tolerance for this level of social integration stemmed in part from the dominance of Moroccan Arabic as the common language in town and from the frequency of social interaction between ethnic groups in rural parts of the province. Although Saharan ethnic groups in both village and town contexts tended to maintain distinct customs and favor in-group marriage, they interacted with each other as friends and neighbors on a regular basis. Even ethnically homogeneous villages bordered the villages of other ethnic groups. Berber, Arab, Rgaiga, and Hurtani farmers attended the same regional markets and their children attended the same schools.

Competition for economic resources and political power had the potential to renew antagonism between the ethnic groups, but I found that regardless of what people said about the other groups in private, Saharans were quick to overlook ethnic differences if it could work to their advantage. This opportunistic form of social networking was especially prevalent in the capital. Knowing someone who worked for government agencies such as the court, the police. or the agricultural extension office was valuable, regardless of that person's ethnicity. Similarly, social connections with pharmacists, health workers, and traditional healers influenced where a household sought health care.

The emphasis on personal relationships above institutional affiliations shaped the character of daily life in the capital. Despite having fluctuating boundaries both in terms of population and geography, Errachidia had the feel of a small town where everyone knew each other's business and commented on each other's behavior. I learned later that this level of scrutiny could work to one's advantage; a positive reputation was a valuable social asset that Saharan households could use to mobilize family and friends in times of need. Shared ethnicity and home village served as a primary way of establishing a social network for this purpose, but Saharans were flexible in their estimation of who counted as family and friend. Cultivating a wide social network—beyond the ties of ones home villages or kin group—was an asset to low-income households. As I describe in Chapter 4, local customs of hospitality, favors, and gifts connected households in a system of reciprocity and moral obligation. These informal systems, which exchanged both material and symbolic gifts, resembled social networks in other parts of the Middle East and North Africa in their reliance on Islamic codes of morality and honor (Meneley 2007, Önder 2007, Wikan 1996).

Because Saharan interpretations of morality were thoroughly intertwined with Islamic principles of practice, a central component of one's social reputation was religiosity. Sunni Islam was the official religion of the nation, but Moroccans interpreted and practiced their faith in a variety of ways. In the 1990s, Saharans had a reputation for being among the most devout Muslims in Morocco. The local interpretation of Islam blended Sufi mysticism with reformist adherence to scripture and the five tenets of practice. The fraternal brotherhoods (i.e., marabouts) and saintly lineages that dominated popular interpretations of Moroccan Islam in the past had a small, predominantly Arab following in Errachidia. Access to national education and television programming from the Gulf States, however, supported a critical view of maraboutism and challenged the socio-religious hierarchy that placed Arab-Sharif holy men above the other ethnic groups. Instead, the more egalitarian reform movement evaluated socio-religious status based on regular adherence to prayer, fasting, and charity as well as the core values of modesty, patience, and sincerity.

The close link between religiosity and social status placed Islamic structures at the heart of Saharan habitus (something Bourdieu overlooked in his theory of practice). The public call to prayer, broadcast from every village and neighborhood minaret (along with the two national television stations) five times each day punctuated the rhythm of daily activities, even for those who abstained from Salat (daily ritual prayer). Although Muslims have some flexibility in scheduling their own fulfillment of this daily obligation, devout Muslims in Errachidia strived to pray "on time," wherever they were when the *muwazzin* broadcast the call to prayer. This practice of praying outside the mosque blurred the division of secular and sacred space in both the household and the public sphere. The ubiquity of religious expressions in everyday conversation, even among young children, added to this impression.

The pressure to adhere to Islamic principles was more reflective of local cultural expectations for comportment than political affiliation with broader Islamic movements. In fact at the time I was conducting research, Saharans seemed reluctant to make any political statements in public because of fear of repercussions from the government.[3] In this light, my connection to a devout family leant me more respectability in *shebi* (popular, common) neighborhoods than my official government stamp of permission ever could. Yussef and his siblings earned a high level of social respect through their observations of reformist interpretations of Islamic practice and values. The women in the family were more dedicated to prayer than the men, but the whole family had a reputation for modesty, sincerity, and generosity to Saharans from all ethnic and economic backgrounds.

Research Design

A few months after I left Morocco in August 1994, Yussef's sisters decided to move back to Errachidia to live with their brothers, Hamad, who worked as a nurse practitioner in the provincial hospital. His income and presence in the household made the move feasible for three divorced sisters and their young children. This composition was unusual for households in Errachidia, where the three-generation patrilocal household was the ideal residence pattern, but it made a convenient home base for my proposed research on household health practices. I joined the household as a guest in February 1996 and became an official member by marrying Yussef at the end of the same year. Even though Yussef continued to live and work in the Western part of the country, his remittances maintained his role as the head of the family. The combination of his high status and my supplemental contributions to the household budget gave me far more power than was typical for a new bride in a rural Moroccan household. I had minimal obligations in daily chores, which freed my time and energy for research. Berber customs of honor, however, restricted my mobility after Yussef and I announced our engagement to the family. I rarely left the house without the company of another family member.

The physical characteristics of the household were more typical of the region than the social characteristics were. We lived in a six room, second floor apartment located in a densely populated neighborhood outside the market center. A nuclear family with several children rented the first floor of the building. In the simple design of cement row houses found throughout Morocco, the second floor had the advantage of access to the roof, which could serve as an extra room in the dry season. We used the roof like a walled courtyard, which provided outdoor space for drying laundry or for sleeping in the hottest months of the summer—although the annoyance of early morning flies convinced me to endure the oven-like heat inside the house. The roof was also the location of our very large satellite dish that, in the absence of strong winds, gave us access to a wide range of international television stations. This piece of technology was typical for households in the middle range of socioeconomic status in Errachidia. We lacked the wealth to afford one of the villas along the national highway, but we did have the conveniences of indoor plumbing, a gas oven, and a telephone.

The household proved to be an excellent base for my research because we had an on-going stream of visitors, many of whom came to consult Mama or Hamad about health problems. Mama provided advice using her knowledge of *dua-l-blad* (country medicine); and for more persistent or severe ailments, Hamad dispensed tablets, injections, and referrals to the provincial hospital.

The consultations were so frequent that I could have put together a research project based just on participant-observation in our front guestroom, but I was also interested in observing social relations in more traditional patrilocal households in the community.

I enlisted Mama and her sisters to help me recruit housewives to participate in my research project. We used a combination of quota and snowball methods to recruit a sample 20 households in Errachidia composed of representatives from each of the four ethnic-linguistic groups. The main criterion for participation in the study was a household composition that consisted of two generations of adult women. Ideally, I was looking for situations involving the co-residence of mother-in-law and daughter-in-law but a few of the households consisted of a mother with her adult daughter. About halfway through the study, I decided to add a comparative sample of 12 more households in Zaouia[4]—a village located further south in the valley. Overall, the majority of the households matched the social norm in both locations in that they were low-income, patrilocal, and religious. The 92 housewives who participated in the interview component of the study, ranged in age from 17 years to 89 years.[5] The original plan was to compare the health seeking behavior of women with different levels of school achievement but too few adult women in the community had attended enough school to construct a comparative sample.[6]

The study employed a range of ethnographic methods, which generated a variety of data. Over the course of 11 months in 1996, I conducted a series of 2–3 semi-structured interviews with junior and senior housewives. For the first census-oriented interviews in Errachidia, I employed a male translator to assist me. I knew the situation was less than ideal given the custom of sex segregation and the nature of my topic, but he was the most fluent and most reliable translator I could find in town. I switched strategies, however, after a few participants advised me to come back without the translator if I really wanted to know about women's health practices. At that point, Mama became my primary research assistant. Even though she spoke no English and had only a first-grade education, she understood the demands of research (from her younger brother) and, more importantly, she understood my Arabic.

Roughly half of the interviews were conducted in group settings consisting of several women living in the household and, occasionally, guests who were visiting them that day. The household interviews in both Errachidia and Zaouia produced core data on women's knowledge of maternal and child health care and introduced me to the complexity of medical pluralism. To complement the household interviews, I spoke also with midwives, herbalists, pharmacists, public health nurses, and US Peace Corps volunteers based in Errachidia. These conversations allowed me to gather diverse perspectives on the range of health resources in the region and how housewives were using them.

Because one of my main goals was to investigate health *practices* in the household, participant-observation was a crucial component of the research methodology. The interviews generated important information about how the participants represented and made sense of their health practices, but I was cautious about taking their words at face value. I knew enough about the potential for hidden agendas in Saharan social interaction to heed sociolinguistic insights about the interactional components of discourse and indirect forms of communication. With this perspective in mind, I took notes on all my interactions with the study participants, including outside of interview contexts. The breadth and depth of those notes increased the more integrated I became in the community and they provided the foundation for my interest in the implicit, non-discursive dimensions of Saharan health culture.

The preliminary analysis of my findings in 1996 provided the foundation for follow-up research in Errachidia during the summer of 1997. This short two-month study gave me the chance to conduct more systematic observations and interviews related to themes that emerged in the notes that I recorded the previous year. My observations focused on the everyday aesthetics of space and time as well as particular forms of cultural sensibility in relation to health and wellness. I also conducted informal interviews with 9 of the original participants about notions of danger, security, and vulnerability. The combination of the two projects generated the data I discuss in this book and the knowledge-in-action approach I use to interpret how culture shapes the experience of vulnerability and art of protection.

I returned to Errachidia again in summer 2005 to update my research and visit family. Although the scope of the trip was limited, my observations of how the culture had changed over time informed my perspective on the aesthetics of everyday life. I mention those observations a few times in the book, but the focus of discussion in the following chapters refers to data collected in 1996 and 1997.

CHAPTER 3

MATERNAL-CHILD
HEALTH IN PERSPECTIVE

Around the time that winter turned to spring, shortly after I settled in Er-rachidia in 1996, news of a birth came to our household. Fatim-Zahra, a long-time friend of the family had given birth to a son and her family invited us to join them in celebrating their good fortune. Saharan customs of *an-nfas* (the post-natal period) entailed a week of events culminating in the *sbuae*, a ritual in which the family officially would name the child on the seventh day after birth. The women in our household were looking forward to the sbuae because the celebration would involve singing and dancing well into the night and would allow them to wear the new outfits they had bought the previous month to mark the end of Ramadan.

I had little idea about what to expect of these events but thought that the invitation would offer me an opportunity to meet other women in the neighborhood and to recruit participants for my study. During my first month in the field, I learned about several Berber health practices through conversations with Mama about midwifery and through observations of treatments that she and her sisters administered to each other, the children, and our many visitors. The nfas presented my first chance to expand my knowledge of Saharan culture and observe the diversity of perspectives on maternal-child health in Errachidia.

Fatim-Zahra's family was *sharif* (honored or titled) — although not true sharif according to Mama's detailed taxonomy of Saharan ethnicity. She explained that true sharif Arabs are descendants of the Prophet Muhammad but this family claimed descent from a local maraboutic saint. In the socio-religious hierarchy of Saharan popular culture, however, the practical distinction between the two Arab groups was minor. Both asserted their high status by secluding women in the household and requiring them to veil their faces on the rare occasions when they did travel into public space. Berber interpretations of the local customs for sex segregation and modesty were far less confining, allowing Mama and me the freedom to accept the invitation without hesitation.

The next day, we set out shortly after the mid-afternoon prayer to represent our household in congratulating the family on the birth of their son. Following the local birth custom, we expected to find Fatim-Zahra close-by at her mother's home, but realized once we arrived that the house was too quiet. We guessed that everyone was gathered at her husband's family household about a mile down the road. The longer walk allowed me to see, for the first time, the crowded architecture of the neighborhood—a characteristic hidden from the main roads I usually traveled to reach the market or bus station. Rows of two- and three-story cinder block houses lined the dusty *pistes* in asymmetric grids with few notable features to distinguish one from the other. The absence of street names or house numbers—not to mention the apparent fondness for identical sky-blue doors and wrought-iron window coverings—made me anxiously dependant on Mama's sense of direction. As it turned out, even she was unsure of the exact location of our destination. Ultimately, the buzz of animated chatter and children running in and out of the doorway guided us to the party.

As a stranger to Fatim-Zahra's family, I felt intrusive when I realized that this initial post-natal gathering was a small intimate affair. Mama dismissed my apprehension and nudged me through the large foyer to a plain room at the back of the second-floor apartment. We left our shoes at the threshold and joined a dozen or so women crowded hip-to-hip on carpets folded along the perimeter of the cement floor. They were talking quietly and eating cookies, peanuts, and *smaida* (a powdered confection of sugar and spices) that were piled high on ornate ceramic plates. The *nafisa* (new mother), covered with three or four woolen blankets, sat on a mattress under a closed window at the far end of the narrow room. She appeared to be in her mid-twenties and had a small but solid build. Her pale complexion revealed her seclusion as well as her fatigue from the previous day's ordeal. I could not see her new son, but assumed he was hidden under the white embroidered cloth that she continuously adjusted next to her on the mattress.

The guests composed a diverse group of women—young and old, black and white—all dressed modestly but fashionably in bright *jellaba-s* (long, hooded robes) and patterned headscarves. My comprehension of Arabic was still shaky at the time, but I could follow the conversation that centered on tales about pregnancy and childbirth. In addition to comparing the effectiveness of rosemary and cinnamon infusions in easing the pain of labor, the guests offered suggestions for protecting the baby during the precarious forty days after birth and for helping Fatim-Zahra recover her strength.

One of the older women advised her to tighten a belt around her waist to regain her shape. Another guest recommended *kuhl* (antimony) to protect the infant's eyes and henna to protect the navel. Mama pointed out that Berbers used to crush dried hedgehog intestine with fresh butter and fennel seed for the infant's first taste of food. An older woman sitting across the room interjected that Arabs say the first taste should be *l-bismillah* (a charm—"in the name of Allah"—that a religious healer writes on the inside of a bowl and dissolves in water). A third woman added that in Azrou, a town in the Middle Atlas mountains, "we just give sugar and water and say '*bismillah*'." Mama insisted that the Berber way was *zwiin* (nice, beautiful) and since she had command of the floor again, added that the *nafisa* should eat hot herbs with milk and eggs and press a poultice of hot herbs between her legs to heal the vagina. Despite agreement from a few of the guests, a rotund middle-aged woman whom I later learned was the *qabla* (midwife) interjected that "we don't do that here." A younger comrade added defiantly that the Imam says "*duk shi haraam*" (that stuff is forbidden) in attempt to deflect Mama's offer to demonstrate her techniques.

Amidst the increasingly shrill cacophony of opposing opinions, Fatim-Zahra sat quietly in the corner of the room, occasionally shaking her head at someone's suggestion. I noticed that the guests seemed to pay little attention to the new mother or her son and found this behavior confusing. I thought that the purpose of this custom was to congratulate the mother and admire the baby. Why did he remain hidden from our view? Why were all these other women describing their birthing experiences, some of which happened decades ago, while Fatim-Zahra and the midwife remained silent about what happened the previous day? My research assistant was the most garrulous of all the guests and I worried that the family would rescind our invitation to attend the other events of the week. Yet, when we stood up to leave about an hour after we arrived, the family begged us to stay and then enthusiastically invited us back for the henna party at the end of the week. My sense that Mama had been rude apparently was incorrect.

On the walk home, Mama explained that Fatim-Zahra had miscarried three times prior to this pregnancy and everyone was worried about the birth. Saharan women of Mama's age (45 years) and older were familiar with the dangers of childbirth, particularly during the first 40 days post-partum when so many infants died in the past. Mama explained that midwives held the responsibility for not only helping the mother and infant through labor and delivery safely, but also keeping them alive in the weeks following the birth. Any woman, regardless of her personal experience with reproduction or educational background was eligible to help with childbirth, but it was the women with expertise in handling difficult births—prolonged labor or breech babies— who gained local reputations as midwives. The strategies they employed came from first hand observations and oral tradition, a process in which women passed knowledge to one another through stories about their experiences.

The narratives I heard that afternoon recommended a variety of herbal medicines and symbolic measures to heal the mother and protect the infant, although the specific rationale of each strategy was unclear to me at the time. Collectively, the knowledge that these ordinary housewives controlled seemed expansive, given the considerable debate about which protocols were effective. What was conspicuously missing from their stories, however, was what I expected to hear—references to public health recommendations. If everyone was so worried about the health of Fatim-Zahra's son, why did she give birth at home rather than at the provincial hospital where there were trained doctors and nurses? Why was no one discussing the option of hospital care post-partum?

The Politics of Home Birth

The simple answer to these questions is that home-based health care was a cultural norm in Errchidia. The circumstances of Fatim-Zahra's labor and delivery reflected a trend in my research sample and in the nation as a whole. A 1997 national survey found that 73.4% of births in rural Morocco took place at home (Ministere de la Sante 2000:107). The trend was slightly higher in my sample, with only 23% of mothers reporting ever giving birth in a health facility. Carla Obermeyer's analysis of data on maternal health behavior in the Demographic and Health Surveys of 1987 and 1988 found that women in Tunisia were 6 times more likely than Moroccan women to deliver in a hospital (Obermeyer 1993:358).

Attention to the location of childbirth in these studies is more than a simple matter of documenting cultural relativism in reproductive practices. Public health interest in local birth customs stems from hypotheses that link them with maternal and infant mortality. Successful public health campaigns to increase prenatal consultations and immunization coverage in rural Morocco contributed to a drop in the infant mortality rates in the past,[1] but maternal death has proven more difficult to prevent. Morocco has the highest maternal death rate (332/100,000 live births) in North Africa (Obermeyer 1993, Johns Hopkins University Center for Communication Programs 2000) and this statistic has made safe motherhood a priority for Moroccan public health.

Although population-level data have identified a number of factors, including previous miscarriage, that increase the risk of maternal death, it is impossible to predict ahead of time exactly which mothers will experience life-threatening complications such as hemorrhage, eclampsia, or infection (UN Population Fund 2008). For that reason, the World Health Organization and the Moroccan Ministry of Health have recommended that skilled health personnel assist all mothers with childbirth (Ministere de la Sante 1995, WHO 2004). Nonetheless, mothers in Errachidia continued to give birth at home.

In the past, public health hypotheses about the discrepancy between medical recommendations and women's behavior would have focused on a lack of knowledge or access to care. These factors, however, had weak applications in Fatim-Zahra's case. First, maternity care was available for free at the provincial hospital, located just a few miles from her home. Secondly, although she and all the other women in her household had no formal education, she had access to public health messages about childbirth through outreach campaigns, word of mouth, and her own past experience. In a later conversation, Fatim-Zahra told me that she had had surgery (presumably a dilation and curettage procedure) after one of her miscarriages. Despite her awareness of the risks of childbirth and services offered at the hospital, she avoided medical care in this circumstance.

An alternative explanation highlights the social and cultural factors that may have influenced Fatim-Zahra's decision. At the time of the nfas, I could only speculate about the reasons why she ignored the Ministry of Health recommendations. Neither Fatim-Zahra nor her midwife ever said much in my presence about the birth. Even in a later interview, she explained her decision in the same vague terms other women used: "when you give birth at home it is better." Over the course of several more months of research, I came to understand the complexity of social norms and cultural values that Fatim-Zahra implied in that statement, but at the time, one factor stood out in my mind.

When I returned to Fatim-Zahra's household for the henna party on the 6th day after the birth, I learned how sensitive the family was about the Arab custom of sex segregation and female seclusion. Fatim-Zahra and her midwife wanted me to photograph them as they positioned the infant to *rkib* (ride) on his mother's back for the first time. This event, which occurs on the day before the sbuae, was a momentous occasion for the household and the two women were excited about having me record it for them. As the three of us were setting up the best angle for a photograph of the baby in Fatim-Zahra's embroidered back-sling, I could hear Mama arguing with a woman outside the room. I had no idea that my camera was the root of the problem. Just as I started to snap the photo, a man's hand appeared in my lens. It was Fatim-Zahra's husband. He wanted to block the view of his wife and son because he feared that I had plans to publish the photographs in a magazine or as a postcard. After several minutes of Mama defending the honor of my intensions, Fatim-Zahra finally was able to pose for the photograph she desired.

In light of the household's strict interpretation of Arab codes for sex-segregation, this social obstacle seemed to be a plausible explanation for why they all wanted

Fatim-Zahra to give birth at home. Aside from a few women among the nursing staff and the Chinese medical volunteers, the provincial hospital was a space dominated by men. The social risk a hospital birth posed to the family may have carried greater weight than the physical risk that home birth posed to the mother. Traditional midwifery accommodated the custom of women's seclusion by assisting the labor and delivery in the mother's home.

I realized later, however, when examining this case in conjunction with all of the data I collected that year—including notes on my own experiences as a bride—that this explanation was far too simplistic, even in Fatim-Zahra's case. Interviews I conducted in other Saharan households confirmed that the preservation of the mother's honor was one factor in the preference for home birth, but all housewives recognized that they should not hold modesty or custom so precious that it endangered the life of the mother or the infant. For example, during a conversation among a group of women from Zaouia, a young Rgaiga woman named Mbarak pointed out that sometimes a doctor was necessary: "if you have no choice, or the pressure (on the body) is great, God protect us, you go to the doctor." Her sister-in-law added, "but if God gives you a soft pain (i.e., an easy labor), what do you want with the Spitar (hospital)? The house is better." The group of friends and relatives agreed with Mbarak, but they debated about how much pain warranted a trip to the hospital. The most experienced midwife among them, a Hurtani woman in her late 30s, compared labor pain to menstrual pain: "if the contractions come for three days, or four, or five, you have to go to the hospital." The other women thought that that time period was too long.

This conversation illustrates some of the ambiguity involved in assessing the social and cultural dimensions of Saharan resistance to hospital birth. Like the guests at Fatim-Zahra's nfas, Mbarak and her friends actively interpreted the health knowledge available to them rather than passively following cultural norms. They spoke like practitioners in their attempts to devise an effective plan for prevention and treatment. The household production of health (HPH) framework, however, pushed my analysis to reduce all evidence of non-biomedical knowledge to the category of "beliefs" that acted as an obstacle to hospital birth. Although the HPH model incorporated a broad range of factors that were relevant to my anthropological research, the core structure of the model was entrenched in standard biomedical definitions of health, illness, and risk. In the context of medical pluralism, the presumption of the universality of those definitions becomes a political statement regardless of the degree of objective science involved in their production.

The use of a biomedical structure for the HPH model made sense given its public health origins, but it clashed with the relativist and interpretive perspectives that dominated my training in cultural anthropology. These perspectives require ethnographers to suspend their own cultural biases in the effort to understand local meanings and practices. The biomedical constructions that shaped my own views about the protocol for a safe labor and delivery did appear in Moroccan health promotion campaigns and clinical settings, but these constructions represented only a small portion of the health knowledge Saharan women employed in the household. The emphasis on what households *were not* doing (i.e., following public health recommendations) was obscuring the cultural logic of what they *were* using to promote health and prevent illness. My own biomedical assumptions about health and illness had to loosen their dominance on my analysis so that I could incorporate the influence of the other cultural meanings of health, illness, and danger in my interpretation of household health behavior. If I wanted to understand why Fatim-Zahra chose to give birth at home, I needed to understand birth from the local perspective.

Saharan Constructions of Danger

The first layer of Saharan medical logic consisted of diverse, overlapping perspectives on the nature of health and causes of illness. Existing alongside the relatively new public health messages about maternal-child health risks was the health knowledge of local healers. Traditional midwives, fuqaha (sing., fqih), and herbalists in the suq offered a wide range of remedies and preventive measures for pregnancy, birth, and post-partum health. International scholarship on Moroccan folk medicine (*Tib at-taqliidi*) provides detailed descriptions of various ways that Moroccan healing traditions conceptualize causality, treatment, and prevention (Bakker 1992, Bellakhdar 1989, Crapanzano 1973, Geny 1979, Greenwood 1981, Westermarck 1968), but I found that Saharan housewives—including those who served as informal healers and midwives—used this knowledge extemporaneously. The housewives in my sample had limited exposure to formal sources of health knowledge because few of them owned books other than the Qur'an and they rarely consulted professional practitioners.

Instead women pooled their knowledge with their mothers, sisters, and neighbors in deciding which medicinal foods, teas, plasters, or rituals would work in a given situation. In other words, they emphasized a practical logic of prevention and healing over understanding the more general classifications of symptoms or body parts. As such, medical pluralism appeared in the household production of health as an eclectic, dynamic mix of knowledge and practices, in which knowledge of one system did not preclude use of another. I refer to the collection of customs, home remedies, and oral tradition I encountered in my study as *Saharan popular health culture*. This informal, fluctuating system of knowledge, resources, skills, and norms guided the strategies Saharan housewives used in their attempts to produce health (see Chapter 4 for an explanation of the local meaning of health).

At its most basic level, the practical logic of Saharan popular health culture linked knowledge about the causes of illness with emergent evaluations about one's susceptibility to those causes at a given moment. The housewives who participated in my study ranked childbirth as the most dangerous time in a woman's life. Although this evaluation concurred with public health notions of risk in childbirth, my observations at Fatim-Zahra's nfas suggested that Saharan protocols for controlling and avoiding danger varied considerably from public health recommendations. The comparison of my observational notes taken during my participation in four nfas rituals and interviews with housewives and traditional midwives revealed a local concern with five main etiologies of illness and death during pregnancy, childbirth, and the first 40 days post-partum.

Although the ultimate focus of household health care was the relief and prevention of physical symptoms, women's discussions about the nature of those symptoms pivoted on the identification of the original cause. This perspective was akin to the way clinicians develop a plan of action for their patients in light of relevant risk factors. Here, however, I use the broader concept of danger rather than risk to encompass the diverse medical constructs in Saharan popular health culture. The sources of danger at the heart of the 5 main illness etiologies that Saharans associated with birth included: humoral imbalance, the Eye, spirit attack, magical curses, and microbes. This list, which encompassed social and spiritual constructions of danger as well as physical constructions, revealed the holistic nature of the Saharan understanding of health and illness. Each etiology, however, depicted health dangers in a slightly different way.

Humoral Imbalance

The most common illness etiology mentioned in my field notes and interviews described maternal and child illness as an imbalance of bodily humors. The theory of *akhlaT al-insaan* (humors of the human body) came to Morocco as Arab medicine, based on the texts of Ibn Sina (Avicenna CE 980–1037), a 10th century Muslim scholar. The principles of Ibn Sina's canon of medicine draw substantially from the Greek philosopher Galen (CE 130–200), who developed Hippocrates' theory of humoral pathology into a formal science of the body. According to Ibn Sina's reasoning, the four main bodily humors — blood, phlegm, yellow bile, and black bile — contain and produce qualities that correspond to the four universal elements: fire, earth, air, and water. In health, the humors intermingle throughout the body in a state of equilibrium: heat balances cold, and dryness balances moisture. When a deficiency or excess of a particular humor causes the body to fall out of balance, the individual experiences telltale symptoms. For example, a fever signifies excess heat and an abundance of phlegm indicates excess wet and cold. The goal of humoral medicine is to administer treatments that will return the body to a state of equilibrium.

Saharan popular heath culture tended to simplify humoral theory by ignoring wet and dry qualities in diagnosis and treatment. The most common home remedies aimed to prevent or treat illnesses classified as *l-bard* (cold). The prevalence of this etiology in the household production of health resulted, in part, from an abundant supply of "hot" therapies. The hot spices, foods, and herbal infusions housewives used to counteract cold were common ingredients in Saharan cooking. Cinnamon, for example, doubled as a spice in Saharan stews and as a tisane to ease the pain of labor during childbirth. A few of the remedies I encountered included rare ingredients, such as Indian flies, which required a visit to *l-eshab* (the herbalist) who specialized in natural medicines. Otherwise, housewives could buy what they needed from spice dealers in the local suq or borrow them from the neighbor's pantry. Many of the remedies women used came from the local environment. Latifa, a divorced mother of three young children told me that she saved money by going to the river to pick wild plants for the household medicine chest. Her family was too poor to afford pharmaceutical medicines or herbs from the market. Even though she had little knowledge about plants because she grew up in town, there were enough knowledgeable women nearby whom she could ask to help her identify the plants.

In addition to the ample supply of remedies for cold illnesses, Saharan interpretations of physiology also drove a demand for them. Humoral science posits that the specific temperament or balance of humors in the body varies according to age, climate, season, and gender (Bakhtiar 1999, Belkhadar 1989). For example, women are more susceptible to cold illnesses because they have colder temperaments than men. Pregnancy, however, generates a hot temperament. According to Saharan midwives, the mother's transition from this hot condition back to her naturally cool temperament during labor and delivery had the potential to trigger a humoral imbalance during the post-partum period. The extra blankets, closed window, and the avoidance of cooling mint tea I observed at Fatim-Zahra's nfas were all strategies to prevent an excess of cold in her body. Similarly, her guests recommended that she eat hot foods to replace some of the heat lost during the birth.

The Eye

In addition to concerns about humoral imbalance, Saharans also worried about the dangers caused by social imbalance at the time of birth. The Saharan construction of l-ein (the Eye) derives from the Mediterranean notion that expressions of envy and admiration have the power to cause harm. Although other cultures focus on the power of the gaze, Moroccans worried more about the power of utterances. As Westermarck (1968) explains in his study of ritual belief in Morocco, the magical law of association by contrast implies that words trigger the occurrence of their opposite. That is, comments about beauty, health, skill, or success cause illness, misfortune, and even death. The object of the envy or admiration can be a person, an animal, or a possession, such as an automobile. Because Saharans viewed utterances as having the capacity to cause harm regardless of the speaker's intensions, words of praise were always dangerous. As I mentioned in the introductory chapter, Saharans commonly added the phrase "tabarak Allah" (may God bless you) to protect the individual from the eye. (Fulana's avoidance of the phrase was a clear indication of her malevolent intentions toward me).

This component of Saharan popular health culture helped to explain why the women at the nfas conversed about their own birth experiences rather than Fatim-Zahra or her son. The family took precautions to avoid even an accidental strike of l-ein by covering the infant with a sheet. Without opportunity to see him, the guests would have no motive to comment on his health or beauty. On other occasions, women reported that they dressed their children in dirty or torn clothing to avoid any possibility that someone would envy them. More commonly, Saharans used amulets in the form of an open hand, a gold ring, or a brass bullet adorned with a black bead or black string to protect themselves and their children from the Eye.

Another danger related to envy and l-ein that was of particular concern to new mothers was the problem of stolen milk (discussed further in Chapter 8). Saharan mothers relied on breastmilk as the primary source of nutrition and protection for their infants, but they worried about the quality of their milk and its capacity to sustain the infant, particularly during the first forty days of life. According to popular health culture, a nursing mother who envied the quality or abundance of another woman's milk (exhibited in her healthy infant) could steal the milk by sharing food with her. The process was more surreptitious than the more usual form of using praise to hit someone with the Eye because the envious mother could deny that she was nursing and render herself safe to eat with the new mother. For this reason, Fatim-Zahra avoided sharing any of the food that her guests were enjoying at the gathering.

Spirit Attack

A third source of danger that was particularly salient in Saharan childbirth customs was spirit attack. In Islamic cosmology, a jinn (pl. *jnun*) is a supernatural being that exists in the part of *eaalam al-ghaib* (the invisible world) that is closest to *ad-dunia*, the material realm of the universe where humans reside. Although jnun are neither good nor evil by nature, they act as pathogenic agents when humans disturb or offend them. Saharan popular health culture associated the jnun with two types of illness: psychological disturbances and the sudden onset of severe physical disability, such as paralysis. Saharans explained the mechanism by which a jinn caused illness as *drub* (to strike) or *darn* (to bother—here, in the sense of haunting) the victim rather than as possession. Both forms required the intervention of a *fqih* or a ritual ceremony to appease the spirit and drive it away. Household health practices focused more on preventing an attack by avoiding the places where the jnun reside or making offerings to them. Local folklore claimed that they live in stagnant water, travel by wind, and are attracted to blood. Any blood shed during childbirth would increase the danger of disturbing the jnun.

Oral tradition included a multitude of ways to protect mothers and infants from spirit attack, but it took me awhile to gather these data. Housewives referred to jnun using indirect and even cryptic speech to avoid summoning them or offending them. Once I realized that terms such as *mu'miniin* (the believers) or *muulin ad-dar* (the owners of the house) referred to jnun in certain contexts, I gained a deeper understanding of several symbolic strategies women were using to protect themselves and their children. For example at Fatim-Zahra's nfas, the family burned incense of benzoin (*jawi*) to appease the jnun. The debate about what the infant should take as his first taste of food also included protective strategies against spirit attack: Berbers traditionally gave crushed hedgehog intestine and Arabs gave Qur'anic talismans. The guests also recommended putting kuhl around the infant's eyes and henna around his navel to block a jinn from entering his body.

In other interviews, lay midwives told me about the importance of sprinkling salt and *Harmal* (African rue) on the infant at the time of birth to ward off any jnun that might be attracted to blood spilled at the time of delivery. Others insisted that the infant should be swaddled in clothing that was untouched by a knife or scissors because steel frightens or offends the jnun. At the nfas celebration I attended in Zaouia in October 1996, the mother introduced her newborn to the spirits of the house by strapping him to her back and stepping into each room while carrying an urn burning jawi.

Magical Curses

Local concerns about the power of spirits to cause harm also figured in the fourth category of danger in Saharan popular health culture. Local etiologies identified symbolic magic as an illness agent in two ways: *tqaf* (magical curses) and *siHr* (sorcery). According to one Rgaiga grandmother in Errachidia, some women summoned the jnun to assist in their use of magic to cause harm. She was one of the few participants in the study who was willing to talk about magic at all. Devout Muslims shunned such practices and anyone suspected of using them developed a negative reputation. For that reason, it was difficult to assess women's knowledge about sorcery or how protect oneself from it.

Nonetheless, I knew about its existence from chance encounters. For example, a midwife I was visiting advised a young woman to consult a fqih in the center of town about infertility she thought was the result of a curse. The woman, who had come in search of an herbal remedy for the problem, explained that recently her neighbor had been burning strange incense that was wafting over to her house. Because this neighbor was also a cousin of her husband (and thus his ideal marriage partner), the new wife thought that the woman, out of envy, might be attempting to use tqaf to make her infertile. The midwife agreed that this etiology was plausible, but claimed that she had no knowledge of tqaf. I suspected my presence during the conversation may have persuaded the midwife to refer the woman to the fqih instead of handling the treatment herself.[2]

The more feared form of symbolic magic in Saharan society was siHr. According to oral tradition throughout Morocco, siHr involved disguising carrion or parts of an exhumed corpse as meat in a stew. Alternatively, a sorcerer could use the hands of a corpse to prepare couscous. The intent of both practices was murder. Whether anyone ever employed this method in an attempted homicide is unclear, but rumors about the possibility circulated in women's discussions about the cause of severe digestive illnesses with sudden onset.

According to these discussions, the danger of siHr for new mothers was intensified because Saharan birth customs entailed the preparations of special therapeutic food for the mother. This practice of serving the mother an individual meal diverged from the more common style of eating meals where members of the household would take their place around one large plate of food. If meat was part of the meal, one person would divide the meat into equal portions in full view of everyone sitting at the table. Although communal eating provided a form of protection against sorcery, sharing food with other people exposed the nafisa to the dangers of humoral imbalance and stolen breast milk. In attempt to manage all of these dangers at once, the nafisa had to rely on someone *qariib* (close) to prepare her food. This trusted person may be the midwife or a close relative (mother or sister) who ensured that the food was safe.

Microbes

Popular interpretations of siHr and its power to cause harm combined the contagious symbolism of death with popular understanding of germ theory. Although I heard the term microbe frequently in discussions about health, my observations suggested that public health messages about hygiene and contagion tended to fragment and attach to previously existing illness etiologies. In the case of siHr, both scientific and symbolic theories complemented each other and provided a more powerful reason for avoiding meat that was potentially poisonous. In other contexts, however, there was less overlap. For example, I noticed that household members regularly shared the same glass even when someone was sick. In all but a few of the village households I visited, soap was a precious commodity that households reserved for the toilet, bath, and washing clothing. Glass washing was more a process of rinsing with cold water—often from the irrigation canal—rather than sterilizing with soap and hot water.

Aside from concerns about poisonous meat, Saharan popular health culture incorporated germ theory into maternal-child health practices in two primary ways related to tetanus prevention. The midwives who participated in the study all emphasized the need to use a clean instrument to cut the umbilical cord and the mothers in the study mentioned the use of immunizations as a strategy to prevent illness in themselves and their children. In contrast to their resistance to hospital birth, the majority of housewives in Errachidia and Zaouia used immunizations enthusiastically. One Hurtani grandmother claimed in an interview that "everyone in Errachidia immunizes."

Her assessment of the compliance rate had some accuracy with respect to my sample. All but 3 mothers of young children reported that they immunized both themselves (against tetanus) and their children. A neighbor of Fatim-Zahra's mother explained that the older women remembered dangers of measles in the past and could see that immunizations prevented that illness, although they had little understanding of the scientific explanation for their effectiveness. The local association of immunizations as a way to prevent child death motivated a few women to seek more than the medical recommendation for pre-natal immunization. For example, a Berber mother in her late twenties reported that she had been immunized 9 times even though she only had 2 children.

When I asked how they know about immunizations, housewives said they heard from other women, radio, television, or the hospital that they were good for health. Their compliance with public health recommendations, however, was not completely voluntary. A few mothers, for example, said proof of immunization was required to obtain a child's birth certificate. Additionally, the national immunization campaign, conducted every year since 1987 actively recruited participants. Zahra, a middle-aged Berber mother of 5 children said that a car drove through the neighborhoods of Errachidia announcing through a megaphone the upcoming immunization campaign.

A more extreme case of recruitment occurred in Zaouia during the immunization campaign in 1996 (also discussed in Chapter 6). The village nurse enlisted the *mqaddam* (local government official) to locate the women and children whom he identified as needing immunizations and escort them back to the clinic. The mqaddam was an easy-going young man in his mid-twenties from a respected Berber family but his official title linked the campaign to an authoritarian state government that no one dared to resist openly, even in this remote part of the country. Nonetheless, a few young women managed to avoid the campaign by tending the fields on the far side of the river that morning.

Despite the coercive techniques that the public health staff used to increase immunization compliance in the village, the overall feel of the event was relaxed. The dozens of women and children who were waiting their turn in front of the clinic caught up with news and joked with each other about the process. Many of them knew the nurses who had come from the regional health dispensary to help with the campaign and seemed equally familiar with the procedures of biomedicine. These same women who accepted a biomedical version of pre-natal care, however, expressed in later interviews a resistance to hospital birth.

This paradox reflected the complexity involved in the study of health promotion in a context of medical pluralism. My observations in Morocco were similar to the findings of anthropological research in other cultures (Finnerman 1989, Inhorn 1994). The adoption of one aspect of biomedical knowledge did not necessarily lead to acceptance of the whole system. Furthermore, the adoption of a new practice, such as immunization added to previous health practices rather than replaced them. Although the coexistence of belief in microbes and the Eye or humoral imbalance may seem irrational from a scientific perspective, the overlap of diverse etiologies in Saharan popular health did follow a system of cultural logic about vulnerability to health dangers.

As I explained in the introduction to the book, my understanding of this local cultural logic emerged from an excursion outside the usual boundaries of medical anthropology. The 5 dimensions of Saharan medical pluralism that I outlined in this chapter provide a foundation for my interpretation of local health practices, but the link between knowledge and practice was more complex than previous health behavior theories have suggested. The next step in my analysis of household health practices entailed situating women's decisions in the broader social and cultural context of everyday experience.

The importance of examining the broader social and cultural context stemmed from the nature of household health care. The co-existence of multiple ways of identifying and responding to health dangers presented household healers with considerable ambiguity, particularly in relationship to prevention. Traditional midwives had no scientific tests or computer monitors to help them interpret the degree of danger the mother and infant faced during a particular labor and delivery. Instead, they had to rely on more general knowledge about the circumstances that put individuals in danger. The formal, oral and text-based knowledge I described above was abstract and ambiguous when applied to the real life circumstance of pregnancy or labor. Mothers and their assistants had to weigh a number of factors when deciding how to act. Which of the multiple sources of danger applied to the circumstances of that particular pregnancy or delivery? What resources were available to prevent those dangers? What circumstances would increase the mother's or infant's vulnerability to those dangers?

These questions begin to illuminate the reasons why a woman might comply with public health recommendations for immunization against tetanus but resist the recommendation for giving birth in a medical facility. Since microbes represented only one of the 5 main childbirth dangers and medical facilities ignored the other dangers, many Saharan mothers felt safer giving birth at home. In some circumstances, however, Saharan women chose to give birth in a medical facility. To gain insight into the logic Saharan women used in discerning the difference between those two circumstances, the next chapter examines the basic structures of everyday household life that shape the cultural meanings of vulnerability and security.

CHAPTER 4

THE AESTHETICS OF
SAHARAN DOMESTIC LIFE

The five types of illness etiologies outlined in the previous chapter provide a glimpse of how Saharan housewives viewed themselves in the world. The combined constructs depict a precarious environment, full of visible and invisible dangers in the form of unbalanced humors, envious neighbors, jnun, magic, and microbes. The abundance of protective amulets, tonics, and charms I observed in the local suq suggested the extent to which Saharans felt vulnerable to these health threats.

The use of so many different forms of protection struck me as a contradiction with Islamic teachings about Allah's power to control fate. Although Saharans were careful to say *insha'allah* (if God wants) whenever referring to future activities or events, the practical side of the culture was far less submissive. The more I examined the connections between everyday domestic practices and the household production of health, the more I recognized women's agency in the household and the community. In contrast to other anthropologists who have written about Muslim women's manipulation of and resistance to cultural norms as idiosyncratic actions (e.g., Abu Lughod's 1993, Early 1993, Wikan 1996), I noticed collective patterns in Saharan behavior. These implicit patterns or structures guided the way housewives tried to promote health and prevent illness in the household.

This chapter examines those structures by framing them in relationship to Saharan habitus and embodied experience. More specifically, it describes the underlying principles of everyday household practice as they pertain to the lived meaning of health in Saharan culture. The analysis submerges the household production of health framework into the flow of local meanings and social politics by considering what qualities Saharan housewives tried to produce in their attempts to protect themselves and their children from the health dangers described in Chapter 3. In making this analytical shift from past interpretations of the HPH model, my aim is not to dismiss or undermine biomedical definitions of health or risk, but rather to gain a better understanding of the cultural logic of Saharan household practices. While the previous chapter introduced the main components of popular knowledge about health and health dangers, this chapter explains the implicit structures though which Saharan housewives interpreted and applied abstract information from medical texts and oral tradition.

The Lived Meaning of Health

In general, the term *health* is both a positive and negative concept. On one hand, it refers to the absence of illness. On the other hand it refers to a state that represents the positive functioning of the body according to particular subjective and objective measures. For example, biomedicine uses technical instruments to measure bodily signs, such as temperature, blood pressure, or cholesterol levels to evaluate an individual's health in comparison to normative levels in a population. At the same time, the individual evaluates how s/he feels in comparison to his or her normal bodily experience. Saharan households used a similar combination of objective cultural knowledge and subjective embodied experience to assess health status, but they rarely had access to scientific instruments for measuring bodily signs. Instead, housewives relied on shared knowledge about the meaning of *SiHa* (health).

In conversation, Saharan housewives used the word SiHa to mean more than simply the absence of illness. To say *endha SiHa* (she has health)—as Fulanah said to me—was to say in a general sense that the woman was strong and had a hearty appetite. The lived meaning of health, however, had multiple components that pertained to Saharan values and expectations for men, women, and children. These values and expectations structured and were structured by common patterns of practice in everyday life, including: the rhythm of work and rest, the spatial arrangement of activities in the household, and the combination of foods and spices in traditional cuisine. According to Bourdieu's logic of practice, it is through these kinds of habitual practices that culture shapes the subjective experience of the body. The embodiment of habitus, especially as bodily hexis (Bourdieu 1990:69–70) establishes a subjective baseline for interpreting and applying the generalized, abstract information about health (e.g., as a balance of bodily humors) found in popular health culture. Hence, the lived meaning of SiHa stemmed from the extent to which bodily experience corresponded to embodied expectations.

Formal medical knowledge contributed to those expectations through its characterization of particular practices as healthy. Medical texts such as *Medicine of the Prophet* (al-Jawziyya 1998) and Ibn Sina's *Canon of Medicine* influenced Saharan habitus through their recommendations about such things as the components of a healthy diet, the ideal time and duration for sleep, and the procedures for maintaining a sufficiently clean body and household. Few Saharan housewives read those texts, but they heard about them through local healers and television. Medical advice, however, coexisted with and sometimes conflicted with other cultural expectations for the body related to morality, productivity, etiquette, beauty, and security. From the holistic perspective of ethnography, then, the lived meaning of SiHa was intricately connected to Saharan interpretations of concepts such as *la-bas* (fine, all right) and *b-khair* (well, safe) [translations from Harrell and Sobelman 1966:5, 215], which Saharans used in conversation to convey a general state of well-being.

To understand the goal of the household production of SiHa, my interpretation of Saharan health practices emerged from an examination of the basic principles of body, self, time, and space that organized domestic life. I derived these principles from the qualitative analysis of the observational field notes and interview transcripts I recorded in 1996 and 1997. The analysis revealed four main themes in the cultural organization of household and community life: interiority, unity, balance, and purity. These culturally distinct structures appeared redundantly in multiple aspects of the everyday life of Saharan households. Together the themes reflect what Bourdieu would describe as the habitus of Saharan society, but I have chosen to modify the concept of habitus within the framework of cultural phenomenology. Following Desjarlais' (1992) perspective on embodied experience, I characterized these themes as implicit aesthetic structures to highlight the active role Saharan housewives played in composing an environment that promoted health and well-being.

Interiority

Over the course of several months of visiting and conducting interviews in over 30 households, I came to interpret the sincerity of women's comments and stories about health in accordance to where we sat and who participated in the conversation. The households I visited followed a definite pattern of structuring space and coordinating social interaction within that space. The parts of the house closest to the front door served as a transitional space between the public and private lives of the household members. It was here that Saharan households entertained guests, especially those visitors who were socially distant from the family because of either their elite or outsider status. My status as an educated American put me in the category of an honored guest and my visits usually took place in the household's *biit l-diaf* (the room of guests). One of the Arab households in the Errachidia sample was even more cautious and held our interviews in the hallway near the front door.

Because hospitality was one of their core cultural values, Saharans decorated the *biit l-diaf* with thick brocade fabric, foam banquettes, pillows, plush carpets, and serving tables to maximize the guest's comfort. The décor of these rooms gave me a sense of the household's economic status, but it was not a reliable measure of wealth. In summer months, housewives stacked the cushions and rugs along one wall and replaced them with cooler woven mats as floor coverings. Mistakenly, I interpreted that arrangement as a sign of poverty until I gained access to the interior of a few of the households in the study (i.e., as I came to know them better). I learned from those visits that housewives kept their valuable objects, such as silver tea sets, televisions, and stereo equipment closer to the center of the house in the family's private quarters. In my own household, the most valuable items (e.g., jewelry, fancy caftans, sugar, books) were locked in an interior storage room to hide them from all the neighbors and extended family members who visited us on a daily basis.

In addition to restricting guests' access to the interior of the house, Saharan households also restricted family members' access to the guest room. The household members responsible for entertaining the guests with conversation and refreshments were the adult men and senior women. The subordinate members of the household, including the children and daughters-in-law contributed to the hospitality by preparing and delivering the refreshments, which could range from mint tea and bread to a multi-course meal. This arrangement of household space diverged from the more common description of the public-private dichotomy in the Middle East in which women occupy the interior *haram* and men have the freedom to interact with each other in the public parts of the household, village, and city. In Saharan culture, senior women—the age cohort that is old enough to be a mother-in-law or grandmother—had access those public places as well and they had the right to talk with men without compromising their honor. The *agusa* (old woman) was the gatekeeper to the interior quarters of the house and she was as likely to prevent female guests as male guests from entering the household's private quarters.

Khaltii Zahra (Aunt Zahra) was the strictest gatekeeper in my research sample. She was a Berber grandmother in her late 60s who lived on the opposite end of Errachidia from our household. The first time I met her in May 1996, I thought she looked out of place in her son's large modern house. Their guest room, which was unusually large for the area, displayed the family's wealth in the form of ornately upholstered foam banquettes in green and gold that lined the periphery of the room and a deep pile, red wool carpet that covered most of the cement floor. Despite the plush comfort of the banquets, Khaltii Zahra preferred to sit on the floor with her wiry, sunburned legs strait out in front of her. Her traditional village attire of layered cotton dresses, calico pantaloons, black *taharuut,* and long hennaed braids clashed with the modern appearance of the house, making her seem all the more exotic.

Zahra's 25-year-old granddaughter Malika and her husband, both friends of our household, helped us recruit the household into the study. Zahra had extensive knowledge of herbal medicines and bone-setting, plus she lived with one of her daughters-in-law and, thus, fit the criteria for my research sample. The first two interviews with the household produced a wealth of information about popular health culture and maternal-child health practices in the past. Zahra seemed to respond to my questions before I asked them and talked so fast that I trouble capturing all that she said in my notebook. She was the only woman in the study who could list from memory more than half of the 44 herbs in the popular health-promoting mixture called *ras al-hanuut* (head of the shop). She said that she learned about health *b-rasii* (literally, by my head) and from her experience raising 10 children with little money and little help from her husband.

I learned during my third visit to her household, however, that there was a limit to the information she was willing to share with me. The questionnaire for the third interview focused on topics related to contemporary household health practices and the contributions of junior women (daughters and daughters-in-law) to the household production of health. Despite my requests, Khaltii Zahra never let me speak with her 18-year-old daughter-in-law, the second wife of her middle-aged son. She told me that the young woman knew nothing. The only time I saw her was when she brought mint tea and cookies for us at the end of the interview. Before I could ask her a question, she returned quickly to the kitchen at the back of the house. Malika and Zahra's youngest daughter, Khadija did stay for the interview, but Zahra did all of the talking and all of her responses steered the conversation back to Saharan culture in the past. The interview struck me as a kind of performance that showcased her knowledge of health, but prevented me and my research assistant from knowing much of anything about her household's current circumstances.

Khaltii Zahra's decision to safeguard information in this socially distant context reproduced a more general pattern of interiority in Saharan culture. The most prominent symbol of the pattern at the community level was the ksar, the type of walled village found throughout Morocco's southeast region. The architectural design of these traditional villages, in which Khaltii Zahra and the majority of the other senior women in the study spent their childhood, united several two-story adobe households arranged wall-to-wall in a rough rectangle with a courtyard in the middle. This arrangement created ramparts with one common gate, which made it easier for villagers to defend against hostile invaders.

The ksar architecture divided the social world into concrete categories of Us and Them, even in ethnically heterogeneous villages such as Zaouia. Communal property and cooperative labor united the various households of the ksar as a spatially oriented social unit. Women from other villages or nomadic households who married into the ksar created links to external social groups, but even those ties had the potential to be antagonistic. An elderly Hurtani woman who had married at age 13 into a family living in the old ksar in Zaouia told me that her mother-in-law prevented her from going to the gate of the ksar to see her mother when she came to visit.

The need for village ramparts diminished over time as the threat of raiding warriors disappeared with colonialism. With the help of remittances from migrant workers, Saharan families began to move out of the communal ksar building into free-standing houses in the late 1960s. Nonetheless, the opposition of insider and outsider persisted as a prominent theme in Saharan social life and other modes of interiority served to protect households from harm. One of the common modes of protection was deceit. Although this practice contradicted the local cultural value of sincerity, revealing too much information could be dangerous in the hands of an untrustworthy outsider, who might be able to cause harm through the Eye, magical curses, or gossip.

The division of *nahna* (us) and *huma* (them) was a common trope in the suspicious way housewives assessed a social situation and in the strategies they used to protect themselves and their households. They restricted the sharing of information about events and relationships in the household to the members' most trusted friends and family. The technique Khaltii Zahra used to guard information about her household was to steer the conversation to collective memories of the past and popular knowledge of herbal remedies. On the occasions when she did divulge information about her personal experience, it was about the distant past. For example, she told me about her first pregnancy when she was a teenager and a time when her 28-year-old son was a child and hospital medicines failed to cure his terrible case of diarrhea. Strategies other housewives used to avoid disclosing personal information in uncertain social situations included the repeated use of common religious expressions (e.g., Allah is present or praise be to Allah) or the use of superficial ambiguous responses to direct questions. For example, in cases when a family member was ill, women described the condition as *ayan* (tired) or *ghair l-bard* (just cold) rather than using the term mariid (sick) or explaining the particular symptoms. They only discussed those details with close friends and family whom they trusted to assist in the healing process.

Another common way that housewives tried to protect themselves from attacks from the Eye or magical curses adapted the ksar's barrier model to create a style of interiority in their everyday practices. In addition to organizing the space of the household so that all the valuable objects stayed in the interior away from the public gaze, Saharan housewives strived to conceal their bodies and emotions in public contexts. In villages such as Zaouia, women covered themselves with simple black or worn sheets when they left the house. In town, women wore headscarves and jellaba-s over their clothing. These conventional styles of dress also represented the Islamic core value of modesty, but all the adult women in the study wore these coverings regardless of their level of religiosity. Moreover, I noticed that despite the intense heat of the desert, women added more layers of clothing when they were sick or were traveling to another town or village. I interpreted this practice as an attempt to increase their protective barriers in contexts when they felt more vulnerable. The use of amulets, incense, and perfume also contributed to these efforts as symbolic barriers. For example, one of my sisters-in-law brought perfume to protect her father while he was in the hospital. After she sprayed the cheap floral scent around his bed, she noticed my puzzled look and explained that the odor of the sick and dying was dangerous, especially to someone who is weak.

Alternatively, housewives reproduced the aesthetic of interiority through the management of emotion. Women who maintained a pleasant disposition even in times of great hardship—including the loss of their children through death or divorce—earned the respect of other women in their social sphere. Emotional control demonstrated an acceptance of fate, which is a virtue in Islam, and simultaneously downplayed the household's vulnerability. A major part of my socialization into my husband's household was learning to stifle my reactions to family news, whether it was good or bad, to prevent the neighbors from knowing our business. It was fine to express emotion loudly in ritual contexts, such as funerals, weddings, or other celebrations. Outside of those contexts, however, emotional expression risked triggering the negative effects of gossip or envy. Together these practices of constructing a barrier around the household's points of vulnerability were a constant, implicit component of the household production of health.

The aesthetic of interiority was also a dominant force in explicit household healing practices as Saharan housewives rarely consulted practitioners outside their social circle. They preferred to treat illnesses in the house first, keeping any information about the illness within the safe interior of the household. Each household I visited kept a supply of herbal medicines on hand to treat common ailments, such as colds, digestive complaints, headaches, and rheumatism. The time span for evaluating a treatment's effectiveness was 3 days. If symptoms persisted for more than 3 days, most housewives said that they tried another home remedy rather than consult a professional practitioner. The most common choice of alternate therapy was another herbal remedy, but several women in the study used fire cauterization, cupping, religious charms, and offerings to sacred shrines. The wide range of medical pluralism in Saharan popular health culture contributed to prolonged home treatment in some cases. One middle-aged mother of 5 children in Zaouia suffered for a month with pain in her abdomen and frequent vomiting. She thought she had a problem with her *masran* (intestine) but refused to go to the health dispensary for a consultation. Another middle-aged father from Errachidia suffered from abdominal pain for 15 days during which he refused to eat or drink. When finally he agreed to go to the hospital, he died in the emergency room. My brother-in-law who worked as a nurse in the hospital saw cases of delayed medical consultation on a regular basis, despite the availability of free health care. The pattern of avoidance, however, was not universal. Three women in the study reported that they had gone to the hospital for illness in the past, although two said the medicine prescribed did not work and they returned to home remedies. Several other young housewives had consulted the health dispensary staff for birth control pills and 15 women reported giving birth to at least one of their children in the hospital.

The one consistent exception to the pattern of interiority in health care was sickness in young children (under age 5). Two part-time spiritual healers in town specialized in treating children and several participants said they had consulted them in the past. Additionally, both mothers and grandmothers specified the hospital as a resource for treating young children if herbal remedies failed to work after three days.[1] Housewives were familiar with the names of pharmacy medicines for coughs, fever, diarrhea, and eye infections, but they did not always follow the doctor's directions when using those medicines. For example, the antibiotic salve for eye infections doubled as a tisane against diarrhea according to popular health culture. Alternatively, three mothers claimed that it was good to share the medicine prescribed to one child in the household with all the other children in the household to prevent the illness from spreading.

Unity

The practice of treating all the children in the household the same way is an example of a second aesthetic pattern in Saharan domestic life. Similar to the way that the walls of the ksar molded the households of the village into a social unit Saharan domestic practices aimed to create unity in the household. The custom in which family members shared the same large plate at meal times was one of the prominent symbols of social unity in the Saharan lifestyle. Housewives served the traditional midday meal of couscous or vegetable stews on a large round ceramic plate, which they placed on a low round table. The members of the household sat on cushions around the table and ate the portion of food in front of them. They also drank from the same cup during the meal even if the household owned several cups.

Both activities reinforced the notion that the members of the group were connected as parts of the whole even though Saharan households were resolutely hierarchical. Regardless of the household's ethnicity, men had more rights than women, and elders had more privileges than children and young adults. Within each segment of the hierarchy, however, egalitarianism and communal property were the norm. In the village, the men of the house shared the labor needed to cultivate the household's trees and fields, and in town, they pooled their income. Similarly, the women of the house shared just about everything: clothing, jewelry, perfume, make-up, childcare, and housework responsibilities. Some households delegated responsibilities according to individual skills in cooking and cleaning, while others rotated responsibility for chores in attempt to distribute the workload more evenly.

I was impressed by the harmonious coordination of housework among the four women in my own household, but neighborhood gossip indicated that other households experienced more turmoil. The source of tension was often the family's criticism of a daughter-in-law. For example, in Errachidia one Arab family complained repeatedly that the new bride was careless when washing her brother-in-law's laundry and that she hoarded her small income from weaving and embroidery. The household's expectation of unity trumped Moroccan family law, which stipulated that wives had no responsibility to contribute their property and income to their husband's household. In the past, a woman's wealth took the form of livestock or palm trees, which she left in the care of her parents or brothers. The new phenomenon of women's income, however, was an ambiguous category. It resembled men's income, which was a communal resource for the whole household. Although Moroccan law provided women with a source of insurance in the case of divorce, it also increased the odds of divorce in Errachidia.[2]

The addition of a new bride into the traditional patrilocal household in Errachidia Province created a rupture in the aesthetic order of domestic life. Despite the cultural preference for marriage between patrilineal first cousins, brides often came from outside the groom's household and occasionally from another village or town. The admission of someone with outsider status to the private quarters of the household contradicted the Saharan principle of interiority. Uncertainty about a bride's trustworthiness tended to make her connection to the groom's family tenuous at first. This pattern of marginalization indicated to me that unity was a structure that households actively achieved rather than assumed to be an automatic outcome of domestic life. Brides had to establish their place in the unified whole or risk divorce. The primary mechanisms for creating unity occurred through the sharing of blood, milk, and food with household members.

The way that brides established a blood connection with her husband's household was through having children. Blood relationships, particularly in the nuclear family represented the strongest type of social connection in Saharan society. Parents and children had a moral obligation to help each other in all circumstances. Grandparents, paternal uncles and aunts, and paternal cousins also carried secondary-level responsibilities to provide financial and social support when one's parents or siblings were unable or unwilling to help. The obligation increased when the extended family lived in the same household. My research assistant, Mama, explained that friends can help as well in a time of need, but it was not an obligation. In her mind, a family member's refusal to help broke the bond of blood; they were no longer family.

Adherence to the aesthetic of unity left little room for individualism in Saharan families. The well-being of the group rose and fell with the successes and problems of each member. Ideally, members of the nuclear family should share all of their resources unconditionally. Even though Islamic law stipulates that women inherit only half of their brothers' share, Saharan customs obliged brothers to care for their sisters in times of need. In both Errachidia and Zaouia, women who divorced their husbands returned to live with their parents and brothers. In three of the households in my sample, the divorced daughters brought their children with them as well. Technically the children were part of their father's lineage, but Saharan women viewed the kinship bonds that a child had with its mother to be as strong as the bonds with the father because of connections created through milk relationships.

According to Saharan popular culture, breastfeeding created social bonds between a mother and the children she nursed. Saharan housewives viewed breast milk as a substance that established a lifetime of love and respect. Children who nursed from the same woman also shared in this kind of connection. The principle of milk relationships strengthened the sense of unity established through the sharing of blood in the nuclear family and created the possibility of expanding the unit through breastfeeding other women's children. This practice occurred when a neighbor or family member was too sick to feed her own child or when two close friends wanted to link themselves and their children in a family-like relationship. Mothers were careful about offering to nurse another woman's child, however, because that child would become a symbolic sibling with her own children. Since milk-siblings were forbidden to marry, this act of charity could limit potential marriage opportunities for ones children in the future.

A third way that Saharan brides established social ties and moral obligations with their husbands' households was through the sharing of food. The practice of sharing meals from the same plate served as a symbolic statement of equality among members of Saharan households, who described their connection to each other with the phrase *kiif-kiif* (same-same). Similarly, friends and neighbors who shared food created a structure of unity at the community level. This type of bond was symbolically weaker and shorter-lived than blood ties or milk ties, but nonetheless the practice of sharing food served to increase trust in distrusting society. As such, food was the pivotal component of Saharan hospitality.

Bread held the highest symbolic value in creating social equivalence between two unrelated people, but Saharan households prepared a wide range of foods to share with their guests and neighbors. The social contexts for sharing food ranged from sending a gift of cookies to the neighbors during Ramadan to hosting the entire village for lunch at a wedding or infant naming ceremony. Housewives participated in regular exchanges of food through the custom of afternoon visiting (discussed further in the next section). This custom allowed women to maintain social networks despite cultural restrictions on their access to public space. My research assistant, however, frequently commented that the quality of food offered during these visits symbolically reflected the nature of relationship between the host and the guests. In her mind, anyone who served us crusts of bread left over from lunch was telling us indirectly not to return.

Gifts of food also played a central role in the spiritual dimension of the aesthetic of unity in Saharan domestic life. In addition to the desire to create social unity in the household and community, Saharan housewives tried to achieve a sense of unity with Allah and other Muslims though moral and spiritual practices. The moral practices that Saharan housewives associated with the creation of spiritual unity derived from the Islamic concept of zakat (almsgiving). In its most simplified form, housewives gave small gifts of food (e.g., a bowl of sugar or flour) to beggars. Women also used the term *Sadaqa* (charity) to describe gifts given to the sick or in honor of a sick relative or friend to gain spiritual credit. In general housewives said that they served Allah by helping other people, whether that be through their work as midwives, visiting a sick friend, or contributing money or labor to the mosque.

The motivation for accumulating spiritual credit was twofold. Islamic teachings characterize humans as having both spiritual and material components, which struggle against each other during the person's lifetime. To gain access to heaven on the Day of Judgment, each person must demonstrate that *ar-ruh* (the spirit), which connects humans to Allah has prevailed over *l-jism* (the flesh, body). Saharans represented the struggle between ar-ruh and l-jism through a popular analogy in which two invisible angels hover over each person and scrutinize his activities. The angel on the left side symbolizes the lower human drives and behaviors and records all of the sins or errors she commits against Allah and the Muslim community. The angel on the right side symbolizes the higher spiritual self and records all the pious and moral acts inspired by ar-ruh.

In addition to the long-term goal of gaining access to heaven, Saharan housewives also said that the regular performance of good deeds could have short-term benefits. One of the benefits housewives hoped to attain by giving alms and helping others in the community was good health among the members of their own households. It would be blasphemous for a devout Muslim to claim that the kind of reciprocity that created social alliances could also influence the will of God, but the Qur'an does suggest that Allah favors those who follow aS-SaraT al-mustaqiim (the straight path) (e.g., Qur'an 4:65–69). Khaira, the Berber grandmother mentioned in the Introduction understood the rewards of good behavior to come in the form of divine intervention:

> Where you go in this life, you find compassion. It is the compassion that goes with us and comes with us, the compassion of Allah ... You will be number one with Allah and good with Him and with his followers. Where you put your hand, you will succeed. If you want to talk to some people or if you want to go one place, Allah makes it easy ... (October 1996) (MacPhee 2003:73).

For Saharan women like Khaira the straight path included both moral and spiritual practices. When I asked the women of her household what they did to keep themselves and their children healthy, Khaira said that she prayed and the rest was up to Allah. Her statement demonstrated her faith and acceptance of God's will, but it also revealed the centrality of religion in everyday life. Khaira was devout in her performance of *Salat*, the daily prayer ritual. She was among the participants in the study who heeded the public call to prayer, even if it meant interrupting one of our interviews so that she could perform the ritual recitation of Qur'anic verses and praise for Allah. Although few women went to the mosque to pray (Khaira prayed at home), the calls to prayer unified devout Muslims five times each day by coordinating the group in simultaneous activities of bowing, kneeling, and reciting. The prayer ritual also unified the parts of the day into a coherent, cyclical sense of time.

Daily participation in the Salat ritual shaped the lived meaning of SiHa for Saharan housewives in two ways, both of which reflect the cultural aesthetic of unity. First, the timing of the calls to prayer set a rhythm for daily activities. Over time, Saharans internalized that schedule as the normal rhythm for bodily experience. Embodied expectations about the normal times to feel hungry or tired coordinated with the Salat cycle. Salat also required Muslims to perform ablutions to ritually cleanse the body from the defiling secretions of al-jism (e.g., urine, feces, semen, etc.). Hence, the ritual also established embodied expectations about the appropriate frequency and timing of digestion, menstruation, and sexual activity. Saharan housewives were interested particularly in promoting the health of *l-masran* (the intestine) as a way of coordinating digestion with cultural expectations about health and ritual purity.[3] Khaira advocated eating figs for this purpose.

A second way that the Salat ritual shaped the lived meaning of health stemmed from the experience of unity in prayer itself. The Arabic word *tawHiid* (unity) refers to the oneness of Allah (i.e. as opposed to polytheism and the Christian trinity), who Muslims understand to be an all-powerful but compassionate and merciful creator. The mystical Sufi influence in Moroccan Islam emphasized the value of understanding the meaning of tawHiid through meditative chanting (*dhiker*), trance (*hadra*), or mindful submission (*khushu'*) to Allah in ritual prayer. Although the ultimate goal of these practices was spiritual transcendence, they established an internalized connection between particular bodily experiences and the concept of well-being. The achievement of tranquil euphoria, which Saharans associated with spiritual unity, required a focused mind and managed emotions. According to the popular health culture, emotions such as fear, envy, and worry agitated *l-qalb* (the heart) and closed it to the experience of faith. This condition, in turn, could lead to all kinds of illnesses in other parts of the body. Faith, on the other hand, brought *raha-wa-l-khair* (rest and well-being) by enacting divine spirit in the body.[4]

Saharan housewives had difficulty achieving this ideal state of being. Problems related to economic insecurity, illness, divorce, and other disputes within the family and with neighbors interfered with their attempts to focus their minds and manage their emotions. For most women the tranquil euphoria of spiritual unity was a fleeting experience. Nonetheless, it was a vital component of the lived meaning of SiHa because popular knowledge claimed that the negative emotions that produced sickness of the heart made people vulnerable to other illnesses. One set of etiologies that explained how emotions exposed Saharans to other illness blamed the external threats of the Eye and magical curses, as discussed in the section on the aesthetic of interiority. The etiology based on aesthetics of spiritual unity, in contrast, suggested that concealing emotions from the neighbors was an insufficient strategy for promoting health. It was better to drive negative emotions away altogether through spiritual practice.

Balance

Saharans who suffered from emotional distress had a third option for promoting health when strategies based on the aesthetics of interiority and unity were unsuccessful. One of the housewives from Errachidia used an herbal remedy made from *sanuuj* (seeds of *Nigella sativia*) to treat a condition she described as *mqalaqa* (nervousness). Khuzama was a slender Arab grandmother in her mid-40s who lived with her husband and seven children in one of the wealthier households in the study. Her disposition was pleasant but more reserved than other participants in her age-cohort. I was concerned that she would drop out of the study until she revealed her interest in health matters during our first interview in May 1996. She told me that she suffered for 3 years from nervousness. Crowds of people at the suq or at celebrations made her feel agitated and the site of blood made her dizzy. She tried medicine from the pharmacy, but it was expensive (200 Dh, $23.50) and did not help. Finally, tried sanuuj and she recovered.

Sanuuj was one of the humorally hot herbal medicines that Saharans used for a variety of ailments. It was available from all of the spice dealers in the market and it was inexpensive. Like other housewives in the study, Khuzama knew the basic principles of the humoral system. As she explained in our second interview, "do cold medicine for hot sicknesses; do hot for cold sicknesses" (September 1996). She learned which foods and herbal medicines were hot and which were cold from *l-kubar* (the older people), but she said that she also used her own intelligence to figure out what to do. In discussing her nervousness, she never classified the condition as hot or cold. What mattered to her was that sanuuj (which she continued to take each day) was effective. In a later interview, Khuzama explained how she used the humoral system in treating sickness in her household: "If someone doesn't get better, you change the medicine. If you started with the hot medicine, then change to cold" (October 1996). The assumptions embedded in her statement were the humoral principles that a healthy body is balanced body, and that the treatment of illness hinges on a system of matching opposite pairs (i.e., hot and cold).

The system of balance in humoral medicine paralleled the way Saharan housewives strived to achieve balance in their social relationships. Just as an excess or deficiency of a humor in the physical body lead to illness, imbalance in the social body lead to envy, which Saharans viewed as a health threat. Social life involved a complex system of calculating how to nurture trusted relationships and cultivate ties with potential allies given the constraints of ones own time and money.

In the ideal model of an Islamic community, there would be no need to prevent the occurrence of envy. The principle of unity dictates the obligation to respect and provide for the needs of all members. Through participant-observation as a member of my in-laws' household, however, I learned that the aesthetic of social unity was as elusive at the community level as spiritual unity was at the level of the body/self. Even the most devout housewives lacked the time, money, and inclination to show charity and hospitality to the society at large. Furthermore, tales of illnesses caused by the Eye, magic, and sorcery cautioned women to be wary of outsiders and signs of envy. While the cultural aesthetic of interiority provided housewives with a way to avoid dangerous threats that came from external sources, the aesthetic of balance served as a form of prevention within their social networks. Saharan housewives participated in a vast system of balanced reciprocity between households—sometimes located great distances from each other—as part of their effort to promote well-being.

As mentioned in the previous section, the act of sharing food with another housewife could symbolically unify the two women in a social bond that approximated blood and milk relationships, but the bond of food was short-lived. To maintain that social bond over time and avoid the introduction of inequality and, thus, envy into the relationship, women alternated in their roles as host and guest. They measured the state of their relationships based on what each served during the last visit and how many times each one had come to the other's house.

The custom of visiting in the late afternoon facilitated women's efforts to create unity and balance in their social networks. In the regular rhythm of household activity, housewives reserved the time between the third and fourth prayer of the Salat cycle for socializing. The hard labor of sweeping floors, washing laundry, cooking stew, and making bread occurred before the mid-day meal, leaving the afternoon for rest and visiting. After the muezzin broadcast the third call to prayer from each neighborhood mosque, women in Errachidia emerged from their households, wrapped in fashionable jellabas or faded sheets, often with young children strapped to their backs. Their destinations varied each day—sometimes the house of an aunt or cousin, other times a close friend. The custom depended on a policy of open hospitality. Women rarely arranged a visit ahead of time, but instead simply arrived at the door with the expectation that someone would be home. Because sharing food was such a central component of social life, the hosts would provide mint tea or coffee with a light snack, depending on what was available in the pantry or what they could afford from the neighborhood grocer.

My research design took advantage of the custom by scheduling household interviews during the afternoon visiting hours. Despite my efforts to make appointments ahead of time, it was difficult to catch some of the participants before they went out to visit someone else. On those occasions, I started visiting households in the late morning so that I could complete my questionnaire for the whole sample. I knew that this strategy violated the regular rhythm of domestic activity, but I was more focused on the demands of my research than on the social consequences of my actions. Once my interviews had been underway for a few months, my own household started receiving an unusually high volume of guests. The participants in the study came to visit our household, first during the customary hours in the late afternoon, then eventually in the late morning as well. My sisters-in-law were exhausted from the onslaught of guests and my fiancé was upset that his remittances were disappearing so quickly from the expense of our hospitality. He suggested that we pretend that no one was home when guests knocked at the door. We tried this strategy for a day or two to appease him, but Yussef's sisters had such difficulty restraining themselves when someone knocked at the door that we returned to the old pattern of open hospitality. They decided that the social ties that developed during those visits were worth the expense; we might need help from one of their households in the future.

The practice of visiting sick friends and relatives followed the same principle of balance. Those who paid into the system of reciprocity by helping someone in need expected to collect the debt when they were sick. Mama shouldered the responsibility for paying the respect of our household to sick friends and relatives. During the time of my research, these outings ranged from visiting a newly circumcised boy to visiting ailing elderly friends. I offered to accompany Mama on these outings whenever I had the time so that I could learn more about household health practices. She was reluctant to take me along, however, because she thought that these extra household visits (that is, beyond the sample participating in interviews) would tire me and expose me to health threats unnecessarily. Even though Mama was fifteen years older than me and assisted with all my research interviews, somehow she dismissed her own vulnerability to the same fatigue and health threats. She was more concerned with keeping our household on good terms with the other households in our social network.

One of the times I accompanied Mama was to visit an elderly woman who lived in a village near Zaouia. Djo, a Berber in her late sixties, was the mother of one of Mama's childhood friends. We heard through mutual relatives that Djo was seriously ill but the family was unsure about the cause. We set out in the late afternoon to walk to her house, which was far more remote than the others I had visited in the river valley. We had to traverse a narrow ridge between irrigation canals in the palm grove and then find a shallow place to cross the swollen river. When we arrived after a half-hour trek, we found Djo leaning against several cushions on the carpeted floor of her dim-lit guest room. She looked thin and frail in comparison to the four stout young women who had joined her for mint tea and cookies. As we approached them to offer the polite greetings of handshaking and hand-kissing, I saw that Djo's hands and feet were wrapped in old rags, making it look like her limbs ended in stumps. The first thought that came to my mind—perhaps because of Mama's cautions about health threats—was that this woman might have leprosy. In the next instant, I had to decide whether it was worse to expose myself to Djo's unknown and potentially contagious illness or risk offending the family by refusing to greet her appropriately. I opted to hold my breath when I shook, rather than kissed her hand, hoping that the gesture would somehow protect me from whatever she had.[5]

The conversation that pursued once we sat down revealed that Djo was suffering from heart trouble, not leprosy. (My breathing resumed its normal rhythm once that piece of information became apparent). The rags that triggered my alarm were covering henna paste that her daughters had applied to their mother's hands and feet earlier that afternoon. They were waiting for the henna to dry so that it would leave the desired dark red stain on her skin. Henna is one of the herbal medicines Saharans use for skin problems, but in this case the family used it to brighten Djo's mood. Usually Saharan women decorated their hands and feet with henna for feast days, life cycle rituals, or other happy occasions. In this context, the daughters hoped that the association of henna with joy would alleviate Djo's heart distress, reflecting the Saharan notion that the heart is the locus of emotion in the body. The only other remedy they used was red onion, which is a hot food thought to generate more energy in the body.

From a structural perspective, both remedies acted to create balance in the body. In this way, the principles of humoral medicine extended to other practices in the household production of health. For example, Saharan women always decorated both hands with henna, even when amateur folk artists took hours to create ornate henna designs (using a syringe) rather than simply smearing the henna paste over both palms. My American friends had only enough patience to sit through the design of one hand, but the artist would insist on putting at least a dot of henna on the other hand. Otherwise the asymmetry would leave the gesture incomplete and the body open to bad luck.

After months of interviewing, I began to notice than the housewives described just about everything in pairs. They told me that in the past women served dates-and-buttermilk to their guests but today they just offer bread-and-tea. Similarly, recipes for cooking and for home remedies grouped pairs of ingredients: cumin and salt, parsley and cilantro, *shib* (alum) and Harmal, and onion and henna. The rationale for these pairings was not humoral in the ingredients (i.e., hot with cold or wet with dry); often the pairs combined two hot spices or herbs. Instead, the pattern seemed to adhere to the local principles of taste. As one middle-aged Hurtani woman told me in response to a question about what she did to keep her family healthy, spices are essential to Saharan cooking: "without the spices, the food is nothing." If one of component of traditionally paired tastes was missing in the pantry, housewives used another recipe.

Other ways that the aesthetic principle of balance appeared in household life included the design of handicrafts, family composition, and the value of patience. The traditional carpets and blankets Saharan housewives wove had symmetrical, geometric designs. The pattern of symmetry also influenced ideas about family size. Young and old women agreed that the ideal number of children in a family was four, so that every boy would have brother and every girl would have a sister. Alternatively, the value of patience applied the principle of balance to local concepts of time and fate. In Islamic world view, the universe is composed of complementary pairs (Qur'an 51:49), such as night and day, male and female, good and evil. Accordingly, every moment of hardship had its complementary moment of success or good fortune. Housewives counseled each other to be patient during difficult times in their lives, reminding themselves that Allah is compassionate and merciful. This is not to suggest that housewives were passive about their fate, but rather that they viewed both good fortune and bad fortune as temporary.

Purity

Saharan Muslims learned to embody patience every year during the month of Ramadan. This holy month, which commemorates the revelation of the Qur'an to the Prophet Muhammad marks the time when Muslims fulfill the obligation of *Saum* (fasting). The observant fast during daylight hours, but are rewarded for their patience and self-restraint after sunset. The Ramadan ritual requires Muslims to abstain from not only all food and drink, but also smoking, arguing, and sexual activity until nightfall. During the time of my research in the mid-1990s Saharans broke the daily Ramadan fast by indulging their ravenous hunger with dates, bread, and tomato soup made with chick-peas and lentils. The customs that followed this light meal entailed visiting, evening strolls, storytelling, and more food. Ramadan was already in progress when I arrived for fieldwork in 1996 and floods blocked my access to Errachidia until the end of the holy month. On the last few nights before the *l-eid as-sghir* (the small feast), we stayed awake past midnight telling stories about the past and eating *shubakia* (a syrupy pastry that resembles a pretzel).

The sharp contrast between daylight asceticism and nighttime indulgence highlighted the struggle between ar-ruh and l-jism, but without denying the needs and pleasures of the body completely. As such, Ramadan was an enjoyable time for Saharan households despite the restrictions of the fast. Toward the end my fieldwork in 1996 as Ramadan approached again, a few housewives commented that they were looking forward to it. They said that their bodies needed to fast again. My sister-in-law explained the sentiment as a desire to cleanse the soul. Fasting provided housewives with a way to create the aesthetic of purity, the 4th cultural structure in Saharan domestic life.

The aesthetic of purity in Saharan culture appeared most frequently and most directly in the Islamic concept of *Tahira* (purity) in Salat (ritual prayer). Before performing each Salat prayer, Muslims must transform the body into a state of ritual purity attained through *wDu* (ablution). The practice of ritually cleansing the body requires Muslims to use water in a sequence of ablutions to remove polluting bodily substances such as urine, feces, or sexual secretions. Menstrual blood constitutes a higher order of pollution which cannot be purified in this way. Hence, menstruating women are exempt from prayer (and fasting as well) and must perform a more thorough bodily cleansing (ghasul) before resuming their prayer practice.

The performance of Salat requires Muslims to maintain the state of Tahira for about 10 minutes at five points in the day. Some Saharan housewives, however, tried to extend their state of ritual purity over the span of 2–3 prayers (MacPhee 2004). The practice of extending bodily control over several hours allowed housewives to avoid the need to repeat the ablution ritual for the next prayer. This adjustment of the Salat ritual to coordinate with other social and economic demands on women's time made the aesthetic of purity a central concern for the health of the body. Any bodily processes that prevented a woman from maintaining ritual purity for several hours became a health concern. Housewives complained about symptoms such as vaginal discharge, intestinal gas, or frequent urination and sought home remedies to prevent the need for multiple ablutions throughout the day.

Although ablution qualified more as a symbolic purification than a hygienic cleansing in a medical sense, cleanliness was the dominant form of the aesthetic of purity at the household level. Among the most common responses to my interview questions about general health promotion practices in the household were references to cleaning. Housewives in both Errachidia and Zaouia specified bathing children, airing the bedding, washing clothes, and cleaning the house. The daily chores of sweeping, washing floors, and airing the blankets were the work of young women in the household. They also shouldered the responsibility for hand-washing the laundry and, in Zaouia, feeding the animals and retrieving drinking water for the household. The girls who were industrious in their housework, especially in producing sparkling laundry, increased their eligibility for marriage—at least from the future mother-in-law's perspective. Cleanliness was a way for a household to increase its honor and socio-religious status in the community. The symbolism was partly socio-economic—not everyone could afford soap and laundry detergent—but also external cleanliness served to represent a state of internal purity.

Keeping the house and the family clean was a challenge because the dirt roads and desert winds covered everything with dust and sand. The rough texture of Saharan housewives hands was a testament to how dedicated they were to cleaning. This aspect of domestic life seemed to correspond well to public health messages about hygiene, but as I mentioned in Chapter 3, the understanding of germ theory was incomplete in most of the households I visited. Saharans in the popular quarters of Errachidia and its outlying villages were more concerned about the contagious nature of bad smells and symbolic pollution than about viruses and bacteria.

Management of symbolic pollution was an important aspect of housewives' efforts to create purity at the community level. My attention to this form of the aesthetic of purity arose through my curiosity about the multiple contexts in which Saharans uttered the term *hashak*. In Modern Standard Arabic, hasha means except; save; God forbid; or far be it from you (Hans Wehr 1974:180). The addition of the personal pronoun "you" (signified here with k) expressed deference to another person. I learned to use the term as part of the hand washing custom Saharans performed before formal meals. A member of the host's family would pour water from a pitcher over a basin for each guest. Rather than saying "thank you," Saharans said "*hashak*" to convey deference to the person pouring the water, a task one might relegate to a servant. Saharan housewives also used the term after they referred to an unclean act, substance, animal, or person in conversation. For example, they said hashak immediately after uttering words for menstrual blood, urine, diarrhea, or vomit. As I became more sensitive to the use of the word, I noticed that Saharans also used it after referring to donkeys, dogs (but not cats), and even women when men spoke to each other. The term provided a way of indexing the kinds of things Saharans viewed as polluting.

The vigilance with which Saharans tried to diffuse references to defiling acts and substances demonstrated both the shamefulness of those topics in social life and their potential to cause harm. The same bodily substances, acts, and animals that rendered a person ritually polluted were common elements in narratives about magic and sorcery. For example, during an afternoon visit with a Rgaiga household in Zaouia, a woman told the story of how someone from another village tried to control her husband by serving him donkey kidneys for lunch. Upon hearing the reference to this vector of sorcery, all of the other women in the room shouted in unison "ah, microbe!" I was amused by their conflation of germ theory with the laws of magic. The perceived danger of donkey meat had more to do with its ambiguous cultural classification than its susceptibility to microbes, but reference to the scientific link between pollution and harm seemed to reinforce the women's disgust.

The symbolic purity of meat was a central concern in Saharan households. Qur'anic guidelines (5:3) stipulate that carrion, blood, and the flesh of swine are *haraam* (forbidden) to Muslims. It is permissible to eat the meat of other animals (e.g., sheep, goat, camel, chicken) provided that they are sacrificed in the name of Allah and drained of their blood. Men in the household or professional butchers held the responsibility for slaughtering livestock while women were responsible for preparing the meat for cooking. Donkeys fell under the category of animals of burden (Qur'an 6:142) rather than animals of slaughter, but the Qur'an does not forbid Muslims from eating them. Like other animals (e.g., snakes and rodents) that were neither haraam nor *halal* (permissible, lawful), donkeys were part of the sorcerer's arsenal.

As both Bourdieu (1990) and Douglas (1988) have pointed out, social groups tend to view the symbols that fall outside or between the boundaries of their cultural categories as having destructive power. That power, however, is not always negative. One of the common remedies Saharan housewives used in the past to treat whooping cough was the blood of a lizard. Alternatively, the use of the mother's urine to treat a severe diarrheal illness called *mard shim* (sickness of smell) was still common in the mid-1990s. These remedies harnessed the power of pollution to combat some of the most feared illnesses. Housewives, however, were cautious about contact with polluted substances and places. According to the popular health culture, blood attracted the invisible and unpredictable jnun that lived in dirty places such as the bathroom. There was always the possibility of prolonging the illness or contracting a new one. As such, the idea that pollution is dangerous implied the sense that purity is not just virtuous, but also safe. In this way, the domestic practices of cleaning and bathing played a role in the household production of health.

Discord and Change

The examples included in this chapter illustrate how the four underlying cultural structures of interiority, unity, balance, and purity influenced Saharan thought and practice, but it is a mistake to view them as determinants of behavior. Discussing each structure in its own section clarifies how it shaped everyday domestic life and the lived meaning of health, but this format is misleading. In reality, the structures overlap with each other and co-exist with other aesthetic patterns that are more tangential to health practices.

In some contexts, the core structures outlined here contradict each other, causing a cultural dilemma for the people involved. For example, in interviews about general strategies for health promotion the majority of housewives listed bathing as one of main activities they used to keep their children healthy. Few households had the means to bathe everyday, but mothers said that they would take the children to the public *hammam* (bath) and scrub them clean a few times per month. This practice reflects the importance of the aesthetic of purity in shaping the lived meaning of health, but according to the popular health culture bathing also posed a danger to children's health. The public hammam was stifling hot and women feared that the abrupt change in temperature on the walk home, particularly in winter, could trigger an imbalance in the child's bodily humors and cause illness. Alternatively, cleanliness enhanced a child's beauty and made him or her more susceptible to the Eye. I noticed that the children who accompanied their mothers to weddings or sbuae parties wore filthy clothing in an effort to prevent an envious gaze from someone at the party. One of my sisters-in-law turned the children's t-shirts inside out and preferred to dress them in old, ripped clothing when she worried about the intensions of people they would encounter that day. In those social contexts, the aesthetic of interiority trumped the aesthetic of purity.

In other contexts, new aesthetic structures imported from Europe and other Western societies challenged or undermined traditional Saharan structures of everyday life. Young women desired the kind of Western make-up, flowing hairstyles, and tight clothing they saw in television soap operas and music videos even though these external standards of beauty contradicted the traditional Saharan aesthetic of interiority. The housewives in the study characterized Western styles as *chiqui* (elitist, derived from the French term *chique*) and cautioned their daughters against wearing them. But, that style was beginning to appear among a few young office workers in town in the mid-1990s. The youngest sister in my own household, a college student, followed the custom of interiority most of the time, but she saw the custom of hijab cumbersome. One morning Hyatt argued with her older sisters for 20 minutes about whether she could walk across the alley to buy eggs without putting on a jellaba. Finally, they compromised and allowed her to leave the house with just an old taharuut draped over her head and shoulders.

When I returned to Errachidia in 2005, the cultural restrictions on women's dress had relaxed considerably. I was shocked to see young women walking down the main road wearing sleeveless tops and tight jeans. Even some of the middle-aged participants in my study had stopped wearing headscarves in public. Hyatt now rolled her headscarves into fashionable headbands, which showed off her shoulder-length hair. In a parallel shift, new construction in the capital included vast open plazas and large windows. Hyatt thought the new styles conveyed a desire to be more open and transparent, which would have seemed unreasonably dangerous ten years earlier.

These changes show how cultural structures fluctuate over time and caution against the construction of deterministic models of practice. Instead, the application of cultural phenomenology in the study of household health behavior provides a method for analyzing patterns in qualitative data. These patterns follow a practical logic that allows individuals to create health strategies that make sense in their local social and cultural contexts. There are other aesthetic patterns that I noticed in Errachidia, such as a preference for ornate design and a 5 segment rhythm of time, but the structures I outline here provide a basis for understanding how housewives approached health promotion and illness prevention in their households. In Part II of the book, I examine how the aesthetics of everyday life illuminate the cultural logic of maternal-child health strategies. Through an examination of how basic structures of the body, household, and community form the tacit foundation of embodied experience, three case studies offer a phenomenological assessment of when and how housewives put objective knowledge about health into action. The cornerstone of that phenomenological interpretation of health behavior rests on an embodied theory of vulnerability and security, which I explain in the next chapter.

Figure 1 Ziz Valley, Errachidia Province panorama.

Figure 2 Central market, Errachidia.

Figure 3 Errachidia neighborhood.

Figure 4 Ksar ramparts.

Figure 5 Girls at the village water tap.

Figure 6 Saharan newborn.

Figure 7 Berber bridal costume.

Figure 8 The author showing hennaed hands before her engagement party.

PART II

THE ART OF PROTECTION

CHAPTER 5

VULNERABILITY AND SECURITY

The effort to produce SiHa in Saharan households was an on-going process in which housewives were the primary contributors. As much as the aesthetics of interiority, unity, balance, and purity shaped the lived meaning of health and well-being, the contingencies of everyday life introduced disruptions into the ordered environment that housewives strived to create. Some disruptions, such as the birth of an infant or the incorporation of a new bride into the household, triggered explicit concerns about the vulnerability of household members to illness or other kinds of misfortune. On those occasions, housewives took precautions to prevent any harmful effects associated with the disruption. Local customs enacted for births and weddings aimed to protect newborns and brides from the Eye, magic, spirits, cold, and even microbes. These customs revealed a cultural connection between changes in social status and threats to health. Saharans enacted similar strategies of protection in response to less predictable disruptions to the order of everyday life such as lost income or a conflict between family members. They wore amulets, burned incense, invoked God's blessings, took herbal tonics, and cleansed their bodies and households to protect themselves from danger. These kinds of protective practices and constructions of danger, when taken at face value, seem to coalesce rather easily as a cultural domain of health beliefs. In interviews, housewives listed the protocols for protective customs with ease because they had seen them or enacted them so many times. A closer analysis of the circumstances in which they put that knowledge into action, however, revealed that Saharan notions about danger and vulnerability were less formulaic than they seemed in interviews.

The cultural consensus in popular knowledge about the multiple sources of and potential exposures to danger masked considerable variation in the way Saharan housewives used protective practices for themselves and their children. Sometimes housewives ignored popular culture warnings about danger in a particular circumstance or saw no need for an amulet or incense even when local custom called for them. The chapters in this section of the book ex-

amine the relationship between underlying cultural patterns of those variations and the aesthetics of everyday life. Case studies describe ways in which
Saharan women interpreted and responded to cultural knowledge about danger in particular contexts to illuminate how cultural sensibilities and embodied experience shaped the household production of health.

Close attention to the contexts when housewives used protective practices
revealed common patterns in their expectations about the social, emotional
and environmental conditions that caused an individual or household to become vulnerable to danger. My appreciation of the conditions that triggered
Saharan women's concerns about vulnerability derived from three sources. The
first of these sources was the haphazard information I encountered in my attempt to learn how to protect myself after Yussef and I became engaged. When
someone said "*endak, ghadi t-mard*" (watch out, you are going to become sick)
or advised me to use protective herbs or incense, I interpreted the comments
as an indication that those conditions met the local criteria for vulnerability.
My vigilance in trying to apply Saharan strategies to protect myself also raised
my awareness of how and when Saharans were using similar practices. My field
notes on the customs and protective strategies housewives enacted at ritual
events—such as weddings and infant naming ceremonies—complemented
my notes on my personal experiences.

The third source of data was housewives' descriptions of specific situations
when they or their children were in danger. The analysis of these data illuminated how Saharans placed local constructions of danger (as described in Chapter 3) into the concrete context of everyday domestic life. I examined the social
and aesthetic structures of the contexts in which women enacted local forms
of protection against the Eye, humoral imbalance, magical curses, spirit attack, and microbes. Most of the descriptions I examined arose in response to
my systematic interview questions about pregnancy, childbirth, breastfeeding,
and childhood illnesses. Additional information came from women's spontaneous narratives about their past encounters with dangerous situations and
from interviews with three key consultants about Saharan constructions of
danger.

The key consultants—all grandmothers who were reflective and articulate
in previous interviews—emphasized the dangers of childbirth, cold, the change
of seasons, summer fruit (for children), and acute illnesses (for adults). My
other interview transcripts and field notes indicated that Saharan women also
associated increased vulnerability with weddings, fright, social isolation, night
time, breastfeeding infants, contact with things that were dirty, traveling to a
new place, and excessive worrying in which feelings *tudugu fi-l-qalb* (pound in
the heart) like spice in a mortar and pestle (MacPhee 2003:66).

At first glance, the Saharan construction of vulnerability seemed multifaceted and expansive, but there was consensus about the most serious threats to well-being. Childbirth ranked as the greatest danger for women and mard shim (sickness of smelling) posed the most serious threat to infants and young children. Women's dramatic narratives about the fear and pain they endured during a difficult labor and delivery or their struggles to save children with cases of severe diarrhea reinforced the shared impression that these situations were dangerous. Similarly, common knowledge about the variety of household practices that aimed to prevent illness and death during childbirth and early childhood led Saharan housewives to anticipate danger in those situations.

My observational notes, however, revealed that housewives sometimes ignored those precautions. For example, Fatim-Zahra (Chapter 3) ignored the custom of hiding newborns from strangers when she asked me to photograph her with her son on the day of his naming ceremony. Similarly, on several occasions I observed young children eating melon and grapes, summer fruits, which emit a scent that Saharans viewed as the main cause of mard shim. These examples and many others from my field notes illustrated the mismatch between abstract cultural knowledge about danger and real life responses to the situations implicated in that knowledge. A comparison of childbirth and mard shim with all the other forms of danger housewives described, however, revealed an underlying pattern that shed some light on when and how individuals responded to general knowledge about danger and protection.

The types of situations that Saharan housewives identified as dangerous shared characteristics with the core aesthetic structures of domestic life described in Chapter 4. For example, housewives viewed exposure to cold as a situation that increased a person's vulnerability. The practical logic underlying this association corresponded with the idea that disruptions in the balance of bodily humors cause illness. Alternatively, situations that created social isolation increased feelings of vulnerability because they detached the individual from the culturally desired state of incorporation into the unity of the household or community. A comparison of the various ways Saharans described danger and vulnerability with respect to states of being-in-the-world revealed four main themes that contrast directly to the core aesthetic structures of Saharan domestic life. Saharan housewives viewed the conditions of openness, isolation, imbalance, and defilement as qualities that increased ones susceptibility to harm, illness, and misfortune. A fifth theme in the data indicated that Saharans had a heightened sense of vulnerability in situations involving transition from one status to another. The way housewives interpreted the cause of vulnerability during such transitions corresponded to one or more of the above four conditions that increased the sense of vulnerability. The identification of these themes and their oppositional relationship with the aesthetic structures of everyday life provided a foundation for analyzing Saharan constructions of vulnerability. But, the way housewives put this embodied knowledge into action entailed a more complex and dynamic process. Three cultural anthropologists—Mary Douglas, Mark Nichter, and Michael Jackson—help to clarify how culture shapes the process of experiencing vulnerability and responding to that feeling.

Vulnerability as Embodied Experience

The consistency with which housewives associated the conditions of openness, isolation, imbalance, and defilement with vulnerability to danger revealed a common cultural sensibility to particular kinds of disorder. This interpretation of the findings of my study resembles Mary Douglas' (1994:29) argument that culture filters the difference between important and unimportant dangers. Her comparative study of the perceptions of risk and danger in pre-modern African societies and modern Western societies holds a prominent position in social research on risk and culture. She shows how social institutions, symbolic systems, and local notions of power and morality influence the cultural construction of danger (Douglas 1966, 1994, Douglas and Widavsky 1983). Douglas points out that individuals live in worlds in which there are multiple risks to consider at any given moment and decisions about how and when to act often involve social others who share common cultural assumptions about how the world works. These assumptions include the local general understanding about the causes of illness and misfortune as well as shared interpretations of the relative importance of social, physical, spiritual, emotional and economic risks in specific contexts.

By situating the cultural construction of danger in the overall symbolic and sociopolitical order of the society, Douglas' socio-cultural perspective on risk perception reinforces my observation that Saharan constructions of vulnerability provided counterpoints to the core aesthetic structures of domestic life. Her perspective, however, sheds little light on the variations among Saharan housewives in their interpretations and responses to danger from one context to another. The functionalist orientation of Douglas' theory oversimplifies the mechanism through which culture influences behavior by depicting the structural connections between belief and behavior as automatic. She argues that beliefs about danger and rituals of protection serve "to protect society from behavior that will wreck it" [Douglas 1994:4]. In contrast to Douglas' view that social institutions use individuals to maintain social order, my understanding of the common themes in Saharan constructions of vulnerability concurs with more recent theories in anthropology which recognize the individual's capacity to manipulate cultural beliefs and practices (within limits) for her own ends.

Even though my study found that Saharan housewives shared a heightened awareness of particular kinds of disorder, individual women responded differently to similar types of danger. Moreover, individual housewives varied in the ways they responded to similar contexts of danger at different times. For example, a Berber mother from Zaouia used all the traditional protective measures when her first son was circumcised but used none when her second son was circumcised a year later. Nichter's (2003) description of constructions of vulnerability in South and Southeast Asian societies shows a similar trend of intra-cultural variation. These variations highlight the contrast between population-level constructions of risk or danger and individual feelings of vulnerability to those threats. He identifies 5 types of vulnerability, which arise from exposure to risk information or from local ideas about individual constitution, preexisting health problems, environmental conditions, and the accumulation of toxins or impurities (Nichter 2003:14–18).

Nichter's insights on vulnerability and his later call for attention to social risk as a pivotal component in popular strategies for risk management (Nichter 2008) have inspired other anthropologists to consider vulnerability in their research. Launiala and Honkasalo (2010), for example, use an innovative research design that revealed how pregnant women in rural Malawi ranked the severity of health threats depending on the availability of treatments and their control over exposure to those threats. Women felt less vulnerable to malaria in comparison to witchcraft and AIDS, even though malaria was more common. Two other recent studies of vulnerability (Leatherman 2005; Ribera and Haussman-Muela 2011) emphasize how conditions of poverty limit the ability of poor households to cope with illness. These later studies conceptualize vulnerability as a state of being susceptible to health risks rather than as feelings of susceptibility. This realist view of vulnerability offers valuable insights to the study of health promotion and disease prevention (which I discuss in Chapter 9) but the assessment of health and risk statuses was beyond the scope of my research. My discussion of vulnerability fits more closely with subjective interpretations of the concept.

The overlap between my observations in Saharan Morocco with ethnographic research on vulnerability in SubSaharan Africa and South Asia indicates the existence of some cross-cultural patterns in the construction of the experience of vulnerability. For example, sudden changes in weather heighten awareness of vulnerability in both Morocco and South Asia. Similarly, there is a common concern cross-culturally about the dangers in lifecycle transitions, such as weddings and pregnancy. Strategies of protection also follow common themes cross-culturally. Healers in Mozambique attempt to symbolically close openings in the body and the household to protect pregnant women from the threats of envy and sorcery (Chapman 2006). Similarly in Morocco, Saharan housewives used kuhl and henna to protect vulnerable body openings at the eyes and navels of infants. The similarities weaken, however, as the analysis moves from abstract concepts to the concrete level of local culture. Constructions of vulnerability in Malawi compare pregnant women to a fragile egg, which make them vulnerable to witchcraft and infections. They often choose to give birth in a hospital to avoid witches in their community (Launiala and Honkasalo 2010). In contrast, Saharan women avoided hospitals because they feared exposure to strangers at a time when their bodies were in an open, vulnerable state. Alternatively, Sri Lankan mothers worry about children who are prone to sinusitis (Nichter 2003:15) while Saharan mothers paid more attention to symptoms associated with diarrheal illnesses. The components of Nichter's 5-dimensional model emphasize the importance of the particular elements of culture and subjectivity in health research, but he stops short of proposing a theory of how those elements interact in the contexts of people's lives.

The concept of embodiment offers a heuristic for taking Nichter's cultural perspective on health vulnerabilities a step further. Nichter's 5 types of vulnerability emphasize subjective interpretations of danger but focus more on ideas about causes of susceptibility rather than feelings of susceptibility. The difference between these two dimensions of subjectivity became apparent to me through the experience of feeling vulnerable to the Eye. When I felt the force of Fulana's comment strike my chest, I gained a visceral appreciation of what Saharan women meant when they said that they were hit by the Eye. The concept of embodiment accounts for bodily dimensions of awareness by portraying the body as the central axis of individual experience. The focus on bodily experience shifts the emphasis of analysis away from symbolism and discourse and toward modes of feeling and being.

From the perspective of cultural phenomenology, the crucial point in the concept of embodiment is the need to situate bodily experiences in the context of culture. Culture shapes bodily feelings, such as those related to vulnerability, in particular ways. For example, Saharan housewives used the terms *maHlul* (unbound, open), *khaf* (afraid) and *tdigidig* (prickly) to convey their sense of vulnerability. Although the emotion of fear may be a universal component of vulnerability, the other two forms are culturally specific. Saharans internalized these ways of feeling vulnerable through participating in social life and learning to interpret these particular kinds of bodily sensations as significant.

The phenomenon of embodiment, however, involves more than conditioning bodies to experience emotions or physical sensations in culturally significant ways. That view of embodiment is too simplistic. The individual's interactions with the social and physical environment add a dynamic character to the concept of embodiment. As Geiser explains "being cannot be reduced to the subject or to the material body plus the mind. Being is always being-in-the-world" (2008:302). Drawing on the insights of phenomenologists such as Heidegger (1975) and Merleau-Ponty (1962), he points out that individuals incorporate a full set of meanings and relationships (i.e., culture) into their perception of objects and contexts in everyday life. From this perspective, embodiment is more than a passive internalization of cultural structures over time. It also involves an active engagement of mind, body, and environment. Social and material environments are dynamic, changing from one moment to the next (c.f. Ingold 2000), and embodied actors constantly assess the situation in order to gauge how to act in culturally appropriate ways. To understand Saharan feelings of vulnerability and the protective practices they catalyzed, it is necessary to consider the significant relationships (i.e., among people, objects, and events) that shape the local interpretations of particular environments.

Michael Jackson's discussion of vulnerability in *Minima Ethnographica* (1998) suggests a model for understanding the multi-dimensional interaction of body, mind, and environment using perspectives from cultural phenomenology. Jackson describes vulnerability as a form of intersubjective experience, which he views as the two-fold interplay of embodied subjects and objects (e.g., other people, amulets, places, etc.) on one axis with general knowledge and particular social dynamics on the other. He argues that this complex dialectical relationship "is steeped in ambiguity and paradox" (Jackson 1998:8). One of the main ambiguities of intersubjectivity is that it is "shaped as much by unconscious, habitual, taken-for-granted dispositions as by conscious intensions and worldviews" (Jackson 1998:9). Hence, discourse about danger—including my interviews on the topic with key consultants—yielded only a partial picture of the intersubjective experience of vulnerability. The analysis must also incorporate observations of social interaction and strategies of protection to gain a more thorough sense of a person's embodied sense of vulnerability in specific contexts.

The conceptual foundation of Jackson's cultural phenomenological view of vulnerability emerged from his study of fetishes in Kuranko (Sierra Leone) health culture. Like Bourdieu, Jackson was interested in how embodied subjectivity influenced behavior. He argues that for the Kuranko, fetishes "seal off, enclose, safeguard and protect" (1998:77). They act to restore autonomy and increase one's "sense of substantiality" (1998:28) in the existential struggle for balance between self and other, a vast category, which includes people, spirits, animals, and objects. Jackson describes vulnerability as a particularly meaningful kind of intersubjective interaction because it "implies an inability to physically combat the will of the other, sensed as a palpable force invading or engulfing one's own body-self" (1998:79). This visceral experience of weakness and susceptibility arises through the juxtaposition of abstract cultural constructions of danger with specific contexts of subject-object interactions.

The components of Jackson's discussion of fetishes overlapped well with some aspects of my observational and interview data on Saharan protective practices but not others. For example, Kuranko culture shares a pattern of interiority with Saharan Morocco. His emphasis on the concept of loss to convey the existential conditions that give rise to a desire for protection, however, is less applicable to Saharan culture. Although one could describe isolation as a loss of unity or defilement as a loss of purity, the concept implies that aesthetic order is the usual condition of everyday life rather than a goal of everyday practice. Moreover, the term "loss" creates confusion in situations when personal gain triggers feelings of vulnerability because of a loss of balance in Saharan communities. Nonetheless, Jackson's cultural phenomenological perspective provides a way of adapting Douglas' and Nichter's insights on the social and cultural construction of danger to the micro-level context of individual experience and behavior.

Variations in the Context of Transition: A Comparison of 3 Weddings

The contexts in which Saharans emphasized the importance of physical danger most explicitly encompassed a set of life cycle events that involved transition from one social status to another. For housewives, the most significant transitional statuses included marriage, pregnancy, childbirth and the 40 days following delivery, the circumcision of sons, divorce, and the death of a loved one. The local customs associated with these transitional statuses employed an array of symbolic techniques and ritual practices intended to protect the initiate from illness and misfortune. Although these customs established a cultural link between transitions and the threat of danger, the potential for this general knowledge to trigger individual feelings of vulnerability depended on a confluence of other intersubjective factors affecting the immediate circumstances of the transition. These factors might include the woman's position in the family, her recent interactions with other members of the household or community, the perceived effectiveness of amulets and other forms of protection, and her past experiences with similar transitions in her own life or observations of other women's transitions. Hence, the Saharan construction of vulnerability was far more complex than the construction of danger. Saharan housewives conveyed this complexity in interviews about pregnancy, childbirth, and breastfeeding through their narratives about their past experiences and individual adjustments of taqliid (custom). The analysis of these narratives in combination with my observations of ritual events and my own experience of transition in the field illuminated basic cultural patterns that shaped variations in Saharan responses to the threat of danger during transitions from one status to another.

The range of practices I observed at weddings during the summers of 1996 and 1997 illustrate some of those variations and provides a framework for the cultural phenomenological interpretation of women's health behavior that I present as case studies in Chapters 6, 7, and 8. Saharan wedding rituals varied between ethnic groups as well as within a single ethnic group, depending on the residence and economic status of the participating households. Each of the 4 ethnic groups in the region had its own wedding customs, although they all shared a common structure that included the night of henna, the transition of the bride to the groom's home (where the weddings took place), and the consummation of the marriage. During the course of my fieldwork, I had the opportunity to attend 3 Berber weddings, one in Errachidia and 2 in outlying villages in the province. The town wedding was remarkably different from the village weddings, both in terms of the behavior of the bride and the guests. Although I observed the town wedding first (in the summer of 1996), the village weddings I attended a year later reflected the Berber tradition more closely.

Berber weddings in rural Errachidia Province in the late 20th century simultaneously commemorated the past and created ties for the future. The participants ate food, wore costumes, and performed songs and dances that represented the heritage of their kin-based social identity. The custom on the first day of the wedding required the groom's household to serve a lunch of couscous and grilled mutton to the wedding guests. Traditionally, the wedding lunch and subsequent celebration was open to everyone in the village, but at the weddings I attended the groom's household extended verbal invitations to specific family and friends both in and outside of the village. After lunch, the groom's mother and sisters would gather gifts for the bride while the guests sang and danced outside the house. The traditional dance for Saharan Berbers is a line dance called the *haaduuz*. Men arranged themselves shoulder-to-shoulder in one line and women faced them in the same formation in another line. The lines moved sideways then back and forth as the performers responded to each other in song accompanied by hand drums. By late afternoon, the wedding party would set out to commemorate the journey of the *isnan*, when men from the groom's lineage would travel to the bride's household to bring gifts and accompany the bride back to the groom's household. The isnan, who wore fig necklaces over white robes and pantaloons, guarded the *waziir* (the groom's attendant and advisor) as he transported the wedding gifts by mule. Along the way, men from the bride's lineage would challenge the isnan to mock battles and contests of strength. In the past, men made this journey alone but now women from the groom's lineage followed along dressed in traditional black taharuut-s and sang wedding songs.

The symbolism of the pageant conveyed the Saharan construction of marriage as a social and economic exchange between two lineages or households rather than a romantic partnership between the bride and groom. First-time marriages in the Sahara, particularly in the villages were arranged by the parents and the formality of this arrangement prevented the bride and groom from knowing each other intimately before the wedding. To preserve the honor of both families, the bride had to maintain her virginity until the wedding. (The community did not hold the groom's sexual status to the same level of scrutiny). In the past, when girls married in early adolescence, brides had little knowledge about sex before their wedding. The increase in female education and the influence of population control policies in the late 20th century, however, shifted the age of marriage to late adolescence. This change meant that brides (usually) knew something about sex on their wedding day, but the continued importance of family honor ensured that modern brides had as little experience with sex as their counterparts from the past. Additionally, the wedding ritual initiated the bride's move from the familiarity of her natal household to a low status position in the groom's household, or to the isolation of new nuclear family household in fewer cases.

For these reasons the wedding ritual entailed as much trepidation and sadness for the participants as it did happiness. Young brides certainly enjoyed their wedding gifts of jewelry, new clothing, blankets, and kitchenware. For most girls, their wedding was the first time they received individualized attention and private ownership of material goods. The lyrics of the wedding songs, however, curbed the excitement about this transition. Guests at the weddings I attended sang good wishes for a handsome husband who would give her food to eat and not hit her. Later in the ceremony, as the bride departed with the isnan for the groom's house, the guests sang sad songs of farewell: "goodbye, father. Thank you. You were good to me." In the past, brides in Zaouia made the journey to the groom's house on a mule but so many brides had fallen off the mules—once into the irrigation ditch—that everyone agreed to use a car to transport the bride to her new home. At the other end of the journey, the groom's family worried about the incorporation of a new woman into their household. The groom's mother, in particular, faced the chance that the new bride would interfere with the mother-son bond and undermine her power to direct the activities of women and children in the household.

Uncertainty about the result of a wedding transition led most Saharan households to take precautions against the possibility of a bad outcome. In many ways, the focus of concern about misfortune was social and emotional in nature, but the recognition of social and emotional agents in Saharan illness etiologies caused concern about health as well. For example, disappointment in the groom's lineage about the bride chosen as his wife could instigate the use of sorcery against her. Alternatively, a neighbor's envy of the bride's good fortune could cause an illness through the mechanism of the Eye. The strategies for protection against these agents of harm took different forms depending upon who or what needed protection: the groom and his household, the bride, or the guests.

One of the common protective practices at Saharan weddings was the use of white paint to deflect against the Eye. Families splashed the paint on the front door, exterior walls, and sometimes the interior walls of the guest rooms. The first time I noticed the practice was at a Berber wedding in Tinii, a village near Zaouia, in the summer of 1997. The groom's family had used white wash to paint the message "*ars saiid*" (happy wedding) in large letters on the mud-brick wall behind the platform where the bride sat. I noticed that there were a few other haphazard splashes of white paint on the walls and support columns of the out-building at the edge of the family property where the wedding took place. The family's use of paint was minimal in comparison my observations at a second Berber wedding I attended in Zaouia a month later. For that wedding, the groom's family covered the entire front door and most of the exterior wall of their household with white wash. The hosts of both weddings were wealthy by village standards. The family in Tinii had considerable land holdings in the valley and the family in Zaouia acquired wealth from remittances sent from France. The only noticeable contextual difference between the two weddings was social in nature. The bride in the Tinii wedding was a first cousin of the groom, which Saharans considered to be an ideal match for marriage. In the Zaouia wedding, the bride was a neighbor in the village rather than a relative of the groom.

The customs enacted to protect the brides were similar at the two village weddings. The preparation of the bride took place at her natal home on the first day of the wedding. The traditional wedding dress consisted of layers of white satin and tulle, which created an illusion of girth to the slender bodies of the adolescent brides underneath all that material. Heavy jewelry in the form of silver (or nickel) pins linked by a metal chain and a necklace made of large orange beads made of resin adorned the dress. The last part of the bride's preparation occurred on the evening of the first day, also known as the night of henna. After the groom's attendants applied henna to his hands and feet, they sent the paste to the bride so that they could share henna from the same plate. On the previous day, the brides applied a more elaborate geometric or floral design of henna to enhance their beauty, but the sharing of henna with the groom served as a central symbolic act during wedding ceremony.

The last stage of preparation for the bride focused on her head. The braiding of her hair and the construction of her headdress and veil took place in front of the guests, although the brides covered their faces during this ceremony. At the wedding I attended in Zaouia the headdress ceremonies took place late at night and took over an hour to complete (I missed this portion of the ceremony at the Tinii wedding). While the women guests sang songs, the bride's attendants oiled, brushed, and braided her hair. Then, they placed a skein of yarn on top of her head and fastened a green cloth over it. A veil of striped red and yellow woolen cloth then covered both the head and face of the bride. Lastly, the attendants pinned clunky metal chains and braided ropes onto the headdress to match the jewelry worn over the dress.[1] The thick material of the veil was opaque, which blinded the bride from seeing more than slivers of her surroundings.

The custom on the second day of the wedding required the bride to sit on display in full costume at the groom's home for hours, usually after staying awake the previous night. Once she arrived at her new home, the bride had to rely on her attendants—aunts, sisters, and close friends her age—to guide her to the cushioned platform where she would sit for most of the day. In addition to the multiple layers of cloth, the brides at the weddings I attended also surrounded themselves with incense and attendants. I noticed that the bride in Tinii also wore an amulet sack of herbal medicines around her neck for added protection. The obstacles of the veil and prohibitions against sharing food with any of the guests interfered with the bride's opportunity to eat during this part of the wedding. Several women told me that the felt like they were going to faint at their weddings. After the consummation of the marriage that night, however, the bride could remove the veil and eat with her new household.

In contrast to the village customs, the Berber wedding I attended in Errachidia during the previous summer (1996) followed a completely different set of customs for preparing the bride. Prior to her debut at the party (which took place at night) the bride's attendants were responsible for decorating her face with Western-style make-up rather than constructing the elaborate Berber headdress. Furthermore, these preparations took place in a private room in the house rather than in view of the other guests. The young bride's arrival to the party—held under a tent in the side yard—followed the modern national wedding custom, which is an adaptation of the Fassi tradition. She sat in an ornate wedding carriage carried by 4 young men in traditional white shirts, puffed cotton trousers, and red Fes hats. The bride's face and long brown hair were visible through the window of the carriage. Only a gold tiara adorned her head, which seemed small in comparison to the oversized green caftan she wore as a wedding dress. The women guests clapped and ululated as the band accompanied her circuitous route to the stage where the nervous groom, dressed in a Western suit and tie, and a throne-like chair awaited her.

Although this style of wedding was popular across urban and western Morocco, I had heard Saharan Berbers associate it derogatorily with Arab culture. The bride's family, however, were recent arrivals in Errachidia, which may explain their atypical attraction to the ostentatious aesthetics of the Fassi tradition (i.e., given their Berber ethnicity). Both families involved in this wedding were from another rural province in the Middle Atlas Mountains. The decision to hold the wedding at the bride's home rather than the groom's village in the mountains also suggests that the family saw the wedding as an opportunity to demonstrate their achievement of a socio-economic status above the rural poor. The open display of wealth in the form of gold jewelry (mostly rented for the occasion) and ornately embroidered caftans was common among wedding guests from the same social class in Errachidia, but it contrasted sharply with the traditional Saharan Berber customs of protection for the bride. In this case, however, the bride was marrying her maternal first cousin and the guests at the small wedding were family and close friends. Still, I did observe some of the trepidation Saharans associate with transitional rituals. The bride was silent and visibly tense when Mama brought me to see her before her debut and her senior attendant became agitated when she realized I was American. She asked me to give them money in exchange for the privilege of seeing the bride.

My attendance at that wedding also raised concerns in my own household. Yussef and I had planned to celebrate our engagement with a private family party the following night and that event seemed to amplify the family's usual worries about my potential vulnerability to sorcery and the Eye. Out of concern for his own safety, Yussef declined the invitation to attend the wedding and stayed home even though he was a close friend of the bride's uncle. He wanted me to stay home as well, but I thought that observing a wedding ritual would enhance my knowledge of Saharan culture. Reluctantly, he agreed but he assigned two of his sisters to act as my *gardes du corps* and instructed me to avoid eating, drinking, and using any henna while I was there. His nervousness that night was out of character and it convinced me to increase the vigilance I usually employed when visiting other households during my fieldwork. At the same time, however, I did not share his sense that the wedding exposed me to any more danger than I encountered on a typical day conducting household interviews. Nonetheless, I stayed only long enough to observe the preparation of the bride's hair and make-up and to join the other guests in celebrating her arrival at the wedding tent.

One of the patterns I noticed among the female guests at the wedding was the bold display of jewelry and ornamentation on their caftans. Women who usually covered their bodies and heads with modest scarves and plain robes were wearing gold belts, cuff-size bracelets, and dangling earrings. A few young women emulated the bride by wearing gold tiaras instead of headscarves. The younger female guests also acted in a conspicuous way, especially once the musical group began to play. Each girl improvised her own style from the sensual dance of swerving hips and arms I had seen at other gatherings of women. In this case, however, the male guests could see the dancing from the adjacent seating area. Their proximity gave me the impression that the girls were dancing for the men, which challenged the strict codes of modesty and gender segregation in Saharan culture. The behavior of the female wedding guests would have been remarkable enough in contrast to my observations of women in everyday life, but their attention-seeking stood out even more in contrast to my own cautious disposition that night. If weddings were so dangerous, why were the other guests taking liberties with the usual codes of modest behavior? In ordinary circumstances, such displays of wealth and beauty raised concerns about envy and the Eye. Why were the women ignoring the risk of those dangers in this situation?

My observations of children at the village weddings a year later shed some light on my questions. At the wedding in Tinii, I noticed that the children were dressed in dirty, torn clothing and their faces were left unwashed. When I commented on their filthy appearance and asked if the people in the village were poor, my companions from Zaouia laughed. They advised me to look at their mothers dressed in gold belts and ornately embroidered caftans. They said that mothers took precautions to protect their children from attracting the envy of some untrustworthy guest. The guests, like us, came from other villages and distant towns in the province. The mothers were not worried about the danger of envy for themselves, but rather saw their children as vulnerable to it. The ritual context was sufficient to protect the adult guests because everyone took part in the dancing and dressed in fancy clothing and jewelry. No indi-

vidual woman would stand out enough to attract the envy of an untrustworthy woman. In contrast, mothers feared that a beautiful or healthy child would
stand out among other thin and sickly children at the party.

These variations in the way Saharans acted at weddings highlight some of
the complexity inherent in the local understanding of vulnerability. Even though
weddings encompassed many of the contexts that Saharan housewives associated with danger—transition from one social status to another, night, social
isolation, traveling to a new place—the degree to which individuals felt vulnerable to that danger varied among the participants and from one wedding
to the next. As such, vulnerability was not a straightforward embodiment of
cultural constructions of danger. In practical terms, the cultural classification
of marriage and weddings as one of the most dangerous situations for women
was contingent upon a number of factors that shaped the perceived character
of the immediate context. Although many of the customs Saharans used to
protect themselves from danger in transitional contexts (as well as in everyday
life) were an overt part of popular health culture, the experiential conditions
that triggered feelings of vulnerability were less obvious. A closer examination
of the cultural structures underlying the contexts in which Saharan households
employed, altered, and ignored traditional customs of protection provides
some insight into the implicit cues that shaped Saharan feelings of both vulnerability and security.

Embodied Structures of
Vulnerability and Security

Jackson's (1996) discussion of vulnerability and protection in terms of intersubjective experience and the relationship between the universal and particular proposes a conceptual link between context and behavior. Although Jackson
focuses more on the significance of loss in the dialectic of being and nothing-
ness rather than on the experience of vulnerability, his insights on how feelings
of diminishment trigger protective behavior provide a foundation for a cultural
phenomenological theory of vulnerability. The overlapping dialectics of self-
other and subject-object in his theory of intersubjectivity point to a model of
vulnerability that entails the interaction of embodied subjects, general knowledge, and particular social and material contexts. This model highlights the re-
lational character of vulnerability and security, but the discussion needs to move
beyond Jackson's theory of loss to explain how culture shapes subjectivity.

Bourdieu (1977, 1990) argues that culture conditions individual subjectivity, including bodily experience through participation in the structured activ-

ities of everyday life. Culture—in the form of norms, customs, rituals, and classifications—organizes social interaction and the activities of everyday life in time and space. Individuals, in turn, embody those ordered patterns of work and relaxation, public and private, self and other, and sacred and mundane as a learned, but taken-for-granted orientation in the world. Although the concept of habitus constitutes the foundation for Bourdieu's theory of practice, it provides only a limited view of how embodied subjects interact with and within culturally constructed contexts. Bourdieu suggests that individuals negotiate the contingencies of real world contexts by enacting practices that conform to basic underlying principles, which unite the various oppositional structures in a particular culture. In 1960s Algeria, the basic oppositions of social and economic life included pairs such as inside-outside, male-female, and night-day. The nature of the underlying principles uniting these structures, however, is vague in Bourdieu's theory of practice (1977, 1990) other than to say that they generate common patterns of practice among the members of a social group.

Desjarlais' concept of the aesthetics of everyday life takes Bourdieu's perspective on embodied subjectivity a step further and offers a way of describing those underlying cultural principles and how they shape embodied subjectivity. One of the important changes that Desjarlais introduces to the study of embodiment and practice is the idea that individuals not only conform to the structures of their social milieu (i.e. as automatons), but they also try to create those structures in their everyday lives. Villagers monitored their feelings and actions in attempt to maintain a particular type of social and cultural order.

Desjarlais' (1992) ethnographic study of embodied subjectivity in relation to Yolmo illness and healing in the Nepali highlands revealed situations in which the structures of daily life broke down. The work of healing, in turn, involved an attempt to repair the integrity of the basic underlying structures of experience. For example, he provides an in-depth account of a young mother suffering from pain, dizziness, and malaise. Yeshi carried the burden of caring for her two young children, her husband, and her elderly father-in-law in a poor household. Desjarlais viewed her symptoms less as metaphors or idioms of her emotional distress and more as "simply a response to it" (1992:150). Nonetheless, like Bourdieu, he views that response as shaped by underlying structures of everyday social life. Instead of focusing on the symbolic structures of space and economic activities, Desjarlais examined illness experience in relation to common patterns in the way Yolmo villagers composed their bodies, households, and social life. He argues that Yolmo structures of being and feeling emerged from basic aesthetic values of presence, balance, purity, and control.

These values, which organized everyday life, generated particular cultural modes of experiencing both illness and healing. The divination ritual for Yeshi attributed the illness to the loss of her spirit (*bla*) and a weakened life span (*tshe*) (Desjarlais 1992:171). The shaman's remedy for this problem entailed a ritual exorcism of ghosts from both Yeshi's body and her home (Desjarlais 1992:185). The common aesthetic principles that structure the body, the home, and the cosmos in Yolmo culture link all three forms as a practical foundation for subjective experience:

> There is a goodness of fit between the kinetics of healing and Yolmo experiences of form. Healing rites catalyze an ontology of experience patterned by a play of flow and stoppage, ingress and egress; ghosts are thrown, life-forces retrieved, and body surfaces cleaned and protected (Desjarlais 1992:194).

Both the divination and the healing ritual reveal the complexity in Yolmo understanding of illness, which imagines pain and malaise to derive from a combination of physical, social and spiritual disorder. The healing process restores that order through a series of symbolic and experiential practices.

The observation that illness disturbs the taken-for-granted rhythms and parameters of embodied experience reflects other scholarship in medical anthropology from the same time period. Scholars such as Good (1994) and Scarry (1985) have argued that illness disrupts, breaks-down, or unmakes the familiar pattern of everyday activities which allow awareness of the body to fade into the background of consciousness. The bodily sensations of pain, fatigue, and nausea reveal the subjective body as an object that cannot be ignored or taken-for-granted. My perspective on the experience of vulnerability in Saharan households expands on this literature by applying the same contextual, embodied theory of health behavior to the study of health promotion and disease prevention. The sense of disruption that arises from the experience of vulnerability is more subtle than it is in illness, but it derives from the same awareness of a shift away from the familiar patterns of everyday life. Like Desjarlais, I view the implicit aesthetic structures of everyday life as generating particular sensibilities of both unsettled (illness, danger) and coherent (healing, protection) experience. Feelings of vulnerability arise in contexts involving a disruption in the culturally desired order of everyday life or in the capacity to create that order.

Common patterns underlying the techniques that Saharan brides, households, and wedding guests used to protect themselves from threats to their well-being reveal local sensibilities that shaped individual experiences of vulnerability and security. The oppositional structures of openness and enclosure, isolation and incorporation, imbalance and equilibrium, and defilement and purification in the composition of Saharan protective practices juxtapose the aesthetic everyday order with its dialectical opposite. Participation in weddings (and other kinds of transitional experience) conditioned Saharans' sensibilities to these kinds of oppositions (cf. Kapferer 1986), but the way that Saharans interpreted the configuration of oppositional pairs in a particular context varied. As illustrated in the description of the three weddings I observed, Saharans employed cultural forms of protection, such as amulets, incense, ritual costumes, and dance, to different degrees in attempt to establish aesthetic order and compose the body or household as a calm, contained state of equilibrium. The variations depended in part on the intersubjective assessment of the type and amount of protection needed for that wedding, given the participants' level of exposure to openness, isolation, imbalance, and defilement. Through participation in *multiple* rituals and customs marking the transition from one social status to another, Saharans internalized a capacity to assess the relevant degree of threat in subsequent transitional contexts, and in comparative contexts in everyday life.

To clarify how Saharans transformed their abstract knowledge about danger into a concrete set of protective strategies, I have broken down the analysis of ritual and symbolic protection at the three weddings in terms of the dialectical structures of vulnerability and security, or put differently, of disruption and aesthetic order. It is important to note, however, that an individual's disposition toward these experiential structures was an implicit rather than an explicit component of the protective strategy employed.

Openness and Enclosure

The opposition of openness and enclosure was illustrated most clearly in the traditional wedding costume of the Berber bride. The enveloping of the bride's body in layer after layer of material constructed her as simultaneously vulnerable to harm and protected from it. The bridal costume for Saharan Berbers opened the bride to the threat of envy by enhancing her beauty in the forms of bodily plumpness (a sign of fertility) and spiritual modesty. At the same time, the costume doubled as a mechanism of protection through the embodiment of interiority. The layers of cloth acted like the ramparts of the ksar in creating a physical barrier between the bride and any external agents of harm. The role of enemy invaders in the context of the wedding took the form of disgruntled members of the groom's family, envious wedding guests, or even the resident spirits in the groom's household. The practices of surrounding the bride's body with several layers of textile, jewelry, incense, amulets, and trusted companions when she made the transition from her natal household to her marital household reinforced the cultural construction of that part of the wedding as dangerous. Moreover, the elaborate design of the headdress and veil drew attention to the head and face as a heightened locus of the bride's vulnerability during the transitional (or liminal) middle stage of the wedding. The removal of the headdress and veil on the 3rd day of the wedding, after the consummation of the marriage, signaled the formal incorporation of the bride into the groom's household and the diminishment of her vulnerability.

The contrast between the costumes in the two village weddings and the town wedding illustrated different levels of concern about the bride's openness as a source of vulnerability. The bride in Errachidia employed a minimal style of interiority for her wedding. The heavy eye-liner and lipstick she wore covered her body's vulnerable openings at the eyes and mouth, but the make-up also drew attention to her face rather than hiding it behind a veil. The caftan she wore, however, was so big that it concealed the true form of her slender body from the neck to her ankles. Similarly, the wedding carriage and the stage where the bride and groom's thrones were located created another barrier between the central participants in the wedding and the guests.

The style of dress the brides wore at the village and town weddings differed from the pattern of interiority Saharan women followed in everyday life. None of the participants in the study, from any of the ethnic groups veiled their faces on a regular basis.[2] Similarly, at the other end of the spectrum, none of the participants wore make-up in public outside of ritual occasions. As such, the effort to create interiority through the bride's costumes was not a reflection of the taken-for-granted order of everyday life but rather an attempt to restore that order in response to its disruption.

The way weddings disrupted the ordinary pattern of interiority in Saharan household life was through crossing the boundaries of body, household, and sometimes communities through marital exchange. As Jackson points out, "passage across these very borders is vital to life and livelihood" (1998:50). Like the Kuranko of Sierra Leone, Saharans strived to monitor and control interactions between self and other (a category that included humans, animals and spirits), but too much emphasis on the practice of interiority cut off opportunities that entailed gestures of openness. The Saharan wedding ritual required the bride to cross the boundary of the groom's household and the groom to cross the boundary of the bride's body to create new opportunities for the birth of children and alliances between affines. When the marital arrangement crossed the boundaries of two communities, new opportunities for economic and political cooperation arose. At the same time, however, the crossing of boundaries involved the disruption of the preferred style of interiority in social life. Weddings exposed the participants to strangers whose intensions were uncertain. As such, participation in weddings heightened a desire for added forms of protection.

The desire for protection varied depending upon the degree to which participants felt exposed to danger during the transitional ritual. The bride in the Errachidia wedding married her maternal cousin and the wedding took place in her natal household's side yard. Her wedding entailed the crossing of fewer boundaries than either of the village weddings. In the Tinii case, the bride had to move to a new household and a new village even though she was also marrying a cousin. The Tinii bride was the only one of the three that I noticed wearing an amulet in addition to the traditional wedding costume. The bride in the Zaouia wedding had to move to a new household, but it was within sight of her natal household, located further down the road in the same village. Moreover, the groom's parents lived abroad, so her new household would consist of just her and her husband for most of the year.

My observational notes of the weddings revealed that the guests also responded to the danger of openness. The sense of this danger was heightened when the wedding involved the merging of two communities and among guests who were also in a state of transition. The placement of betrothed couples and young children in similar categories of vulnerability suggests that transitional social statuses exposed bodies (and households or communities) to harm over an extended period of time. That is to say, the Saharan construction of vulnerability encompassed not only the ritual activity of crossing a boundary, as in the consummation of marriage or the entrance of a bride into the groom's household, but also in gradual states of transition between two social categories. When I attended the wedding in Errachidia, I was neither single nor married and, according to Saharan health culture, this status increased my vulnerability to harm from sorcery and the Eye. Young children in Saharan culture occupied a similar intermediate state of being because infant mortality was so high in recent collective memory. Exposure to strangers with uncertain intentions at weddings was less dangerous for other categories of guests, provided that they conformed to the customs of sharing food, giving gifts, and participating in group performances of song and dance.

From the perspective of guests, these wedding customs allowed for the relaxation of the everyday interpretation of interiority and created new openings for social ties between households and communities. Weddings provided a contained context for young women to display their beauty and their mothers to display the household's wealth through jewelry and ornate caftans in the hope of attracting marriage proposals. The relaxation of the everyday aesthetic of interiority allowed both young and old women to dance in a seductive hip-swerving style, to decorate their faces with make-up, and to wear colorful caftans with sparkling metallic embroidery. The festivities were full of laughter and excitement and I heard no warnings about the need to be careful or the potential for danger (with the exceptions of young children and engaged couples I mentioned above). The degree of openness among wedding guests was greater in the Errachidia wedding than in the village weddings, where women covered their heads and shoulders with a taharuut when in the presence of male guests. Nonetheless, women in both contexts participated in public dancing and singing as well as sharing food with women from other households.

Isolation and Unity

The mechanism that protected Saharan wedding guests from harm, according to the implicit assumptions in popular health culture, was their participation in social acts of equivalence and obligation. As described in Chapter 4, the act sharing food from the same plate with other people—even strangers— unified the group in a social bond of trust and obligation that approximated the bonds of blood in a family. With everyone contributing food and eating from common serving plates, there was little chance for a sorcerer to single out one person to harm. Similarly, there was little chance for a guest to become an object of envy as long as her appearance and behavior stayed within the boundaries of custom.

The village weddings I attended hosted approximately 100 guests, at considerable expense to the groom's family. Saharans viewed the extension of generous hospitality to be an essential part of not only hosting a good wedding but ensuring a good marriage. The prevalence of divorce cast a shadow of uncertainty over Saharan weddings and adherence to the aesthetic of unity in both social and spiritual forms provided Saharan households with a strategy for protection against the threat of envy, magical curses, or simple bad luck. Elder housewives from Zaouia said that in the past all the women in the village worked collectively to help the groom's household make couscous and bread for the wedding. The ksar would try to celebrate 2 or 3 weddings collectively to economize the work and expenses involved in hosting a wedding. This collective sentiment had diminished by the mid-1990s when I was conducting fieldwork, but wedding guests continued to contribute gifts of sugar and bread to the groom's household. In return, the Muslim value of unity compelled the host family to share their good fortune with everyone in the community. The wedding feast, like all other lifecycle feasts served as a gesture of thanks to Allah, demonstrated explicitly through the sacrifice of a ram or a calf for the occasion. Few households, however, had the resources to feed an entire village or neighborhood. The village of Zaouia managed this dilemma in the summer of 1997 by holding 4 separate weddings at the same time so that each host would have fewer guests.

Although the customs of sharing food offered a sense of protection to the wedding hosts (i.e., the groom's household) and their guests, they extended little protection to the bride. The role of the bride in the Saharan wedding ceremony isolated her from the other participants. The customs that took place over the first two days of the wedding drew attention to her as an individual through her distinct clothing, the activities of preparing her headdress (either as a veil or make-up), and the display of her wedding gifts. In the town wedding, the public attention on the bride as an individual was brief. The preparation of her make-up took place in a private room away from the wedding guests and her wedding carriage only had to travel a short distance from the house to the tent in the side yard when she made her debut. For the remainder of the evening the bride sat on stage with the groom. In contrast, the bride was the sole focus of the village weddings for the better part of the first two days. The groom appeared briefly for the first part of the henna ceremony, but a white tarp shielded him from public view when his attendants applied henna to his hands and feet. Otherwise, the groom stayed with his friends away from the festivities until the consummation of the marriage. The bride, in contrast, had to sit alone on display, first outside her natal home, then at the groom's home.

Most of the attention extended to the bride at the village weddings took the form of congratulations, praise, and wishes for good fortune, but the attention itself could be unsettling in a culture that avoided any form of isolation. Prior to their weddings, young women in the Sahara rarely owned any private property. For example, Saharan parents gave gifts to all the children in the household at the end of Ramadan or to boys on the day of their circumcision, but no one celebrated individual birthdays. The avoidance of isolating activities helped to preserve a sense of unity and solidarity in households, and from the perspective of the popular health culture, they helped to prevent feelings of envy in the household or community.

Of all the participants in Saharan wedding rituals, brides had the highest degree of isolation, not only because their costume and gifts set them apart but also because of the local post-marital residence patterns. This custom, which required the bride to move from her native household to her marital household, isolated her temporarily during the wedding ceremony. This transition occurred in the village weddings but not in the Errachidia wedding, where the bride stayed in her natal household. As such, she required less protection. The village brides, on the other hand, spent one day in an in-between, transitional state when they were separated from their childhood household but not yet incorporated into the groom's household.

To protect the bride during this middle stage of the transition, Saharan custom relied on composing her body in terms of the aesthetic of interiority, as described above, as well as creating an aesthetic of unity through the henna ceremony. The sharing of henna from the same plate symbolically unified the bride and groom before their actual unification as husband and wife when they consummated the marriage. Saharan tradition invited the guests to share the henna as well, creating a temporary social unit during the wedding. In this way, the sharing of henna reproduced the aesthetic of unity established through the sharing of food, but in a minimal, precarious way. The henna ceremony, which took place on the first day of the wedding, initiated the bride's separation from her natal household. After that point, the cultural construction of her vulnerability to harm increased. Traditionally brides avoided sharing any food or drink until the consummation of the marriage after the second day of the wedding. Once the bride and groom unified their social statuses through the act of sexual intercourse, the bride was free to remove her veil and to partake in the feast on the last day of the wedding. At one of the village weddings I attended, however, there was an attempt to provide food and drink for the bride before the last day. My research assistant worried that the bride would faint from hunger and exhaustion and advised the bride's attendants to bring her something she could eat under the veil when the rest of the guests were eating. This advice conflicted with the traditional precautions for avoiding harm, but made sense to the bride's attendants given their knowledge of biomedical concepts of health promotion. The compromise the young attendants made between popular and biomedical health knowledge, per Mama's advice, was to take portions from the food they were eating themselves rather than asking for a special plate prepared by the women of the groom's household (who may have harbored envy or ill will).

Imbalance and Equilibrium

A third aesthetic pattern I noticed in Saharan wedding customs was the arrangement of paired relationships in the design of the bride's costume and in the dance performances. This structure was a less prevalent theme in my field notes, but nonetheless the opposition of imbalance and equilibrium in wedding celebrations was densely integrated with the other aesthetic structures of vulnerability and protection for the bride, the groom's household, and the guests. Weddings disrupted the balance that Saharan households tried to create with other households in the community. The good fortune of the bride, the groom, and their respective households introduced a form of inequality into the community and increased the chance that feelings of envy would arise among the less fortunate households. The resulting imbalance in the community exposed the couple and their households to harm in the form of the Eye or sorcery. This threat was amplified when a member of the participating households objected to the match or when other households had aspired for a marital arrangement with either the bride or the groom.

To counteract the imbalance, Saharan wedding customs composed an aesthetic structure of balance at the level of the bride's body and at level of community through the wedding feast and haaduuz dancing. The composition of equilibrium was less evident in the Errachidia wedding than in the aesthetics of the village weddings. The only prominent structures of balance I noticed at the town wedding were the four young men who carried the wedding carriage (two on each side) and the henna tattoos on the bride's hands. The deliberate creating of symmetry in the preparation of the bride's costume in the village tradition was more explicit. At the Zaouia wedding, the bride's attendants plaited her hair in 2 braids on either side of her head.[3] The arrangement of bride's jewelry also followed a pattern of paired symmetry. The brides wore 2 sets of triangular pins: one set connected a metal chain on over her headdress and the other connected a larger chain from one shoulder to the other.

Two ritual activities in the village wedding also constructed an aesthetic of balance among the participants. The pageant on the first day when the isnan delivered wedding gifts to the bride and her household served as a symbolic compensation to the bride's family in anticipation of the labor and progeny the bride would give to the groom's household during the marriage.[4] The second way of constructing balance occurred in the traditional Berber haaduuz dance. The two lines of the haaduuz arranged the men and women of the two families and the guests in a balanced, cooperative ritual performance of the Berber tradition. As the two lines moved and sang in unison, each man and woman (of all ages) faced their counterpart in the other line, but at a respectful distance and in modest dress: women wore taharuut over their heads and shoulders (with some concealing their faces) and men wore long gandura shirts. The dance embodied the balance of men and women in a marriage, in the household, and in the community. The Berber participants in my study enjoyed this type of dancing to such an extent that at various points during my fieldwork women (young and old) said wistfully that they needed a wedding in the family so that they all could dance the haaduuz.

Defilement and Purification

The final dimension of the cultural aesthetics of vulnerability and security in the context of weddings took form as the opposition of defilement and purification. The bride's transition from a virgin to a wife through the ritual consummation of the marriage marked the apex of Saharan wedding customs. In other parts of the Arab world (Abu Lughod 1993), including other parts of Morocco, the display of a blood stained sheet or undergarment after the consummation serves as proof of the bride's virginity. In the Saharan custom, however, verification of the bride's pure, honorable status was a private matter between the bride and groom and their senior attendants. Not only did Saharans view the public display of hymen blood or any other bodily substance as defiling (cf MacPhee 2004), but also they avoided discussing the topics of sex, blood, and coital fluids in public contexts, particularly in the company of respected elders and members of the opposite sex. Even in conversations among close friends, Saharan women used the term hashak (explained in Chapter 4) to remove the polluting effect of the topic.

Although the popular health culture depicted the defiling substances produced during sexual intercourse as harmful to both the participants and others they encountered outside the context of the bedroom, Saharans viewed sex as an important and pleasurable part of marriage. The notion of defilement in relation to sexual activity reflected a cultural preference to separate private and public activities as a means to maintain social order, rather than a condemnation or distaste for the act itself. To maintain social order at weddings, Saharans allowed the bride and groom privacy when they consummated the marriage. Only the waziir and waziira (respected attendants of the groom and bride) were privy to knowledge about the successful completion of the consummation and the bride's virginity. For the other guests and family members, the appearance of the bride the next morning without her veil served as an indication that everything had gone well.

Another custom that counteracted the disruption of the aesthetic order of purity (that is, the separation of defiling substances and topics from social life) at weddings was the prevalence of the color white. In the traditional Berber wedding custom, both the groom and the bride dressed in white. Similarly, the isnan wore white robes and trousers. The paint on groom's house was also white. The cultural association of white with the concept of purity extended to other Saharan customs as well. Saharan Muslims who completed the pilgrimage to Mecca, for example, wore white clothing upon their return home to represent the cleansing of their soul. I was unable to observe the other wedding customs that involved purifying activities, such as the bathing rituals before the wedding and after the consummation or the practice in which the groom says "bismillah" (in the name of Allah) before penetrating the bride for the first time. As such, I cannot comment on whether or how the participants adhered to any of these customs at the weddings I attended.

One of the paradoxes of the aesthetic of purity at weddings was the practice of leaving young children in a dirty state as a form of protection from the Eye. At the Tinii weddings a few mothers even left their toddlers (and the rest of the guests!) to endure the odor of soiled diapers during the festivities. Although young children were exempt from the standards of purity that adults upheld for both social and spiritual activities, a mother who ignored the standards would be the object of ridicule and gossip in ordinary circumstances. Indeed, housewives listed bathing and washing clothing as principal strategies they used to keep their children healthy. My observance of children with dirty faces, clothing, and diapers at weddings revealed the extent to which mothers feared inciting feelings of envy from other guests.

The Aesthetic Underpinnings of Vulnerability Management

Participation in the protective customs enacted during life transition rituals conveyed practical knowledge to Saharan housewives about how and when the body was vulnerable to danger as well as the mechanisms that protected it. Through customs that protected the bride during the wedding ceremony or the mother during childbirth, Saharan women learned to associate particular feelings, relationships, and body parts with danger. In turn, this embodied knowledge shaped the way that they interpreted and responded to less predictable disruptions to the order of everyday life. As demonstrated in the discussion of weddings, the source of disruption could be positive in nature as well as negative because the local sense of well-being hinged on the maintenance of the overall aesthetic order of interiority, unity, balance, and purity. Any change to those structures—whether it was a marriage, a child's illness, or neighbor's hesitation to return a favor—could trigger concerns about vulnerability to illness and misfortune. Because the dimensions of both the disrupting and the stabilizing qualities of experience combined and expressed themselves in multiple ways, the evaluation of vulnerability in specific contexts was challenging for a cultural outsider such as me. For women who grew up in Saharan culture, however, their participation in everyday life and in ritual events enabled them to develop an internal subjective index for evaluating the difference between vulnerability and security in culturally appropriate ways.

As shown in the description of variations in Saharan wedding practices, women's strategies of protection sometimes diverged from the dictates of local custom. The groom's family in Tinii minimized the use of white paint at the wedding. In Errachidia, the family opted for a modern wedding ceremony that revealed the bride's hair and face. Although each individual had a slightly different index of the external conditions and internal feelings that triggered a sense of vulnerability, the social nature of Saharan health practices—both in discussing the significance of bodily sensations and in enacting therapeutic strategies—established common structures of knowledge and experience. Those internalized structures contributed substantially to the overall Saharan habitus because life cycle rituals were large communal affairs which dominated women's conversation for weeks before and after the event. Through informal evaluations about the appropriateness of someone's behavior or the health consequences of failing to follow tradition, the women of the community established the cultural limits of individual interpretations of custom. At the weddings I attended, for example, my companions criticized the clothing of some young female guests as being too revealing (one dress was so transparent that the girl's underwear was visible).

Saharan housewives attempted to compose aesthetic order in all kinds of transitional contexts including illness and travel, but the remaining chapters in Part II focus on transitions related to maternal-child health. The following chapters present case studies, which explore how particular Saharan women managed their vulnerability to danger during the transitional contexts of pregnancy, childbirth, and breastfeeding. The analysis of women's behavior in relationship to the aesthetic structures of embodied experience helps to illuminate the cultural underpinnings of the health seeking strategies they employed.

I discuss how particular strategies hinged on managing learned sensibilities to the local aesthetics of vulnerability and security rather than on direct adherence to protocols specified in Saharan popular health culture. Even when the protocols had direct relationship to the prevention of illness and death, managing vulnerability in Saharan households was more of an art than a science. Although the popular health culture incorporated modern and ancient medical knowledge, it also included social and symbolic interpretations of illness and healing. Moreover, housewives relied on gut feelings and common sense rather than scientific tests when deciding which aspects of health knowledge to use at a given time. Saharan customs for pregnancy, childbirth and breastfeeding established protocols for reducing vulnerability and preventing illness, but medical pluralism and ethnic diversity in the region introduced several variations for each protocol.

The case studies described in Part II highlight how the complexity and ambiguity that arise from contingencies faced in everyday life added even more confusion about the best way to reduce one's vulnerability to danger. For Saharan housewives, the art of protection included social, spiritual and symbolic practices in place of or in conjunction with medical protocols. The way that these various factors combined in particular contexts illuminate the role of cultural aesthetics and embodied experience as housewives put their health knowledge into action.

CHAPTER 6

NAIMA'S PREGNANCY

The emphasis on prenatal care in the Moroccan Ministry of Health agenda for rural populations in the mid-1990s pushed pregnancy to the forefront of my research on medical pluralism and maternal-child health. My research interests encompassed a broad view of maternal-child health that included family planning and female education, but prenatal care and immunizations dominated public health activities in Errachidia Province, especially in the rural villages. At the time of my research, the rate of prenatal consultations, including immunization against tetanus was low in Morocco overall. The geographic region that encompassed Errachidia achieved a rate of 50.5% for prenatal consultations according to a 1992 survey (Direction de la Statistique 1994:211).[1] My brother-in-law, who had worked as a traveling nurse in rural parts of the region said that prenatal care was the dominant aspect of his work. One initiative required him to go to women's houses to conduct prenatal check-ups. This emphasis on prenatal care in the national public health agenda motivated me to use questions about pregnancy as a starting point for my interviews with housewives. My primary goal at the time was to elicit housewives' responses to public health messages and assess the extent to which they incorporated scientific advice into their own practices. But, I was also interested in learning about how the popular health culture constructed pregnancy with respect to health. Although both the local health culture and public health perspectives viewed pregnancy as a status that increased a woman's susceptibility to illness, household strategies of protection did not always conform to biomedical advice.

The question that launched my exploration of Saharan household health practices in Errachidia asked housewives about pregnancy in *zman* (time-past). The decision to focus the first round of interviews on past practices was strategic. I predicted, correctly, that the senior women in the households that I had recruited would do all of the talking during the first interview and I hoped to build a rapport with them. I assumed that these mothers-in-law and grandmothers would find it easier to answer a question about the traditional ways that women protected their health during pregnancy in the past than to describe the more recent biomedical concerns about birth control technologies and prenatal care.

The question succeeded in putting housewives at ease, but much to my surprise, the participants in Errachidia, and later in the Zaouia sample had little to say on the topic of pregnancy. Instead, they responded to the question by describing their experiences with childbirth. Pregnancy, it seemed, had a far less prominent place in women's narratives of the past.

The silence about pregnancy stemmed in part from the dearth of explicit therapies for pregnant women in Saharan popular health culture. Public health initiatives in recent years introduced new prenatal protocols for immunizing against tetanus and monitoring the progress of the pregnancy. In contrast, midwives offered little advice until the onset of labor. My interview with two neighbors in Errachidia, however, revealed some of the implicit practices embedded in Saharan customs for pregnancy, particularly in relation to the aesthetic of interiority. Their comments along with my notes on more casual conversations with other senior housewives helped me to understand the cultural tactics a Berber mother employed to cope with a difficult pregnancy during my fieldwork in 1996. Naima's pregnancy (discussed at the end of the chapter) serves as a case study on the way one Saharan woman adjusted her interpretation of popular health knowledge to fit her particular social and experiential situation. Although her actions seemed to demonstrate resistance to biomedical advice, a deeper level of analysis showed that she viewed biomedical health services as a resource for her household. Her health care strategy for this pregnancy, however, reflected a contingency response to reduce her vulnerability in accordance with local aesthetic structures.

Pregnancy Customs

Before I delve into the details of the unusual context of Naima's pregnancy, some background on the common Saharan patterns of practice during pregnancy is needed. The two neighbors who helped me understand the household art of protection during pregnancy were among the first women who volunteered to participate in my study. I met Lalla Aicha and Arquia at Fatim-Zahra's nfas (described in Chapter 3) and recruited them to participate in my study shortly thereafter. My first official interview with both of them occurred in the late spring of 1996. Lalla Aicha, an Arab widow, lived with her divorced daughter, two sons, and a new daughter-in-law at the end of an unpaved alley on the outskirts of Errachidia. She was in her early 50s and had lived in Errachidia for about 15 years. Arquia, who was a few years younger than Lalla Aicha, lived next door with 8 of her children and 2 daughters-in-law in a new cement block house. The family was still in the process of constructing the second floor, which had walls but no roof. Arquia was the de facto head of this large Rgaiga household; she considered her husband to be a member of the household but he was absent more than he was present.

It was impossible to visit Lalla Aicha without someone from Arquia's household knowing about our arrival, especially on warm afternoons when the young women would sit in the doorways in search of a cool breeze. My original plan was to interview Lalla Aicha alone during the traditional late afternoon visiting hours, but when Arquia—not realizing the visit was a formal one—came over a few minutes later I decided simply to interview them together. The decision to interview two women at once was ambitious in light of my rudimentary comprehension of Moroccan Arabic at the time, but I relied on Mama and a translator to fill in the gaps on both sides of the conversation.

The formality of my notebook and list of questions contrasted with the informality of the setting. We all sat on a large, frayed plastic mat on the floor of Lalla Aicha's front guest room. The winter décor of wool rugs and brocade banquets were stacked against the far wall in attempt to make the room cooler. That afternoon, however, there was no escaping the intense heat of late spring in the desert. I was not surprised when Lalla Aicha complained of feeling hot. The perspiration on her pale face and hands drew my attention to the knit sweater she was wearing over three other layers of clothing. When I commented that the weather was too warm for a sweater, she replied that her *masran* (intestine) had been bothering her since Ramadan. This response was her way of explaining that her layered attire was therapeutic. The herbal infusions and pharmacy medicines that she had tried were ineffective in relieving her abdominal pain, but she said she felt well enough to proceed with the interview. I feared that the interview would be too taxing, but hoped that it might distract her from her illness.

When I asked Lalla Aicha and Arquia what a woman did to protect her health during pregnancy in the past, both women laughed. They said that young brides were ashamed to say that they were pregnant. They used the expression *kiif-kiif* to explain that nothing changed and each woman took a turn describing her own experience. Arquia said that when she was pregnant she walked 4 kilometers carrying heavy sacks. She also had to grind wheat and carry water when she lived with her husband's family in a small village south of Errachidia. Arquia, who was in her late 40s at the time of the interview, was tall and had the smooth complexion and strong physique of a much younger woman. It was easy to imagine that she was capable of such strenuous labor as a teen during the first of her 14 pregnancies. Lalla Aicha told a similar tale of hardship, although it was harder to picture her cleaning the house, preparing soup and bread, and then giving birth the next day. As a shurfa Arab, Lalla Aicha's family had enough wealth to dig a well in the household, but she said the women still had to grind the wheat by hand. She was much shorter than Arquia and had a weary disposition and wrinkled complexion, which made her appear much older than her neighbor.

Although both women endured the difficulty of raising children in premodern conditions with little help from their husbands, their narratives reflected the pride of survival rather than complaints about injustice. Lalla Aicha boasted that she carried one child on her back and another in her "*krsh*" (stomach) while her husband did nothing. Arquia agreed that the men knew nothing about pregnancy or raising children; her husband just ate and went to work. New mothers learned from other women that eggs, boiled okra, and tea with black pepper were good for pregnancy but the leaf of apricot and caraway were dangerous. Otherwise, pregnant women ate the same diet as they usually did unless they experienced *l-luHam* (cravings). Arquia explained that if a pregnant woman craved a particular food, her husband's family had to give it to her:

> Don't hide anything from the pregnant one. The mother-in-law has to give the bride a little of whatever she has. The women crave what is in the palm grove (May 1996).

According to popular health culture the consequence of denying such cravings for scarce foods such as fruit or meat was that the child would be born with a blemish in the shape of the food the mother craved. Birthmarks served as a permanent sign of the mother's mistreatment by her husband's family but also of her resilience.

In past decades prior to the aggressive promotion of prenatal care in rural Morocco, the phenomenon of l-luHam was the only public indication that a woman was pregnant. On several occasions, middle-aged and senior women in the study remarked that they disguised their pregnancy under a taharuut or *lizar* (sheet worn as a cloak). The explanation they gave was that they felt ashamed to reveal the pregnancy to their in-laws, even though children were valued highly in Saharan households. The shame came from the association between pregnancy and sexual relations, a topic that breached the principle of purity in the structures of social respect between a new bride and her mother-in-law.[2] Concealing the pregnancy also protected the mother and fetus from the harmful gaze of an envious neighbor or visitor. Anthropologists have reported similar customs of hiding pregnancy as a form of protection in other African cultures with personalistic explanations of illness and misfortune, including Malawi (Launiala and Honkasalo 2010) and Mozambique (Chapman

2006). These practices stand in sharp contrast to public health recommendations for prenatal check-ups, vitamins, and immunizations that called attention to pregnant women.

I imagined I would hear about similar therapeutic or health promoting practices for pregnancies when I interviewed midwives, but there were few explicit protocols. The one professional midwife in town (i.e., the only one who charged a fee) advised that pregnant women should avoid shock, carrying heavy loads, and herbal medicines that were *Har* (humorally hot), such as cloves or chili pepper. She said in an interview that a woman should consult her 15 days after she knows she is pregnant to estimate the due date. Otherwise, she specified no other protocol for prenatal care. Household customs were even less explicit. Aside from a few women who mentioned in interviews that they had lost their appetite or had suffered from cramps during pregnancy, there was little commentary about pregnancy among any of the participants, young or old. The majority of participants said that pregnant women simply continued their regular routine of housework.

On the surface these comments suggested an attitude of indifference toward pregnancy, but underlying the interview responses was common knowledge that pregnant women rarely revealed their status to anyone outside their immediate family. The current practice in the 1990s was less extreme than the past trend in which young brides were ashamed to tell their in-laws about the pregnancy, but the pattern of silence was the same. Only two participants in my research sample disclosed their pregnancy to me (Naima, discussed in this chapter and Fatiha, discussed in Chapter 8). Both were in their 3rd trimester and the pregnancy was obvious. I learned of two other pregnancies among the participants after the mothers gave birth. One of these women spoke with me about reproductive health several times during the first four months of her pregnancy (her 6th child), but never mentioned her own status. I was stunned when I returned to Errachidia in the summer of 1997 and met her 6-week-old daughter. Similarly, the responses of three other young participants to my questions about immunizations and contraception led me to suspect that they were in the early stages of pregnancy, but none of them admitted it directly. In this light, I came to view a woman's continuation of her regular housework routine during pregnancy as a ruse to avoid the dangers of the Eye, magical curses, and sorcery. In the same way that Saharan households concealed both good and bad news from the neighbors, pregnant women employed a strategy of interiority to prevent the kind of social imbalance that might lead to envy. The interpretation of when a mother was socially and physically (i.e., in terms of gestation) vulnerable to the danger of envy, however, could fluctuate over the course of the pregnancy.

Pregnant and Divorced

The experience of Naima, a Berber woman in her twenties from Zaouia, helps to illustrate how one household improvised a strategy of interiority in their effort to cope with the overlap of three types of vulnerability: pregnancy, illness, and divorce. I met Naima in September 1996 when I interviewed her mother Rbia about pregnancy and children's health in the past. Other women in Zaouia had been pushing me to meet Rbia because she had lived as a *rHala* (nomad) in the mountains before settling in the village for her old age. The unpainted walls and lack of furnishings in her 4 room mud-brick house gave the impression that she had settled in Zaouia recently and that her household was on the lower end of the socio-economic range in the village. Shortly after Rbia moved into her new house, her two daughters and their children moved to Zaouia to live with her. Naima, the younger of the two, arrived that year after divorcing her husband, who lived further south in the valley.

It was unusual for the villagers to welcome strangers into their community, so I was intrigued by their insistence that I visit Rbia. No one encouraged me to speak with the share-croppers who recently settled in the old ksar on the periphery of the village. Some women went so far as to warn me that it was dangerous even to go into the old ksar (where most of the villagers lived as children). Rbia, however, lived in the new part of the village and more importantly, she represented Berber nostalgia for the past when their nomad ancestors controlled the trade routes and politics of the region. Her leathery skin, blackened hands (from repeated use of henna), facial tattoos, and striped woolen cape in the traditional colors of red, white, and black reinforced the association. For the village women, Rbia also represented rHala expertise with traditional medicine and they were certain I would learn a wealth of knowledge about plant medicines from her. My visits to her household and the stories she told about her past revealed that she had extensive experience with using herbal remedies to treat illness, but she struggled to manage her family's health problems just like the other housewives in the study. The local characterization of Rbia as a traditional doctor was an overstatement of her knowledge.

That autumn, Rbia's household suffered a long string of illnesses. Autumn was a time that Saharans worried about *bdl-l-jau* (the changing of the weather), which caused people to catch cold and to be "hit" by the sun. Headaches and coughs were common complaints in the other households in the village, but Rbia's household was suffering from more serious symptoms when I came to visit for the second time in mid-October. When Rbia greeted us at the front door, Mama and I explained that we wanted to talk with the young women of the household, but the house was so quiet I feared no one else was home. Rbia, however, led us to an unfurnished room at the back of their house where we found Naima and her 2 year-old daughter sleeping on the floor. We offered to return another time, but Naima and her mother insisted that we stay, showing their gratitude for the 2 cones of sugar we brought as compensation for the interview. Naima explained that she and her daughter had been sick for 3 days with diarrhea and fever, and the daughter had been vomiting. I noticed also that Naima had a congested cough. She thought that the illness may have come from the sun or the wind, but at that point she had not consulted any medical practitioners, including the public health staff, who had been in the village that week for the national immunization campaign. Instead they used simple home treatments of soup and rest. Naima said that she was afraid to use any herbal medicines for herself because she was pregnant. Her usual fever remedy of soup with chili pepper and cumin was too hot for a pregnant woman to eat.

I was surprised that Naima spoke as openly about her current pregnancy as she did about her first birth experiences. She was the first participant in the study to do so. The custom of wearing layers of loose-fitting dresses and robes allowed Saharan women to conceal a pregnancy well into the third trimester. Naima, however, had a tall wiry build that seemed to emphasize her pregnancy under the flowered dress and cotton leggings she was wearing. With the exception of the fetus itself, I suspected that she had not gained much weight since she became pregnant. Nonetheless, the interview was general enough that she could have avoided discussing her condition or asked her older sister to participate in the interview in her place. For some reason, she trusted Mama and me with the information even though she had met us only a month earlier when we interviewed her mother.

We learned during the interview that this was Naima's third pregnancy. Her first two children were born in the tent where she lived with her husband and his parents. Her mother-in-law served as a midwife and they followed traditional Berber customs of washing the mother's face after the birth with barley and *smin-l-Har* (clarified butter) and eating dates cooked in oil on the seventh day post-partum. When I asked about immunizations, she told us that her children had been immunized but she had not. As I mentioned in Chapter 3, the Moroccan Ministry of Health made an extensive effort to immunize all women of child-bearing age against tetanus. Mobile immunization campaigns helped the Ministry of Health reach the most rural populations, but the rHala traveled in such remote parts of the desert and mountains that their access to biomedical care was minimal. Naima, however, did have past experience with biomedicine when she took the contraceptive pill after the birth of her first child. She consulted a doctor because the pill had caused irregular bleeding. She said that once she stopped taking the pill, she was fine and had not seen a doctor since that time.

By coincidence, the national immunization campaign came to Zaouia 3 days prior to my interview with Naima. I asked if she had gone over to the village health dispensary that day but she said she did not hear about it. I, too, had missed the announcement even though I was in the village the day before the campaign. But, the commotion on the day of the campaign made it difficult to miss hearing about the event. Dozens of women and children were gathered all afternoon at the health dispensary, located the center of the village not far from Naima's house. Their laughter and excited conversations as well as the screams of children who were afraid of the injections created substantial noise in an otherwise quiet little village. It is possible that Naima had been out in the fields on the other side of the river like two other young women I had spoken with that week. Alternatively, she could have heard the noise and thought it was related to the schistosomiasis eradication campaign that had come through the village the previous week. Even though the village nurse had sent the muqaddam to summon personally all the women and children who needed vaccines, it is likely that his records overlooked Naima because she was new to Zaouia. Knowing that she was pregnant and sick at the time of the interview, however, I was surprised that she did not seek out medical attention, particularly because she was worried about taking herbal medicines.

When I visited Naima's household again 2 months later, her motivation for avoiding the immunization campaign became more apparent to me. Mama and I stopped by their house just before the midday prayer on our way back from another household interview. Rbia answered the door and led us to the roof where Naima was sleeping against a far wall in the sun. On our way across the roof we spotted Naima's daughter squatting to urinate among the dozen sheep clustered on the other side of the roof. Despite the chill of the mid-December air, the sheep and their dung attracted a thick swarm of flies, which dissuaded us from staying for lunch. We visited just long enough for an update on Naima's pregnancy.

Naima's abdomen was much larger than the last time we saw her, suggesting that her due date was imminent. She looked pale, tired, and disheveled. Her dress and cardigan sweater were covered with dust, and her long dark curls had fallen out of her headscarf. When Mama teased lightheartedly that Naima still had not given birth, Rbia said that they were worried: "We don't know if this baby is going to be born. We have been waiting two months." I asked if they were sure they had counted the dates correctly, not realizing the insensitivity of my question until after I had voiced it. Because Naima was divorced, the timing of her pregnancy had implications for her honor. I was unaware of the exact timing of her divorce, but Rbia's and Naima's insistence that she became pregnant during *l-eid as-sghir* (i.e., the "small" feast at the end of Ramadan) led me to conclude that she separated from her husband close to that time (the last week in February). By that estimate, Naima was overdue by 2 weeks at most, not 2 months.

One of the ways that Saharan popular health culture explained delayed birth in the past was through the illness construct of the sleeping baby. When gestation took longer than 9 months, housewives said that the baby was sleeping in the womb. The sleeping could last as little as a month or a long as several years. Married women who had experienced this phenomenon explained that they had stopped menstruating and thought that they were pregnant, but the baby did not start growing in the womb until several months later. Prolonged amenorrhea was the main sign of the sleeping baby, but one woman reported also having l-luHam, which was a telltale sign of pregnancy in the local culture. When I heard about this phenomenon, I thought that it would help to maintain the reputation of divorced women who became pregnant after they separated from their husbands. The timing of Naima's pregnancy was so close to her divorce that I wondered why the family did not raise the sleeping baby as a possible explanation for the delay. Instead, they seemed to focus more on medical explanations.

The conversation on the roof that day put me in an awkward position as I realized that the family was looking for medical advice, something that happened occasionally over the course of my fieldwork. My educational background and Western identity on top of all my research questions about health gave some Saharans the false impression that I had medical expertise. I assured Naima and her mother that I was not a doctor but I asked a series of questions to try to assess if the delay was a mix-up with the dates or a health problem. Naima's responses to the questions revealed that she could still feel the baby moving and that she felt fine except for feeling tired and sleeping more than usual. She had not tried anything to encourage labor because they viewed that to be against Islamic law. Instead, they were just waiting day after day for the contractions to start. She said that she had no difficulties with her previous births, so I thought they had miscalculated the dates. Nonetheless, I suggested that she try going for a walk to stimulate labor and if there was no change within a few days that she should go to the hospital in Errachidia. We stopped by the house two days later to ask about Naima and her older sister, who had been ill with a cough and a fever during our previous visit. Rbia said that both were fine but she did not invite us to stay for a visit.

Intersections of Health Behavior and Vulnerability Management

The household's sensitivity about the timing of Naima's pregnancy shed new light on her avoidance of the immunization campaign in October. Attending the event would have called attention to her pregnancy in a way that increased her exposure to social scrutiny. Naima was new to Zaouia and had yet to establish the protective social ties that developed through balanced reciprocity with the other women in the village. Simply attending the clinic would have broadcast her pregnancy as it had for another participant in the study. Mina, who was married with 3 children, laughed when her neighbors shouted "You? You?" as she approached the dispensary steps with the muqaddem. Their surprise was a reaction to the need for immunization at her age (early 40s) but the laughter and broad smiles conveyed that everyone, including Mina was happy about the pregnancy. Naima's circumstances were different. Her divorce ruptured the socially appropriate context for pregnancy, that is, within the unified structure of the paternal household.

This rupture isolated Naima in a cultural sense even though she was living with her mother and sister. Although their household practiced social unity in their solidarity with Naima's dilemma and offered her more security than living alone would have, its composition diverged from the dominant cultural pattern of the male-headed household. Rbia's husband was the official head of their household but he spent little time with his second wife and her children. I never saw him nor heard them talk about him in the four times I visited, but he must have supported them financially, at least minimally, because none of the women worked outside the home. In an aesthetic sense, the household's lack of balance between men and women compromised its capacity to construct a secure family unit according to the local cultural criteria. Saharans followed an Islamic world view that considered marriage to be a natural foundation for family life in which husbands and wives represented complementary parts in a unified whole. Rbia and her husband satisfied that cultural criterion in a nominal way but only minimally in a practical way, leaving the women vulnerable socially and culturally.

There was one other all-female household in the village, but this widow and her unmarried daughter had lived in the Zaouia their whole lives. Their long term integration into the unified whole of the community compensated for their vulnerability at the household level. As newcomers to Zaouia, Rbia and her daughters had a more tenuous connection to the community. They had to rely on maintaining an honorable reputation to win the respect of their neighbors whereas long-term residents could rely on the protection that arose from years of participation in social networks of reciprocity and moral obligation. The presence of imbalance in the bodies of Rbia's daughters and grandchildren, who were suffering from some illness or another each time I visited, reinforced the sense of their imbalance and isolation at the household and community levels. The combination of all these disruptions to the expected order of everyday life, in turn, heightened the family's awareness of Naima's vulnerability to other kinds of misfortune.

According to popular health culture, the social and emotional disruption of divorce increased a woman's vulnerability to illness and other misfortune. In Naima's case, her pregnancy added to that vulnerability and complicated her options for protecting her health. Any consultation with the public health staff at the event would have raised questions about the timing of her pregnancy. Such questions put her honor as well as her child's honor at stake. The source of the shame was not the divorce itself, which was common in rural Morocco, but rather the scandal of a child born outside of marriage. Moroccan law stipulated that any pregnancy that occurred within three months of death or divorce would be considered the progeny of the mother's former husband. A pregnancy identified after three months would require another marriage to legitimize the child's status. In this light, the timing of Naima's pregnancy had serious social implications.

The connection of honor and reputation to Naima's management of her health was both direct and indirect. Her avoidance of the immunization campaign put her and her baby directly at risk for tetanus at the time of delivery. At the same time, her decision to stay at home that day aimed to protect her health indirectly. She enacted the Saharan cultural aesthetic of interiority by keeping information about her pregnancy inside her household. Her strategy, however, diverged from the more common reason that Saharan women employed the practice of interiority. Naima's unenviable situation was unlikely to raise the typical pregnancy worries about the Eye, usually blamed on envious outsiders. In this case, Naima was the outsider. A more pressing reason for Naima to practice interiority was to prevent gossip. Speculation about her honor would have compromised her potential for building a social network in the village. Her best option for social, economic and health security in the long term was to marry again. Another option was to rely on assistance from other households in the community. Both of those prospects would diminish substantially if gossip spread about the possibility that she had sex outside of marriage. Although Saharan culture valued charity and hospitality to a wide range of social others, full participation in the unified community of the village hinged on moral behavior. Hence, to gain acceptance into Zaouia's unified moral community and all the protection it could offer to a poor, single mother, Naima had to manage knowledge about her pregnancy. Her social status was so fragile that even the local health construct of the sleeping baby seemed to be unavailable to her. The strategy of interiority provided Naima with the simplest way to prevent gossip and strengthen her overall state of well-being.

The effectiveness of practicing interiority as a health strategy, however, was questionable in Naima's case. When I interviewed her in October she was sick and later in December she was fatigued and worried about delayed labor. In the short term, at least, her reluctance to consult health practitioners outside the household was an insufficient strategy for preventing illness. Furthermore, Naima had far less faith than the other villagers in her mother's expertise as a traditional healer. When I asked her who in the household was responsible for administering medicine (*tdawii*—i.e., treating illness), Naima said that her mother did not know much about herbal medicines or illness: "if someone gets sick, we go find someone who knows and do what they say—make tea of cumin and eat garlic for cold." According to this statement, Naima's decision to self-treat the illnesses she experienced during pregnancy was unusual for her household. Nonetheless, Naima applied common knowledge about the principle of balance in her attempt to cope with the symptoms she had in October. She avoided the humorally hot foods and medicines that had helped her recover from coughs and diarrhea in the past because she considered those treatments to be dangerous for pregnant women, who have a hot temperament. This strategy followed the logic of Saharan popular health culture to protect her pregnancy, but it failed to relieve her symptoms. Her body, like her circumstances, remained in a state of imbalance. Zaouia offered a number of other health resources, including the village nurse, several experienced midwives, and a fqih in a nearby village. Naima, however, was reluctant to consult anyone outside her household, that is, until she asked Mama and me for advice.

Speaking with us about her condition constituted an improvisation from her previous adherence to the aesthetic of interiority. Apparently, Naima viewed us a less dangerous than the local medical practitioners or the other housewives in the village. Together we represented a resource that combined biomedical and popular health knowledge without the associated social risks. On one hand, I was more of an outsider than she was and I was bound by the ethics of social research to maintain the confidentiality of their interview responses. (I had explained their rights orally during the first interview). On the other hand, our visits to the household for the research project resembled local forms of reciprocity that bound Saharan women in networks of moral obligation. Naima helped me by participating in my research interviews and then cashed in the debt when she asked for advice about her pregnancy.

From our conversations, I gained the impression that Naima wanted a healthy pregnancy and safe birth, and was open to using biomedical care. She had immunized her older children and mentioned doctors as a good health resource in her description of treating illnesses. The complex nature of her vulnerability for this pregnancy, however, constrained the range of strategies that were culturally feasible. The social stakes for this household were so high that Naima avoided Mama and me after our conversation on the roof that day in mid-December. I heard later that winter that Naima gave birth to a healthy baby before the end of the month. The only other time I saw her was from a distance at a wedding the following summer. She was walking and laughing with other women her age, which gave me the impression that she had found a place in the village community. Perhaps her strategies worked after all.

CHAPTER 7

THE BIRTH OF FATIHA'S SON

The socially sensitive circumstances of Naima's pregnancy highlight the need for a knowledge-in-action approach to examining individual health behavior. Many of the simple explanations for why someone ignores health recommendations fail to account for Naima's behavior: she had knowledge of prenatal vaccines, she had access to them, and she acknowledged their value in protecting the health of her children. Her reluctance to seek prenatal care stemmed from her concern about the social danger that her precariously timed pregnancy posed for her and her child. Naima applied the resources available to her in a way that fit her unique circumstances and increased the chances of a good outcome with respect to her overall well-being. The same dynamic analysis is appropriate for the examination of Saharan childbirth practices even though the customs for birth were far more explicit than the customs for pregnancy. The interview responses and observational notes I recorded indicated that households improvised in their use of traditional safety protocols for birth depending on several factors, including past experience, resources available at the onset of labor, and other complicating dangers to the household.

One of the households I observed in 1997 demonstrated how childbirth could be a routine event involving minimal precautionary measures. It was a large Berber household located in one of the older neighborhoods of Errachidia. The family's small grocery business afforded them the modern luxuries of a telephone, satellite television, and shower, but still they followed the traditional patrilocal residence pattern. Four married sons shared the same roof with their elderly parents, wives, children, and unmarried siblings. The daughters-in-law estimated that 24 people lived in the household at the time I conducted my first interview in May 1996. The 25th member arrived the following summer, about an hour before Mama and I stopped by for an unannounced visit. The youngest of Haja Abicha's daughters, an attractive teenager with a slight build and an ivory complexion, answered our knock at the door and extended a hushed welcome. She whispered that her sister-in-law Halima had just given birth upstairs. I feared that we were intruding on a private event as we followed the girl to the foyer at the top of the narrow cement stairway, but I realized straightaway that the family had a nonchalant attitude about this birth. The mother, Halima, draped in a flowered sheet was lying on folded blankets arranged as a twin-sized bed on the floor adjacent to the bathroom. Her newborn daughter was next to her covered completely with a clean white cloth. The only sign that she was alive was the kicking of her legs midway through our visit. The grandmother, Haja Abicha, was sitting on a folded blanket near-by winding yarn into a ball and talking with another set of guests, a young mother and her two toddlers. The other women of household were busy downstairs preparing afternoon tea for us.

The scene had none of the commotion that I expected to see after hearing so many women's stories about birth. I knew from previous interviews that the women of this household, especially Haja Abicha, had extensive knowledge of herbal remedies and Berber customs for birth and the nfas period, but I noticed only minimal protective practices that afternoon. In addition to my observation that Halima and the infant were covered with lightweight sheets, I could smell the pleasant aroma of incense lingering in the air and saw that the floor of the foyer was spotlessly clean. Shortly after our arrival Halima asked her sister-in-law to close the windows to keep out the cool wind. These constructions of interiority and purity were far less elaborate than the practices Fatim-Zahra's household (Chapter 3) enacted to protect the health of the mother and infant. Nonetheless, I could tell that this baby had been born just hours before we arrived. Halima looked pale beneath the black scarf that covered her hair and she sighed every so often from fatigue but participated in the conversation as if nothing unusual had happened that afternoon. Giving birth to her fifth child seemed to be a routine event for this 35 year-old mother. She spent more time talking about her oldest son (8 years of age) who had been seriously ill with a fever for two months. The family had taken him to the national hospital in Rabat for specialist care, but he was still sick. We heard the following week that the family decided to postpone the newborn's sbuae until after her brother had recovered fully from his illness.

Childbirth Customs

The sbuae ceremony that publicly declared the name of the child and sacrificed a ram in the child's honor usually took place 7 days after a birth. The timing of the event followed Muslim tradition but also reflected historical uncertainty about infant death in the first week of life. Immunizations against tetanus and public education about the importance of hygiene during the birth process have reduced infant mortality rates in Morocco, but the prevention of infant and maternal death remained a central concern in Saharan birth customs. As Arquia said in her interview with Lalla Aicha, however, Saharan women have different ideas about what the best practices are:

> Everyone wants a good birth. Each woman is different. Some call for the midwife (but) usually the birth happened already before she arrives. The first time there is a midwife, then they do it themselves. Now they don't call anyone. It is enough to have a woman close to you. You learn by watching your own births and (those) of other women (May 1996).

In a country with a high fertility rate,[1] childbirth was a familiar subject to most Saharan women whether they lived in town or in a village. Housewives learned about childbirth from listening to other women's stories, watching their mothers or sisters give birth, or as Arquia pointed out, from their own experiences. In some cases, adolescent daughters served as midwives to their mothers. At gatherings to celebrate a birth during the first week of the nfas, women would exchange knowledge about the effectiveness of herbal infusions, incense, and symbolic rituals in helping to ease labor pain and expedite delivery. The elder women I observed on such occasions described their experiences in the past giving birth at home with only the help of other women or, on occasion, their husbands. Some women boasted that after giving birth, they got up and made dinner or breakfast for the rest of the household, adding that they had no chance to rest like the young mothers today. Other women described dramatic tales of prolonged and painful labor, breech babies, and infant death. The juxtaposition of housewives' accounts of these vastly different experiences created an ambiguous view of birth in the popular health culture: it could be dangerous or ordinary.

Since housewives had no way of predicting in advance whether a given birth would be easy or hard, they took precautions. All of the mothers participating in the study mentioned using protective birth customs to some extent. As outlined in Chapter 3, Saharan popular health culture specified multiple sources of danger and associated protective practices for childbirth. The number and type of practices the mother and her midwife employed depended on the extent to which they felt vulnerable to those dangers during labor and during the first week post-partum. The following description of Saharan birth customs, many of which were mentioned in Chapter 3, highlights the practical logic and aesthetic structures that shaped women's attempts to reduce the sense of vulnerability and promote a good birth outcome.

The most common protective practices Saharan housewives used during labor and the nfas followed the aesthetic of interiority. As I observed when I visited Halima on the afternoon of her daughter's birth, the family used pleasant incense (usually a mix of rosemary, cedar, ambergris, and sweet myrtle), and textiles to create a protective aesthetic barrier around the mother and the infant. Similarly, the custom of sprinkling salt and Harmal on the designated site of the birth and on the baby immediately after birth aimed to block potential attacks from spirits in the vicinity. Protective customs immediately after birth focused on symbolically closing off the infant's body from potential sources of harm. These protocols included putting kuhl or henna with olive oil around the stump of the umbilical cord, kuhl under the eyes, and olive oil or *miswak* (a red root) on the lips. Then the midwife or mother would swaddle the infant's body with a clean white cloth and tie another cloth around the head with a bandana. Precautions against the Eye varied from covering the infant entirely with a white cloth (as both Halima and Fatim-Zahra did during the first week of the nfas) to adorning the infant with amulets. These items included gold rings with a black stone, bracelets made of black and white string, and pendants in the form of an open hand or a brass bullet. Traditionally, Berber mothers who went to work in the fields a week after the birth made an elaborate sash of amulets to protect their infants. In addition to the items listed above, Ait Atta mothers would add salt, Harmal, a strand of their hair, and pieces of meat from the ram slaughtered at the sbuae party.

Another way that childbirth customs employed the aesthetic of interiority as a form of protection was through confining news about the onset of labor to trusted allies. When Haja Abicha's teenage daughter answered our knock on their door, she whispered to tell us that Halima had given birth. We were far enough away from the newborn to discount the interpretation that she meant to avoid startling her with too much noise. Instead, I interpreted the whisper to be an attempt to prevent the neighbors and passersby from knowing the household's good news. Even though the labor and delivery had been easy, the health of the mother and baby remained uncertain during the first few days post-partum. Other housewives in the study spoke about the importance of choosing a qabla who was *qariib* (a close relative or friend) as a strategy for assuring an easy birth. My research assistant thought that the reason for this practice was that the moral status of all the people who knew about the onset of labor would affect its duration: all the sins of the people who knew would have to be erased (i.e., balanced with good deeds) before the baby could be born. Her explanation was unique among other women's descriptions of birth customs, but it captured the sentiment of distrust in Saharan culture and the social orientation of local etiologies of illness. The secretive nature of home birth conformed to the broader logic of Saharan popular health culture, which warned about the dangers of revealing information to people outside the trusted confines of the household.

The aesthetic of interiority had further social and cultural implications for cases involving hospital birth. During one of my visits to Zaouia in the autumn of 1996, I asked a group of women whether they preferred home birth or hospital birth. The six women of mixed generation and ethnicity who gathered for afternoon tea that day all agreed that the house was a better place to give birth. Rachida, a traditional midwife visiting from Errachidia, explained: "We do it (give birth) quietly. We don't divulge our honor to anyone (*kandiru saktin. ma fidah had aeraaDna*). We cut the cord ourselves and sleep with the child." In her statement, Rachida touched upon ways that the shared aesthetic of interiority dissuaded Saharan women from giving birth in hospitals. Hospital procedures for medically attended childbirth required the mother to expose her body—her honor—to strangers. The danger associated with this aspect of hospital birth fell into 2 categories. First many of the medical and nursing staff at the provincial hospital and outlying health dispensaries were male. The idea of exposing one's body to any male other than one's husband conflicted with all that Muslim women learn about shame and modesty. Second, hospital birth increased the chance that the mother and infant would be exposed to strangers with unknown backgrounds or intentions. According to the logic of Saharan popular health culture feelings of envy among the other patients or even the hospital staff would expose the mother and infant to danger. Additionally, the hospital's practice of taking the newborn for examination after birth exacerbated housewives' concerns about the infant's safety. Traditionally, Saharan health practices required a family member to stay with infants constantly from birth until they cut their first tooth.

Although the aesthetic of interiority dominated the design of Saharan birth customs, the aesthetics of balance, unity, and purity also contributed protective structures during labor and after delivery. For example, the aesthetic of balance influenced the type of herbal infusions that women chose as medicine to ease the pain of labor. The warm quality of rosemary, cinnamon, and cumin taken as a tea or with food followed the logic of humoral theory in attempting to manage the cooling process of labor.[2]

The principle of balance also structured the customs of the nfas and the sbuae celebration on the 7th day after birth. The tradition of visiting during the first week post-partum was usually limited to family and close friends. Halima's openness to accepting social distant guests within hours of her daughter's birth demonstrated their low level of concern about danger and vulnerability. I had met the family only twice before and Mama only had a connection with one of the daughters-in-law, who was out of town that day. They family easily could have said that none of the women were home or they could have visited with us in the guest room downstairs without revealing any information about the birth. Instead, they invited us to sit with the nafisa, but enacted a few precautions—such as whispering the news and preventing us from actually seeing the newborn.[3]

More commonly, the sbuae ritual was the time when households invited the more distant parts of their social network to celebrate the birth. In this custom, the household would invite extended family, friends, and neighbors to share a feast of grilled mutton and couscous or vegetable stew in honor of their good fortune. In exchange for this generous hospitality, the guests would bring token gifts of sugar or cash to show their good will toward the family. Although the reciprocal gestures of hospitality and gifts attempted to bind the participants in a single, balanced community, most Saharan households took extra precautions against the Eye during the festivities. At the sbuae parties I attended only close family and friends were permitted to see the infant and new mother, who would remain in the private quarters of the household during the party. The mother, however, would share food with the family and guests for the first time since the birth, representing her incorporation into the unified household and community.

The aesthetic of unity also structured Saharan customs for protecting the infant after birth. All ethnic groups participating in the study followed the custom of saying "Allahu akbar" three times at the moment of birth to welcome the baby to the Islamic community. Arab and Hurtani ethnic groups also asked a fqih to write "*bismillah, ar-rahman, ar-rahiim*" in a bowl or on a piece of paper placed in the bowl. The mother would then pour water into the bowl and place a drop or two on the infant's lips using her finger or a date before giving him or her anything else to eat or drink. These customs and variations of them enacted a spiritual connection with Allah and placed the infant under divine protection. One young Hurtani housewife said that the hospital staff told her that is was bad to give her newborn sugar-water as his first taste because of microbes in the water. She did it anyway because it was their tradition (a variation of the above custom) to say l-bismillah while placing sugar water infant's lips. In this case, the family viewed the aesthetic of unity in its spiritual form as offering greater protection than the aesthetic of purity in a secular form. A few families compromised and boiled the water before placing it on the infant's lips. In the past, the fqih also provided a protective resource for mothers who experienced difficult labor. Two elderly women said that the local fqih wrote a verse from the Quran as a talisman dissolved in water to help hasten their labor. Another woman said that the fqih burned the paper on which he wrote the talisman and she stood over the smoke to help the labor progress.

Because vaginal discharge during and after birth placed new mothers in a state of ritual impurity, they were prohibited from performing the Salat ritual for several weeks post-partum. Nonetheless, the aesthetic of purity contributed to the logic of childbirth customs. All of the mothers in the study described a ritual in which they cleaned their bodies after giving birth. This ritual involved the mother rinsing her mouth three times with clarified butter or oil and then using it to wash her face, breasts, and other parts of the body. Some women said that the process removed dark spots that had appeared on the skin during pregnancy. Others emphasized the importance of cleaning the breast before feeding the infant. Rachida claimed that the mother will itch forever if she ignores this custom, even if she gives birth in the hospital. Other senior housewives mentioned the importance of cleaning the vagina after the birth, usually with water and herbal infusions. This practice, however, had diminished by the time of my research. Fear of jinn and cold persuaded new mothers to avoid bathing with water until several days after the birth.

Medical pluralism offered Saharan women a wide range of ways to protect themselves from the dangers of birth, but these strategies were not always successful. Even some of the younger generation of housewives participating in the study experienced the tragedy of infant death. Despite the dissonance of hospital birth with the aesthetic of interiority, young women increasingly saw it as a potential resource for ensuring a good birth. Only one participant who had a secondary school level of education chose hospital birth as a strategy for preventing complications. She viewed the hospital as offering a cleaner place for birth. A few other housewives preferred having access to the hospital's pain medication. Several other women, however, described the hospital as a resource they used when they encountered problems with home birth. Their dramatic narratives began with accounts of complications with labor at home and ending with an emergency trip to the provincial hospital in Errachidia.

Fatiha's Hospital Birth

One of participants who experienced a late-night emergency trip to the provincial hospital was Arquia's daughter-in-law Fatiha. Her situation was unusual in comparison to other Saharan women of her generation. She married and became pregnant for the first time at an older age than other women in her cohort in the study. Additionally, her ethnic-linguistic identity was different from that of her in-laws. This kind of mixed marriage was unusual in Saharan society, but Arquia said that her sons had their own ideas about whom they wanted for wives. Economic contingencies sometimes led to arrangements outside of the more common ethnically insular marriage trends in the region. Fatiha's parents had died when she was young, making it harder for her to arrange a marriage in her own ethnic group. Arquia's son, on the other hand, had a small but successful business, which made him a desirable match across ethnic groups. Although I had met Fatiha twice during my fieldwork in 1996, I knew little about her life until the birth of her first child in the summer of 1997.

During my first visit to Arquia's home in the spring of 1996 (before her interview with Lalla Aicha), Fatiha joined us later when she brought tea, cookies, and *milwi* (fried bread) for the guests. No one introduced her and she remained silent during our visit, but I assumed she was a daughter-in-law and not a daughter because her physical appearance was significantly different from other women in the family. I learned more about Fatiha's knowledge and attitudes about health care during my third visit to the household. On our way to the interview in mid-October, Mama and I saw Fatiha as she was leaving for the palm grove with the family donkey to gather herbs for the household's livestock. She was dressed for hard work with her dusty skirt hiked up to her knees revealing her cotton pantaloons and plastic sandals. A faded yellow and threadbare sheet thrown hastily over her head and shoulders served as a token of modesty. Although Fatiha was intent on getting to her chores, we convinced her to stay and talk to us for a half-hour. Arquia met us at the front door and invited us into their guestroom, where we sat on pillows arranged around a woven mat on the floor. Their more formal furniture was stacked against the far interior wall waiting for cooler weather.

In the interview, Arquia and her teenage daughter dominated the conversation. Fatiha contributed only a few responses to my questions. She had the quiet, serious disposition of a new teenage bride, despite her strong physique and advanced age. My questions were aimed toward understanding what knowledge and resources the household employed for addressing illness as well as gaining a sense of whether household members converged or diverged in their ideas about health and healing. Arquia's daughter and Fatiha said they used aspirin from the shop near the house to treat simple symptoms like dizziness or feeling tired, but that Arquia treated most other illnesses in the household: "She knows. We don't." Their comment referred to Arquia's knowledge of herbal medicine and fire cauterization (*kawi*). Arquia's daughter added that home remedies were better if the illness was *khafif* (light). For more serious problems that continued for "2, 3, or 5 days," they went to the hospital.

I knew from previous interviews with Arquia, however, that mother and daughter had different views on seeking health care outside the home. For example, when I told Arquia in our first interview that my research concerned matters of health and medicine, she responded by saying, "We don't need a hospital ... all the medicine we need is here. If the children have cold, I rub chicken fat on their chests." This view reflected her confidence in her own healing abilities and the Saharan pattern of interiority more than a complete rejection of biomedicine. In her joint interview with Lalla Aicha, Arquia remarked that she thought that the colonial medicine she remembered from her youth was good, but "people had shame to go to the hospital unless the sickness was heavy, unless you were going to die." In light of Arquia's views on healing, I was surprised when I heard that her daughter-in-law gave birth at the provincial hospital.

I had not seen Fatiha for eight months when I returned to Morocco in the summer of 1997. A few days after my arrival in Errachidia, I walked over to Lalla Aicha's house to visit with her family and found Fatiha, very pregnant, talking to her neighbors. The shurfa women were sitting in their doorway, in search of a cool breeze on a hot July afternoon, and Fatiha was standing next to them. Her rosy cheeks made her look healthier and more relaxed than she did during our last two meetings. It was the first time I had seen Fatiha laugh as she told us the news that she was eight months pregnant. I had heard earlier that week that there was a divorce in Arquia's household, so I was happy to see that her position as a daughter-in-law was becoming more secure with this pregnancy.

News of the birth came to our house on a Sunday morning a month later. Lalla Aicha's oldest daughter brought us the story as an excuse to visit my sisters-in-law. She said that Fatiha had gone to the hospital late at night and gave birth to a son. We were all concerned that there may have been problems with the birth, assuming that Fatiha would have chosen a home birth like so many other women we knew. My brother-in-law frequently returned from his night shifts at the provincial hospital with stories about emergency cesarean sections and maternal hemorrhage, but he was off duty that weekend. Aicha's daughter said that she did not know any details of the birth, only that the family said the sbuae party would take place the next weekend.

The next day, Mama and I took the opportunity of the afternoon visiting custom to pay our respects to the new mother and to bring the household traditional gifts for the nfas. We wanted to bring two cones of sugar but they were difficult to find as the garage grocers were sold out because of a high volume of neighborhood weddings that summer. We could have given Fatiha money, but sugar was a more appropriate gesture for our new friends. We stopped at no less than six shops before we finally found the customary 2 kg cones of sugar, wrapped in blue paper. When we arrived at the house long after the mid-afternoon prayer, 2 other guests had gathered with the women of the household in a small bedroom near the front entrance to the house. It was a scene that had become familiar to me; everyone was laughing and telling stories while the new mother stayed on the periphery of interaction.

The room was decorated in a Western style with furniture in matching blonde wood. Fatiha sat upright on the double bed pushed against the wall, while everyone else crowded below her leaning against cushions on the floor. She was wearing a white polyester caftan and her wavy brown hair was falling loose from her matching headscarf. Just one light blanket covered her from the waist down to protect her from the late summer breeze. Her newborn son was lying next to her facedown, uncovered but hidden from the guests. In comparison to the measures Halima and Fatim-Zahra took to surround themselves and their newborns with protective barriers (using textiles and incense), Fatiha behavior suggested that she had little concern about her vulnerability as a new mother. Arquia seemed to share the same sense of security as her daughter-in-law as she invited the guests to sit in Fatiha's small private bedroom and told the story of her grandson's birth. No one at Halma's nor Fatim-Zahra's nfas celebration revealed any information about the labor and delivery to the guests. This level of openness was unusual, but as the details of the story began to unfold, it became clear that Arquia wanted to air her views about Fatiha's decision to give birth at the hospital.

While passing around a plate of cookies and another plate piled high with powdered spices mixed with sugar, the proud grandmother said that the labor pains had started after *al-eSr* (3rd) prayer and they planned to have the birth in the house. Arquia, who had given birth fourteen times, did not see a need for any other assistance. The mother-in-law is an atypical choice as the midwife for a woman delivering her first child. The Saharan tradition allows a daughter-in-law to return to her mother's home for the first birth experience. This option, however, was unavailable for Fatiha because her mother had died years ago and her sister, who lived in a nearby town, was busy with her own family. Fatiha had to rely on Arquia as a midwife if she planned to give birth at home. Although Fatiha respected her mother-in-law's knowledge of health care, my previous interactions with the family suggested that there was also a respectful social distance between the two women.

Arquia explained to the guests that as the labor pains became worse, Fatiha started to ask to go to the hospital. Fatiha interjected that she knew a nurse at the health dispensary, where she had obtained birth control pills during her first year of marriage. Arquia, however, told the guests: "if I was giving birth, I would want to stay in the house." Fatiha responded by explaining that the pain in her krsh (stomach) was very difficult and getting worse: "*dazt eliia tamaara*" (I was suffering). Contradicting her daughter-in-law, Arquia told the guests that it was fine. She knew that the head of the infant had dropped and thought that the birth was imminent. Arquia said that she tried to convince her daughter-in-law to be patient, but Fatiha insisted that the pain was too great and she wanted to go to the hospital. Arquia feared that the birth would happen in the car on the way to the hospital (something that happened to two other young mothers participating in my study), but she agreed to let her daughter-in-law go anyway.

At this point, Fatiha took over the telling of the story. She said that she thought the hospital would help her but the nurse working that night was mean to her. She wanted Fatiha to hurry and did not respond to any of her complaints about pain. Her dark brown eyes widened as she described her ordeal:

> I thought I was going to die from the pain in my back and my stomach. But she (the nurse) didn't do anything. Just 'Get up,' 'move here,' 'push.' I said 'You have to help me.' But it wasn't her business. If you don't pay them, they don't do anything for you. *Haraam* (forbidden) (August 1997).

The women listening to the story voiced sympathy for Fatiha, but they spent the rest of the afternoon commenting indirectly on her error in wanting to go to the hospital. Rather than supporting Fatiha's assertion that she was a victim of the nurse's mistreatment, the subsequent conversation indirectly characterized Fatiha's behavior as immodest. They spoke about how women had shame in the old days. They showed me how young women would sit hunched in a ball to hide their swollen bellies with their *lughta* (coverings). They told stories about how they knew nothing about birth or sex when they were young and gave birth in the house with their mothers' help. They likened the current lack of shame to adultery and prostitution. One middle-aged woman said that in the old days, if a woman gave birth, the man knew it was his child. Now, she added, people say that women give birth in the hospital and the man says he is not the father. In response, everyone agreed that life was better in *zman* (time past).

Meanwhile, Fatiha sat quietly on the bed listening but not participating. She abandoned her previous effort to tell her perspective on the story and retreated to the more typical silence of a new daughter-in-law. Saharan norms of respect for elders required Fatiha to endure the disapproval that these friends of her mother-in-law expressed about her trip to the hospital. After awhile, however, Fatiha selected a cassette of Berber folk music from the bookshelf next to the bed to play on the tape player. I wished I could have understood the words to the song, but the music alone was sufficient to construct a wall between Fatiha and the judgmental guests. The hospital birth, and perhaps more importantly the social assessment of it, interfered with the sense of unity that should have developed between Fatiha and her husband's family after the birth of her son. I had never heard Arquia speak critically about Fatiha or anyone else prior to that afternoon. She was a devout Muslim who projected a calm, optimistic attitude in other circumstances. Just a few weeks before the birth, Arquia described her relaxed approach to managing the household chores:

> I don't worry about *ad-dunia* (this world). If *l-arusaat* (daughters-in-law) make ten or twelve loaves of bread, it is not my business. I do not watch everything that they do. They have *eql* (intelligence). In the house, everyone can do what she wants (July 1997) (MacPhee 2003:67).

Even though her description of Fatiha's birth experience had a teasing quality, Arquia's silence during her friends' chastisement of her daughter-in-law indicated that there was a limit to her policy of freedom in the household. The hospital birth ruptured Arquia's attempt to create an aesthetic of interiority in her household and the conversation that afternoon conveyed that message to Fatiha. The decision to play a cassette tape while the guests were talking—something I had never witnessed in other households—seemed to indicate that Fatiha's sense of vulnerability increased over the course of the afternoon. The recent divorce in the household may have amplified that feeling.

Post-Partum Complications

A week later, we heard that Fatiha was having trouble adjusting to motherhood. The news came to us via the neighbors again—the most common way that information spread among women in Errachidia. They said that Fatiha had become *majnuuna* (crazy) and did not remember having given birth. Their explanation for the cause of this condition emphasized her social isolation; no one was helping her through this important transition in her life. Shortly after the sbuae (which I missed because of a wedding in Zaouia), Arquia left to visit her natal family in a nearby village, leaving Fatiha at home with her younger, unmarried sisters-in-law. Fatiha's sister came to visit after the sbuae but she stayed only for a day and she neglected to bring any of the ritual gifts for her sister's nfas. Typically, during the first seven days after giving birth, the new mother receives from her family a variety of gifts such as new clothing, food (e.g., chicken, eggs, date syrup, and sweets) and handicrafts, such as an embroidered cloth for carrying the infant. A few days after the sister left, Fatiha's brother arrived and became enraged that their sister had left Fatiha "alone" at a time when she needed her family. The brother sent for the sister, but the commotion was too much for Fatiha. She began to cry uncontrollably, pulling her hair in despair, alternating with periods when she would sit staring at nothing. The absence of all the gifts, symbols, and attention due a new mother from her natal family led Fatiha to claim that she had not given birth. Even though the father's family celebrated the birth, the rituals they performed focused more attention on him and their own good fortune in gaining a new member of the patrilineage. At other sbuae parties I attended, the mother and newborn sat in a private room while the guests sang and danced in the guest rooms or courtyard. I assumed that the same pattern occurred at the party for Fatiha's son.

When faced with Fatiha's frightening behavior, the daughters in the household were at a loss as to how to help the new mother. As one of the daughters explained in an interview the year before, Arquia was the one who treated illnesses in the household and she was away for her yearly vacation to visit her family. The neighbors told us that Arquia's daughters brought Fatiha her son but she said, "I don't have a son." They brought her husband to her, but she said, "I am not married." She refused to nurse the infant, which was usually considered dangerous in Saharan culture. In this case, however, the family thought it was safer to avoid breastfeeding. According to the women who heard about her story, the family feared that Fatiha's state of mind would have caused the infant to become sick. Finally, Arquia's daughters decided to send for a fqih. He wrote a talisman for Fatiha and sent tar for her to smell. Tar is a substance known to repel jinn, indicating he thought she had suffered a spirit attack. Fatiha's recovery shortly after this diagnosis reinforced the popular notion that new mothers were particularly vulnerable to capricious spirits. The additive nature of Saharan medical pluralism meant that within two weeks Fatiha could switch from having a preference for biomedical health care for childbirth to accepting traditional Islamic medicine to treat her emotional breakdown after the birth. What mattered was that both forms of treatment were effective. By the time Arquia returned from the countryside, the household had returned to normal.

I went to visit Arquia again a week later to see how Fatiha was doing. I brought a new outfit for the infant to make amends for missing the sbuae party and to acknowledge the difficult ordeal they had endured. Fatiha was delighted with the gift and for the first time, she joined the conversation I had with her mother-in-law. We sat for almost two hours talking about the dangers mothers and infants faced in the months after birth. Between breastfeeding and playing with her chubby-cheeked son, Fatiha asked me questions about whether women in America swaddled their infants like Moroccans do, and whether Americans knew about the dangers of stolen breastmilk. The comparison steered the conversation to the topic of changes in Moroccan lifestyles in recent years. Arquia commented that young people in Morocco no longer feel shame and Fatiha added that she thought that satellite television was the cause. She

criticized the short skirts that young women wore and their boldness in talking to men. Her comments were more candid than she had been in the past and,
surprisingly, they echoed what her mother-in-law's friends had said at the gathering on the day after she gave birth. Typically, in the other households I visited young daughters-in-law were reluctant to speak openly with guests in the
presence of their mothers-in-law. Fatiha's behavior that evening was one of
the few exceptions to that pattern and I wondered if the change was a response
to her illness.

Despite the commotion about Fatiha's emotional distress a week earlier, no
one mentioned the crisis overtly at this meeting. Arquia, however, used examples from her past difficulties with her husband and children to give indirect advice about managing life's problems. As the oldest of the women gathered
in her newly built second-floor room that summer evening, Arquia had the
power to hold the attention of her audience of 3 young women in transition:
one newly married (me), one recently divorced (my sister-in-law), and one a
new mother (Fatiha). She told us about her husband who left her repeatedly
and her struggles to raise their 14 children, 6 of whom died as infants. At the
end of her story Arquia advised us to have faith in Allah: "Almost everyone has
times when they are cold and hungry. You have to be patient and it comes out
well" (August 1996).

This strategy for coping with hardship invoked the aesthetic of balance in
a long-term perspective and indirectly characterized Fatiha's post-natal breakdown as a problem of spiritual deficiency rather than spirit attack. The etiology of spirit attack seemed to hold little meaning for either Fatiha or Arquia
even though Saharans viewed new mothers as vulnerable to jnun and Fatiha's
condition improved after the fqih treated her. Their silence on the topic may
have been simply an expression of the Saharan aesthetic of interiority, but it
also gave me the impression that Fatiha's recovery had less to do with the fqih's
treatment and more to do with Arquia's return from the countryside.

My interpretation of Fatiha's majnuuna behavior after the sbuae echoes Desjarlais' emphasis on the experiential dimension of illness in his assessment of
suffering from soul loss in Nepal. He characterized the pain and malaise he
observed in a Yolmo patient as a response to distress rather than an idiom of
distress. Similarly, I viewed Fatiha's symptoms of excessive crying, social with-
drawal, and denial of her husband and son as a response to her overwhelming sense of vulnerability. Her claims that she was not married and did not
have a child as well as her withdrawn behavior (when she sat staring at nothing) met the criteria for a victim of spirit attack, but her behavior was less a
performance of well-known sick role than it was simply an expression of her
sense of isolation. The first signs of her sense of isolation arose during the

labor process when she sought help from her friend, the nurse at the provincial hospital. Not only did that strategy prove unsatisfying but also her mother-in-law chastised her publicly for choosing a hospital birth. To make matters worse, Arquia left for her yearly vacation a week after her first grandson was born. The token visits from Fatiha's sister and brother resulted in increasing Fatiha's feelings of abandonment and isolation, which other housewives ranked among the most frightening conditions they could imagine.

The household's decision to consult a fqih about Fatiha's condition contradicted Arquia's more common pattern of treating illnesses in the household. I interpreted Arquia's previous comment about young people lacking shame to be connected to her disapproval of both the fqih and the hospital birth. According to the principles of Saharan popular health culture, Fatiha's spiritual and emotional imbalance combined with the household's exposure to unknown health practitioners and Fatiha's isolation from her natal family increased the threat of danger to the new mother and infant. Arquia's behavior during our visit indicated that her strategy for protecting her household from further danger attempted to create the conditions of well-being in accordance with implicit structures of security. On one hand, she constructed the aesthetic of unity by incorporating Fatiha more fully into the unified whole of their household. On the other hand, she constructed the aesthetic of interiority by remaining silent about Fatiha's emotional breakdown instead of telling the story in detail as she had on the day after her grandson's birth.

My observations that night and during the previous weeks suggested that Arquia's interpretation of the aesthetic of interiority was flexible. Her shifts between openly sharing news about her family to remaining silent about the details of recent events struck me as both an improvisational acceptance of cultural change and an attempt to protect Fatiha and her son. A new trend toward openness in Saharan culture was reflected in the design of the new room where we sat that afternoon. Arquia's sons built the second floor of their home with large windows and an open floor plan, which contrasted with the older enclosed architectural style of the ksar (and the first floor of Arquia's house). This same pattern of openness appeared in Arquia's willingness to allow Fatiha to participate fully in the conversation and to show us her newborn son. The topic of conversation, however, followed the more traditional aesthetic of interiority by strictly avoiding discussion of Fatiha's recent illness. Although Arquia was willing to discuss her own problems from the past, Fatiha and her son were still vulnerable to the dangers of the first 40 days after birth. The emotional breakdown she experienced heightened the relevance of those dangers for Arquia's household, but the pattern of interiority that isolated new mothers from social interaction proved counter-productive in Fatiha's case.

The nature of her distress—whether one characterized it as spirit attack or temporary psychosis—conveyed to Fatiha's in-laws her feelings of confusion and abandonment. Giving birth changed her whole world and the people whom she needed to teach her how to be a mother were unavailable. Her mother had died. Her sister (a mother) left quickly to visit relatives in another town. Even her mother-in-law had gone to her natal village for a vacation. The familiar pattern of chores and prayer that Fatiha knew before giving birth was now replaced with breast-feeding and caring for another life, which according to popular knowledge was vulnerable to multiple dangers. The responsibility was overwhelming and the only social resources she could turn to were her unmarried sisters-in-law, her husband, or a neighbor who had yet to have children. Moreover, the divorce of Arquia's other daughter-in-law earlier that summer loomed over Fatiha and must have added worries about the potential consequences of the disagreement about the hospital birth.

Arquia's return from her vacation, however, reduced Fatiha's sense of isolation in two important ways. First, she relieved some of Fatiha's burden of responsibility for the infant. Grandmothers were primary care givers for infants in traditional Saharan households and Arquia, by far, had the most experience with childcare in her household. Secondly, Arquia made an effort to incorporate Fatiha more fully into the protective unity of the family. On this last day I spent with her before I returned America, Fatiha held a role that was more like a daughter than a daughter-in-law. Instead of staying in private quarters of the household doing chores or making tea for the guests, she served as a co-host alongside her mother-in-law. Most daughters-in-law achieve this status in middle-age when their children have grown and their mothers-in-law become feeble from old age. Arquia's acceleration of this process for Fatiha was a response to her daughter-in-law's and new grandson's vulnerability. The household rallied around her to protect her and the baby and to enhance their sense of well-being. In response, Fatiha adopted her mother-in-law's adherence to Saharan codes of modesty, as revealed in her criticism of young women who dress shamefully. Fatiha's generation was caught in a current of rapid social change, especially with regard to health practices. Public health messages encouraged her and her peers to use contraception, to seek prenatal care from biomedical practitioners, and to give birth in the hospital. Her positive experiences previously with a nurse at the health dispensary cultivated Fatiha's trust in biomedicine, but her birth experiences destroyed that trust. Not only was the labor nurse mean to Fatiha, but her mother-in-law resisted her decision to go to the hospital at all. The additional absence of Fatiha's sister and brother at the time of birth resulted in Fatiha becoming socially isolated, which in terms of the local culture posed even more danger than the social transition of childbirth. As such, Fatiha's best hope for security and well-being in the future was to ally herself with Arquia and to err on the side of practicing interiority.

CHAPTER 8

LALLA KABIRA'S STOLEN BREASTMILK

The most important resource for promoting infant health and well-being in Saharan households was breastmilk. The popular health culture valued breastmilk for its perceived nutritional, medicinal and protective qualities as well as its capacity to strengthen the social bond between mother and child. The multifaceted value of breastmilk, however, placed a burden of responsibility on mothers to produce a sufficient quantity and quality of milk to maintain the health and development of their children. The mother's emotional state was one of the variables that Saharan popular culture associated with the quality of breastmilk. As mentioned in Chapter 7, Fatiha's sisters-in-law and neighbors feared that her emotional breakdown would spoil her milk and harm the baby. In the past, Saharan housewives worried more about losing their milk altogether before their children were old enough for weaning. This chapter examines the Saharan construction of lost milk and spoiled milk along with the strategies housewives used to prevent these conditions and to restore the milk when problems did occur. In parallel with the protective and health promoting practices housewives employed for pregnancy and childbirth, the aesthetic structures of everyday life shaped the Saharan art of healthy breastfeeding.

Breastfeeding Customs

Saharan culture identified breastmilk as one of three vital substances that established social bonds of unity, trust, and obligation. The description of the aesthetic of unity in Chapter 4 provided an overview of how Saharans interpreted the strength of social connections in terms of the sharing of blood, milk, and food. Although blood formed the strongest ties and food the weakest, none of these symbolic mechanisms of embodying social unity guaranteed the production of feelings of unity or the performance of social support. As illustrated in Fatiha's story, the birth of her son failed to yield an immediate sense of unity with her husband's family. Instead, she felt more isolated despite the newly created blood ties through her son. Unfortunately, children did not guarantee Saharan woman security in their marriages. The possibility of divorce loomed in the back of every housewife's mind even after years of marriage, making a mother's bond with her child all the more important. Breastfeeding provided a strategy for strengthening that bond by uniting the bodies of the mother and child through the vital, nurturing substance of milk. Saharan women saw a mother's milk as the substance that established a lifetime of love and respect between herself and her children as well as the children's relationship to each other.

In addition to the social value of breastfeeding, Saharan housewives also viewed breastmilk as having a number of protective and health promoting qualities for children. Nutrition was foremost among these qualities, but the Islamic promotion of breastfeeding added moral mandate to household decisions about nourishing children. According to Islamic scripture (Qur'an 2:233), the ideal period of time for nursing is the first two years of the infant's life. The religious perspective exceeded the recommendation in Moroccan health education campaigns, which advised women to breastfeed for the first 4 to 6 months of the child's life (Ministère de la Santé Publique 1995:24–29). The poverty and remote location of the households in my study sample offered few alternatives for infant nutrition. Hence, breastfeeding was the automatic preference for promoting infant health.

All of the mothers participating in the study nursed their children, but there were variations in their practices. One of the customs that diverged from biomedical advice was the practice of feeding newborns something other than breastmilk as their first taste. As described in Chapter 7, adherence to the custom of l-bismillah, against medical advice, reflected a desire to create an aesthetic of unity between the infant, Allah, and the Muslim community. Parents wanted the words of the Qur'an to be the child's first taste. Berber midwives followed an alternative tradition that mixed dried hedgehog intestine with crushed date pits or date juice and spices. The specific ingredients varied from one household to another. The aim of that tradition was to prevent illness, including from spirit attacks.[1] An Rgaiga grandmother from Errachidia explained in an interview about health practices in the past that the baby would suffer from colic if its mother nursed before giving the hedgehog mixture as a first taste.[2] The ingredients of the first taste have changed over time but the majority of housewives continued to follow the tradition into the 1990s. Only 16% of the housewives who responded to my questions about breastfeeding (out of 51 responses) said that they started breastfeeding immediately after giving birth. Other mothers waited until after the first taste and some waited as long as 3 days because they had trouble producing milk.

The duration of breastfeeding also varied among the women in the sample. The oldest participants in the study breastfed their children longer than the younger participants. Khaltii Zahra (introduced in Chapter 4) boasted that she nursed her children for 2 years and her pregnancies were spaced 2 years apart naturally, without taking the contraceptive pill. Another Berber grandmother who raised her children in a Saharan oasis argued that she prevented her children from growing up with thirst by breastfeeding exclusively for the first year. She said that her left breast contained water and the right contained milk, giving the children all that they needed. More often mothers began to introduce other foods—such as boiled vegetables or spices and crushed nuts mixed with dates—as soon as the infant grew teeth.

The motivation to continue breastfeeding even after the baby could eat other foods stemmed from the value of breastmilk in creating a social bond and from its perceived ability to protect children from health dangers. A Rgaiga grandmother from Errachidia claimed that sprinkling breastmilk over a sleeping infant and saying "bismillah ar-rahman ar-rahiim" would protect against spirit attacks and the Eye. Other housewives mixed breastmilk with herbs to treat childhood fevers. The combination of social, religious and medical support for breastfeeding contributed to its position as both a norm and an ideal in Saharan society, but there were circumstance that forced women to stop before the prescribed length of two years.

When discussing their experiences in the past, the most common reason senior housewives gave for early weaning was insufficient milk. They attributed the problem to the phenomenon of stolen milk when lactation stopped during the precarious first 40 days of an infant's life. According to local oral tradition, the first 40 days after birth entailed a heightened stage of danger for both mothers and their infants. Like other transitional categories cross-culturally, Saharan culture also attributed special powers to initiates who passed from one stage of life to another. In this case, new mothers had the ability to steal breastmilk from another woman as long as both the perpetrator and victim had given birth within the past 40 days. The mechanism of the theft combined the laws of sympathetic magic with notions about the danger of unbalanced reciprocity. Any new mother who took food from the household of another new mother without providing a return gift in kind would result in stolen milk, whether the act was intentional or inadvertent. This popular etiology of insufficient milk depicted lactating mothers as objects of envy and placed them at the center of social relations between households. The etiology was more complicated than the envy associated with the Eye. Onder's (2007:148–149) study of household health care in Turkey observed similar concerns about the power of envy to compromise a mother's ability to nurse. Turkish women protect their milk by nursing the infant away from the gaze of other women. They even avoid talking about breastfeeding in public. Saharan women, in contrast nursed their children in public—even in front of their houses—without fear of the Eye. The danger of stolen milk occurred only during the first 40 days post-partum when another nursing mother with the same status took food from the household without reciprocity.

Because breastmilk was essential for the newborn's health, nursing mothers took precautions to protect their milk during the first 40 days after birth. This post-natal time period was typically marked by a high volume of visitors, who would come to congratulate the family on their new addition. To prevent new mothers from taking each other's breastmilk when visiting each other, Saharan customs required women who had given birth recently to share food, usually splitting a round loaf of bread into 2 pieces. This gesture unified the households in a social bond and symbolically balanced their relationship in an effort to dis-pel any feelings of envy between the two mothers. Women in Zaouia claimed that the custom for protecting breastmilk extended to the nursing animals in the house as well. For example, when Yussef's late mother gave birth to her youngest child, the cow and the dog had also given birth in the same week. Her concern that the animals' potential desire for her milk would compromise the health of the baby motivated her to share food with the animals over the next forty days.

Although Saharan women viewed this strategy of protection to be effective, they suspected that some women here dishonest about their lactating status and others took food accidentally. Hence, the popular health culture included a variety of other universal measures to protect the milk. One method involved having a fqih write verses from the Qur'an as a charm (*sarah* or *Hijab*) to pro-tect the milk. The mother would secure the charm (usually written on a small piece of paper) in a locket or piece of cloth and wear it until she weaned the child. This charm, however, posed a danger to all other breastfeeding moth-ers who shared food with her. Elder housewives told me that it was *Haraam* (for-bidden, or in this sense, unforgivable) for a women who had "written for her milk" to conceal that fact from other women who may be vulnerable to losing their milk because of it.

A less powerful method of protection required women to participate in bal-anced exchanges of food with other women in the neighborhood or village on third or seventh day after birth. A third ritual involved making a charm out of household items. Mothers would take a piece of dough or a bone and cover it with three drops of milk from each breast. They then wrapped this charm in a scarf and kept it with their possessions. Not all women in the region knew about these strategies, but it was common knowledge in Zaouia and among most of the participants in the Errachidia portion of the study sample. A few housewives, however, said that they forgot to take precautions and suffered from stolen breastmilk.

Lalla Kabira's Trouble with Stolen Milk

The most entertaining narrator of stolen milk stories was an elderly Arab woman from Zaouia named Lalla Kabira. She was tiny in stature and her wrinkled face made her seem older than her stated age of 60 years. When I shook her hand, I immediately noticed the softness of her pale, white skin which was a stark contrast to all the other rough, hennaed hands of women I met that year. She lived with her son, daughter-in-law, and 5 grandchildren at the far end of the village road. The plain mud façade of the house and chipped paint on the front door were misleadingly modest. The extent of her family's wealth became apparent when one of the grandchildren led us to the guestroom that opened on to a large courtyard with a dozen fruit trees surrounded by a cement terrace. The guestroom was small and dark, but richly decorated with ornate brocade fabric on the banquettes and lace doilies that matched the carved legs of the 3 small wooden tables. The family's wealth and status was also apparent in the confident way Lalla Kabira described her life. The articulate, elaborative style she used in responding to my interview questions also revealed the intelligence she gained from life experience rather than formal schooling.

Unlike some of the other Arab women in the study, Lalla Kabira's stories recounted her feistiness as she manipulated the custom of female seclusion in her struggle to protect her children's health. Her eyes seemed to sparkle as she told us about her experiences with 14 pregnancies, 8 of which ended in miscarriage, stillbirth, or infant death. Although Lalla Kabira was a devout Muslim who respected God's will, she was proud of the innovative ways in which she faced the challenges in her life. One of the repeated challenges she faced as a young mother was losing her ability to produce breastmilk. She explained that her breasts were small, which she thought made her vulnerable to losing her milk. In the first few weeks after giving birth, she would sleep on her back to prevent the milk from spilling out. As an extra precaution she would also make a charm using a bone sprinkled with her breastmilk (she pantomimed the action as she spoke). These strategies, however, proved to be unreliable:

> One time I didn't do this (i.e., make the charm) and the wife of my brother came to the house. She was in her thirty-ninth day (after giving birth) and she ate with us, soup. The next day my milk went away but the wife of my brother was no longer in her forty days, so

we couldn't just send over for food from their house. I had to go to the *fqih* … but it was a problem because the *shurfa* women did not go out of the house in those days. I had to wear my husband's jellaba and turban so no one would know who I was. It was so big and I could not see, so my brother had to help me.

Another time I gave birth and my milk dried but I didn't know why. But then I remembered that I was grinding wheat with another woman the day before, but she did not eat from us (which would cause Lalla's milk to dry). That woman, however, remembered that she licked her finger and that was all it took (Lalla Kabira licked her own finger to show how it happened). The neighbor woman sent over some bread, we divided it and the milk came back.

The last time, our Black maid sent some yeast (sourdough) from our house to her friend. My milk dried later and we tried to know how. Finally we asked the maid and she remembered that her friend also had given birth. We sent to her house to (ex)change food, and the Haratina sent us soup. They had nothing, the poor things, may God protect them, but she was full of milk. Big. So, they sent what they could. The soup was terrible and dirty and I couldn't drink it. I told my husband to drink in my place, and the milk came back. (September 1996).

Lalla Kabira's explanations of how she lost her ability to lactate after the birth of three different children framed the problem in terms of the aesthetics of balance in the social relations between households. The only references she made to her physical symptoms in the story were simple references to the milk drying and coming back. There were no references to feeling ill, fatigued, or nervous after giving birth. Instead the narratives depicted her body as a barometer of unbalanced relationships between her household and others in the village. This explanation positioned Lalla Kabira as an object of envy in the community, even though she worried about having small breasts. The etiology also deflected the responsibility for the infant's well-being to the level of the household and community rather than solely at the level of Lalla Kabira's body.

The first story highlights Lalla Kabira's ingenuity as a caregiver for her child. The traditional remedy for stolen milk was to share food with the mother who stole the milk in attempt to regain a balance between the households. That protocol, however, was impossible because the sister-in-law no longer had the same vulnerable status as Lalla Kabira. Rather than passively accepting the lost lactation as a matter of fate, she searched for another strategy for regaining her milk. The women in Zaouia described three different strategies for recovering lost milk when sharing food with the thief was impossible. One strategy involved leaving flour at a saint's shrine overnight and then making a soup with it the next day. Another required the mother to gather a leaf from each type of tree in the palm grove and make a soup with that. The third strategy employed the services of a fqih. Lalla Kabira's household had the financial resources to afford the third strategy, but the protocol (like the others) required her to leave the house. At that time, the only legitimate occasions that allowed an Arab woman of her status to leave the house were her wedding and her funeral. Lalla Kabira's determination to preserve her child's health, however, motivated her to defy the custom of female seclusion, which could have put her husband's honor in jeopardy. Her strategy of wearing her husband's dellaba with his turban over her head adapted the aesthetic of interiority well enough to allow her to walk to the fqih's house.

In the second and third stories, Lalla Kabira followed the traditional remedy to restore her milk but the strategy involved searching for the women who had stolen the milk. Lalla Kabira's past experience with lost lactation and the elite socio-religious status of the household amplified the relevance of the stolen milk etiology as an explanation for both cases, but the identity of the perpetrator was unclear. The search for a woman who had eaten at their house, however, involved more than a desire to provide a meaningful explanation for the lost lactation. Several of Lalla Kabira's children died as infants and the stolen milk etiology provided a strategy for preventing another death. The last story incorporated the aesthetic of unity with the aesthetic of balance in the attempt to restore Lalla Kabira's milk. After the household discovered that the maid's friend had taken food from their house, Lalla Kabira could not bring herself to eat the soup that she offered to balance the reciprocity. Instead, she asked her husband to eat it in her place. By that time they had been married for several years and had children together. The Saharan interpretation of unity rendered them interchangeable—or as Saharans put it "kiif-kiif" (same-same)—for the purposes of the symbolic health practice. The return of Lalla Kabira's milk likely reinforced the couple's sense of unity.

The last story in particular strengthened my impression that Lalla Kabira's characterization of her lost lactation as stolen milk was an account of embodied experience more than an expression of social or emotional distress. This etiology contrasts with the cultural construction of luHam, which requires households to give pregnant women valuable food such as meat or fruit to prevent the unborn child from developing a blemish. The cravings drew attention to social inequalities in the household and, as such, could serve as an idiom of distress. In Lalla Kabira's story, however, the remedy required the non-lactating mother to eat whatever the other household offered, even if it was terrible soup. Moreover, the lost lactation in the second two stories had nothing to do with a *perception* of imbalance in the community because Lalla Kabira and her household had difficulty figuring out who stole the milk. Instead, stolen milk seemed to reflect the experience of imbalance in Lalla Kabira's body that was restored by the creation of balance with another household in the community.

In contrast to the prevalence of references to stolen milk and the need to protect it among senior housewives, the topic was absent in my interviews with the younger women in the sample. Fatiha was the only woman who spoke about protecting her milk. Amina, a 26-year-old Berber mother from Zaouia was the only woman who described an experience with stolen milk. Amina had little interest in traditional health practices and offered little elaboration on her birth experiences when I interviewed her in the fall of 1996. I attributed her aloof attitude about my research to her grammar school diploma and the relative affluence of her household in comparison to the others participating in the study. When I returned to visit her household in 1997 the topic of strategies to protect milk came up in the conversation. Amina said that she never did anything to protect her milk, but she did stop lactating when her first child was an infant. They gave him formula from the pharmacy but also tried to solve the puzzle of why she lost the milk. Amina was the picture of health according to Saharan standards. She was strong and plump with ample breasts. Her son was healthy as well. It was easy for the household to suspect that an envious guest might have stolen her milk, but no other lactating women had come to visit during Amina's nfas. Then, Amina explained, "I remembered giving olive oil to a beggar woman who came to the house." The family concluded that the woman must have given birth within 40 days and the other women in the household set out to search for her. The found her in a nearby village and took some of her food for Amina to eat. The strategy worked and the milk returned. The household might have been able to afford to buy formula instead of searching for the beggar woman, but most housewives viewed it as inferior to breastmilk. Moreover, the danger of stolen milk was well known in Amina's household. Her mother-in-law, in a previous interview, told me that she had lost her milk after the birth of one of her children and he died because they did not know what else to feed him. After that tragic experience, she always performed the ritual to protect her milk on the 3rd day after birth.

It is difficult to account for the difference between Lalla Kabira's generation and Amina's generation in my data on protecting milk and experiences with stolen milk. Although I asked about breastfeeding in my interviews with senior and junior housewives, I did not ask specifically about stolen milk in either set. Hence, I can only infer that fewer mothers were taking measures to protect against stolen milk in the 1990s because fewer women suffered from lost lactation (at least in my sample). The biggest change in post-natal practices between the two generations participating in the study was a shift in expectations about a new mother's responsibilities in the household. In the past, new mothers returned to their chores within the first week after the birth. For village women, those chores often involved working long hours in the family's fields. In contrast, the norm in the 1990s was to exempt new mothers from heavy housework for 40 days after the birth. Many new mothers spent this time resting in their natal household. The contemporary custom allowed new mothers to nurse their infants more frequently than mothers in the past could and the new feeding pattern may have helped more women sustain lactation during the precarious 40 days post-partum.

Good Milk and Bad Milk

Although the sense of vulnerability to stolen milk appeared to have diminished among young Saharan women, the dangers of premature weaning remained a central concern in the household production of health. The circumstances that forced the younger generation of Saharan housewives to stop breastfeeding were associated with the problem of bad milk. That is, instead of worrying about the quantity of breastmilk, young mothers worried about its quality. The cultural notion that poor quality breastmilk could harm nursing babies encouraged mothers and grandmothers to evaluate the benefits of breastfeeding based on their interpretation of each infant's state of health and level of vulnerability to illness and death. The symptom that housewives most often associated with bad milk was diarrhea. When nursing infants contracted repeated or severe cases of diarrhea, mothers suspected spoiled milk and faced the decision whether to start weaning. Among all the illnesses children contracted in rural Morocco, housewives feared diarrhea the most because it was a leading cause of infant death. Children of mothers with good milk were more resilient to diarrheal illness, but mothers with bad milk had to resort to feeding other foods to their infants.

Usually, the alternative food took the form of homemade cereals or infusions. The ingredients of these homemade cereals included a creative mix of readily available crushed nuts and spices combined with butter and honey or dates. Latifa, a divorced Arab mother of three children, had difficulty finding a milk substitute that her infant son would tolerate. She tried cow's milk but he rejected it. Instead she alternated between soup and orange juice or tomato juice. Infant formulas were available in all the pharmacies in the region but Amina (introduced above) was the only mother I knew who used it, and that was only temporarily while her milk was stolen. The primary reason Saharan households used homemade pabulum rather than commercial formula was cost, although the women in one household in Zaouia argued that pharmacy formula caused diarrhea. One of my key consultants captured the crisis of spoiled milk for low income households poignantly during a conversation in the summer of 1997. I asked Khaira, a Berber grandmother, whether women with bad milk bought formula from the pharmacy as a substitute. She replied with a sigh and said "Well, what are you going to do? We are poor. You can't buy that milk" (July 1997). Even though homemade pabulum was time consuming to prepare, housewives saw it as the only way to prevent diarrheal illness from becoming more severe.

According to women's responses to interview questions about breastfeeding and child health, the 3 most common factors that compromised the quality of breastmilk were pregnancy, the contraceptive pill, and summer fruits. Pregnancy was the most common culprit in suspected cases of spoiled milk. The consensus among women participating in the study was that pregnant women should wean the older child because continued nursing could harm both the child at the breast and the one in the womb. Nursing mothers had trouble heeding this advice, however, because pregnancy could be hard to detect. In the first few months of nursing it is unclear whether the absence of menstruation is the result of breastfeeding or another pregnancy. One Berber mother from Errachidia thought her pregnancy with her second child may have harmed her first child but she did not realize it in time to wean him. The first child, a son, was healthy until he reached his first birthday when he accidentally fell and hit his head. He died from the injury within a week. The mother, a soft-spoken woman in her late 20s, blamed the accident on a stranger who hit him with the Eye when she commented that he was a quiet baby. After telling me this sad story, the mother said that she realized after his death that she was pregnant with her second child. She wondered if her milk had turned bad and made him vulnerable to the Eye.

Modern biomedicine offered Saharan housewives a way to prevent pregnancy and spoiled breastmilk, but local attitudes about the contraceptive pill were mixed. For example, two Berber women, one a mother and the other a grandmother advised the other women in their households to delay using the Pill until after they weaned their children because they thought it caused diarrhea in children. Other participants pointed out that the hospital distributed a form of the contraceptive pill that was safe for nursing mothers. Nonetheless, Lalla Kabira's daughter-in-law reported that she tried taking the pill after her third child was born and it reduced the amount of milk she produced. She stopped taking it and waited until she stopped nursing before taking it again. These variations suggest that in the absence of authoritative knowledge about the effect of the contraceptive pill on breastmilk and infant health, housewives based their interpretations of the danger it posed on the social evaluation of their personal experience. A nursing infant's episode with diarrhea presented sufficient evidence to persuade the mother to stop taking the pill, but the danger posed by other side effects of the pill was less clear. It was not surprising that Lalla Kabira's daughter-in-law decided to stop using the pill when it reduced the quantity of her milk in light of all the trouble her mother-in-law had with stolen milk.

The third mechanism that linked spoiled milk and infant illness centered on summer fruit. Saharan housewives identified summer fruit as the proximate cause of a life threatening illness they called mard shim (sickness of smelling). Bad milk played a role in housewives' explanations of why some children contracted the illness when others avoided it, but the range of factors that caused the milk to spoil in the first place were unclear to me and the participants in the study.

According to the popular construction of this illness, the odor of summer fruits such as apricots, grapes, apples, plums, and especially melon caused children under 6 years of age to become ill with a severe form of diarrhea. The prototypical symptoms that distinguished mard shim from ordinary diarrhea were weakness or listlessness, folding the thumbs into the palm of the hand, and inability to hold the head upright. The Saharan etiology of mard shim was connected to the local miasmic theory of contagion, which viewed foul odors such as that of garbage, feces, or death as causes of illness. In this case, however, only young children were vulnerable to the dangerous smell of summer fruits. One Hurtani grandmother explained that children were more sensitive to odors. She also pointed out, as did many other housewives, that the illness was contagious. Once one child contracted mard shim, he or she could pass it on to other children. It was the most feared type of illness for young children even though Saharan oral tradition offered a variety of protocols to save the child's life. These treatments combined local plants, household ingredients, and symbolic rituals in different combinations. Additionally, some of the local fuqaha treated the illness by making small cuts on the child's head and face.

Given the prevalence of fruit in Saharan markets and household gardens, I wondered why suspected cases of marid shim were rare. As much as senior housewives warned against bringing melons, apples, and apricots into households with young children, the households I visited frequently offered them as dessert in the summer. A closer examination of the data revealed that the local etiology of the illness characterized some children as being more susceptible it. When I asked housewives to describe the treatment protocol for marid shim,

a few women responded by saying that their children never had the illness because their milk was good. Mama explained that they were referring to a local
analogy in which women compared the quality of their milk to the milk of
dogs and cats. In this analogy, dog milk was hearty. It made children fat and
resistant to illness. Cat milk, in contrast, was thin like the emaciated feral cats
to which housewives fed their stale crusts of bread. The children of mothers
with cat milk were open to the most severe cases of illness, including marid shim.

This association helped to illuminate why Saharan mothers worried so much
about the effect of the contraceptive pill or pregnancy on breastmilk. Those factors, however, were not the only cause of bad milk. Children of mothers who
were neither pregnant nor taking contraceptive pills also became ill with marid
shim. The popular health culture also identified other factors that contributed
to the production of bad milk. In addition to emotional distress (described in
Chapter 7), the nursing mother's diet could also expose the baby to mard shim.
Summer fruit was the primary factor in this etiology. The application of this
general health knowledge into a strategy of prevention, however, was difficult
because of the ubiquity of fruit, particularly in village households. Lalla Kabira's
courtyard, like several of her neighbors in Zaouia was full of fruit trees. Nursing mothers could try to avoid eating summer fruit, but the contagious character of the illness meant that even the children of mothers who vigilantly
avoided summer fruit could catch mard shim from another child.

In contrast to housewives' pervasive references to rituals that protected
against stolen milk, there was little indication that housewives felt empowered
to control the quality of their breastmilk. Aside from warnings that pregnancy,
contraceptive pills, and summer fruit could cause nursing infants to become
ill, the interview results revealed no explicit strategies for producing, maintaining, or restoring the quality of breastmilk. At an implicit level, the structural analysis of the causes of spoiled milk suggests parallels with stolen milk.
All three of the contributing factors in the popular etiology of spoiled milk
had the effect of changing the balance of humors in the mother's body. Summer fruits cooled the body whereas pregnancy heated the body. There was little consensus, however, about the effect of the contraceptive pill. Some women
said it had a cooling effect and others said it had a heating effect. Alternatively,
some women said the pills from the hospital were cold and the ones from the
pharmacy were hot. The direction of the imbalance was less important than
its potential to compromise the quality of a mother's breastmilk, which in turn
could lead to an imbalance in the child's body. While this analysis seems plausible in the abstract, I am unconvinced that it carried significance even as embodied knowledge among Saharan housewives. The observational data I collected
on breastfeeding practices were simply insufficient to understand how (or

whether) strategies to promote good breastmilk reflected the aesthetics of every-day life.

On the other hand, aesthetic analysis did illuminate the contexts in which Saharan mothers viewed their children to be vulnerable to mard shim. I heard many stories about children who suffered from mard shim in the past—20 to 30 years before my research took place—but I had difficulty studying its occurrence in the contemporary time period. Advanced cases of mard shim were obvious to senior housewives in the Sahara. Severe dehydration and wasting, as depicted in a public health handbook I saw at the health dispensary in Zaouia represented a definitive image of mard shim in Mama's mind. We saw a six-month-old boy at the provincial hospital with a similar condition. His ribs protruded from his chest and his limbs were no more than skin and bones. I tried unsuccessfully to stifle a gasp when I saw him and the other visitors in the room whispered "mard shim" to convey the gravity of his condition to me. Earlier stages of the illness were harder to diagnose but local healers and knowledgeable housewives viewed early diagnosis and treatment as the best strategy for preventing death.

One suspected case of mard shim in Errachidia illustrates how the social and experiential context affected the process of diagnosis. During an interview with Fatim-Zahra (from Chapter 3) and her sister in October 1996, the conversation shifted to her infant son's illness. As Fatim-Zahra sat cross-legged on the floor, cradling her pudgy son in her lap and feeding him milk from a bottle, she told the story of how he became sick with vomiting and diarrhea two days after visiting with his cousin, who had mard shim. There was no sign of alarm in her voice as she described his symptoms and her son was content with his bottle during the conversation. Nonetheless she asked the other women whether they thought he could have caught marid shim from his cousin. The baby had no signs of folded thumbs or a drooping head and it was no longer summer, when cases of the dreaded illness usually occurred. As a precaution, however, Mama and Fatim-Zahra's sister advised her to prepare the remedy for mard shim right away; the illness was too dangerous to wait for the symptoms to become worse. Fatim-Zahra was repulsed by their description of the home remedy that required her to mix a paste of red onion and henna with her urine, collected when she woke in the morning. She refused to put that on her son's head and wrists. The alternative protocol was more appealing. It involved consulting a native mountain scrub bush called *mulbiina* (owner of milk) in order to perform a divination to determine whether illness was really mard shim. The remedy required her to take some of the sweet smelling, milky sap from one of the branches and place it under her son's nose and on various parts of the head.

Although the women discussed treatment at length, no one raised any questions about the quality of Fatim-Zahra's milk or suggested that she wean him. One or two episodes of diarrhea were an insufficient reason to wean a baby, particularly at the teething stage (which some mothers blamed for some diarrheal illnesses). Fatim-Zahra was still breastfeeding her son 6 months after his birth, although she had recently started feeding him cow's milk (from the store) as well. The baby's chubby cheeks and legs suggested that Fatim-Zahra's milk was dog-like, which would help her son resist the illness. A few participants in the study even listed breastmilk mixed with herbal medicines as a remedy for diarrhea. One middle-aged mother modernized this remedy by arguing that she treated diarrhea by putting antibiotic ointment for eye infections on her breast and letting the baby nurse. It was only persistent and severe cases of diarrhea that raised the question of bad milk and motivated Saharan mothers to seek alternative foods for the baby. Fatim-Zahra's son's illness had lasted only a few days and it was unlikely that her milk had spoiled. Even though she had had difficulties with pregnancies in the past, everything in her life fell into order once he was born. Despite Mama's warnings about mard shim and her son's exposure to it, Fatim-Zahra was in no rush to embrace that diagnosis or use the treatment for it.

In all the stories I heard about cases of mard shim, I never noticed anyone blaming the mother for producing bad milk. Mothers could try to promote healthy or dog-like milk by avoiding the spoiling factors mentioned above, but otherwise they seemed to attribute the quality of breastmilk to fate. Bad milk was as a matter of bad luck. In cases when housewives suspected a case of mard shim, the focus was on healing the child rather than blaming the mother. Other factors also played a role in exposing children to mard shim and other childhood dangers such as the Eye, spirit attack, and unbalanced humors. Breastfeeding was important, but Saharan housewives were resourceful in devising other foods and protective practices when the milk turned bad.

The cultural association of bad milk with bad luck helped to uphold the cultural value of breastfeeing in general. In addition to its value in enhancing the social bond between mother and child, breastmilk also was part of a broader symbolic association of milk with health, protection, and good fortune in Morocco. Milk was a central symbol in celebrations of good fortune such as a marital engagement or the return of a relative or friend after a long absence. It was also a common gift that Saharans brought to people who were sick. In addition to consuming milk, Moroccans used milk as a means of protection, sprinkling it on the threshold when moving into a new house, or on a bride and groom at their wedding. Although many aspects of Saharan breastfeeding practices reflected the aesthetics balance and interiority to a lesser extent, it was this cultural association of breastmilk with the aesthetic of purity that prevented worries about bad milk from undermining Saharan convictions about the value of breastfeeding. In Islamic symbolism the color white represents purity, but breastfeeding carried an even deeper connection to religious purity. Breastmilk was one of the few bodily substances that did not ritually defile a woman's body and disqualify her from participation in Salat prayer. Furthermore, mothers in Errachidia and Zaouia had no hesitation about nursing their children in public. Two participants even nursed in front of my male translator during my first visit to their households. These same women followed the local tradition of modesty by covering their heads with two scarves and wearing leggings under ankle-length dresses. The openness of breastfeeding contrasted sharply with the bodily shame and caution Saharan customs associated with pregnancy and childbirth. For all these reasons it was far easier for public health workers in the region to promote prolonged breastfeeding than to promote prenatal care or hospital birth.

CHAPTER 9

EMBODIED KNOWLEDGE IN ACTION

The variations in household responses to health dangers described in the previous 3 chapters create an impression that there was little cultural coherence in Saharan Morocco in the mid-1990s. That impression, however, derives from an oversimplified view of the relationship between culture and behavior. The common patterns in Saharan health behavior existed as tacit sensibilities, which shaped experience and practice. In some respects, the variations I observed were an artifact of my comparative research design. The description of participants in terms of their ethno-linguistic, generational and geographic (i.e., town vs. village) identities amplified social differences in the study sample. Similarly, the sorting of illness etiologies and health practices into distinct medical traditions highlighted the presence of medical pluralism in household health practices. The common links between all of the variables I examined, however, emerged through the realization that *diversity* characterized the context of everyday life in southeastern Saharan Morocco. People from different ethno-linguistic groups, different generations, and different parts of Errachidia Province interacted with each other in an orderly, coherent fashion on a regular basis. Shared devotion to the norms and values of Sunni Islam contributed to the maintenance of the social order, but the overall coherence of Saharan culture grew from a broader set of shared customs, traditions, tastes, and assumptions. Together, the various dimensions of Saharan culture created a familiar context in which individual Saharans lived their lives. This context set limits on the kinds of things people could say or do without seeming absurd or deviant, but it also allowed for a considerable range of individual freedom. The recognition of this dynamic perspective on culture and the ability of individuals to negotiate the constraints on what they could reasonably say or do is the cornerstone of my understanding of how culture shaped health behavior in Saharan Morocco.

The idea that individuals have the capacity to manipulate the application of cultural norms, values, knowledge, and meanings in everyday life has been a dominant theme in cultural anthropology since the late 1980s. Critical schol-

arship on the role of culture in the exercise of power in social life has highlighted multiple ways that weaker groups resist domination. Medical anthropologists have focused on patient resistance to discourse that objectifies
individuals as a diseased body or judges individual behavior in terms of compliance with therapeutic recommendations (e.g., Ferzacca 2000, Finnerman
1989). Alternatively, research in Middle Eastern and North African studies has
emphasized women's resistance to the social and cultural conditions of patriarchy (e.g., Abu Lughod 1993, Wikan 1996).

These trends in both subfields of cultural anthropology influenced the way
I examined maternal-child health practices, but the concept of resistance described only one aspect of how Saharan housewives approached the household production of health. As the case studies show there was evidence of
resistance to medical discourse and patriarchy. Naima resisted public health
efforts to convince (and even coerce) all pregnant women in Zaouia to attend
the national immunization campaign's mobile clinic. Similarly, Lalla Kabira
resisted the norms of Arab patriarchy that confined wives in their husband's household when she dressed in his robe and turban to find a remedy for her lost lactation. In other circumstances, Saharan women submitted to the forces of
medical discourse and patriarchy. Within the span of 2 weeks, Fatiha gave birth
in the provincial hospital and accepted treatment from an Islamic spiritual
healer for post-partum emotional distress. Understanding Saharan health behavior requires consideration of all of these disparate responses.

The widespread variation in housewive's adherence and resistance to medical advice—whether its source was biomedical, Arab, Islamic, or folk knowledge—thwarted the creation of categories representing Saharan health behavior.
A more productive strategy was to examine cultural patterns in the *contexts*
in which housewives used protective behavior. Despite the definitive knowledge housewives provided in interviews about the customs for protecting the
health of mothers and children, their application of that knowledge in practice entailed an evaluation of the unique conditions of a particular patient or
illness problem. The decisions household caregivers made about how to fa-
cilitate a safe pregnancy or birth, or how to protect an infant from illness or
death took place in contexts that encompassed multiple, diverse variables,
some of which fluctuated over time. Moreover, these variables reflected several different domains of knowledge in Saharan culture and caregivers had to
weigh the relative importance of each one, often under urgent time constraints. Occasionally, they consulted health professionals for help when a
health threat seemed overwhelming, but most of the time Saharan women
relied on each other to devise a course of action that made sense for the particular problem at hand.

The types of variables and domains of cultural knowledge that contributed to Saharan sensibilities for assessing maternal-child vulnerability appear in the case studies described in Chapters 6–8. The examples of Naima's pregnancy, Fatiha's first birth, and Lalla Kabira's breastfeeding difficulties as well as the experiences of other women discussed in the chapters illustrate the ambiguity inherent in Saharan interpretations of vulnerability to health dangers. In all of the cases discussed in Part II of the book, the assessment of vulnerability was a social process involving not only other members of the household but also other relatives, neighbors, and friends. Although I want to avoid suggesting that any of these case studies represent general trends in Saharan household health practices, an examination of the ways these women managed the threats to their well-being reveals common underlying patterns in the assessment of vulnerability and the culturally appropriate responses to it.

Elements of Vulnerability in Saharan Culture

A comparative analysis of how and when Saharan women enacted strategies to protect health during pregnancy, childbirth, and breastfeeding indicates that 5 domains of information contributed to the assessment of vulnerability in Saharan households. These domains include: popular knowledge of health dangers, the individual's quality of well-being, past experience, the availability of socio-economic resources, and the presence of protective forces. Multiple variables within each of these domains introduced uncertainty into the collective process of evaluating the type and degree of vulnerability for the individual in question, but this situation dissuaded few Saharan housewives from attempting to manage health concerns themselves. The containment of knowledge about one's vulnerability within the household or within a small circle of trusted friends was purposive; the symbolic construction of interiority was one of the multiple strategies that women like Naima employed to increase the chances of a good health outcome.

As I explained in Part I, one of the main sources of complexity in assessing health concerns in Saharan Morocco was the presence of medical pluralism. The co-existence of Arab, Islamic, biomedical and folk knowledge in Saharan popular health culture presented housewives with a wide range of health dangers to consider in their efforts to produce health. As Mary Douglas (1994) has argued, however, each culture emphasizes particular dangers as being more important than others. Saharan popular health culture's focus on humoral imbalance, the Eye, spirit attack, magical curses, and microbes in the assessment of threats to maternal and child health shows the overlapping importance of social, spiritual and physical sources of danger. The relevance of each type of danger in a given situation depended on the circumstances of the individual woman and the social environment. Naima, for example, avoided taking herbal medicines for diarrhea during her pregnancy because she worried that they would create a humoral imbalance in her body and harm the fetus. Fatiha's household, in contrast, feared that she may have suffered a spirit attack after giving birth to her son and they consulted an Islamic spiritual healer for treatment. In the third case study, Lalla Kabira's high status family assumed that envy was the cause of her lost lactation.

The customs that housewives enacted during pregnancy, childbirth, and breastfeeding often attempted to protect against several dangers at once. For example, the custom of hiding pregnancy simultaneously decreased the chances that someone would use the Eye and magical curses to cause the mother harm. Similarly, amulets placed on a newborn aimed to protect against the Eye and spirit attack. The degree to which any of these threats triggered concern depended on the social assessment of the individual's relative vulnerability at a given time. In general, Saharan popular health knowledge stipulated that women and infants were susceptible to all five types of danger, but the example of the birth of Halima's daughter demonstrates that some women felt safe enough to take minimal precautions even in prototypically dangerous circumstances.

One type of information that housewives used to evaluate someone's degree of vulnerability considered the person's overall state of well-being. As explained in Chapter 4, the Saharan concept of health (SiHa) incorporated social, emotional and spiritual dimensions of experience in relationship to the physical state of the body. Disruptions to subjective experience in any of these forms indicated that the individual was maHluul (open to danger). Among the more explicit indications that an individual was maHluul were symptoms of illness or emotional distress. Naima's bought with diarrhea and Fatiha's post-partum breakdown fit into this category. Although both situations constituted health problems themselves, Saharan popular health culture also viewed those conditions as signs of vulnerability to other kinds of danger, such as spirit attack, magical curses, or humoral imbalance. For that reason, Saharans enacted strategies of protection at the same time they employed therapeutic measures to restore health.

The assessment of well-being also incorporated implicit, embodied knowledge which situated subjective experience in the context of everyday activities. For housewives, Saharan culture structured this context in terms of 4 underlying principles. These principles, which I described in Chapter 4 as the aesthetics of Saharan domestic life, include: interiority, unity, balance, and purity.

These implicit structures organized experience in the body, household, and community and mediated the lived meaning of health, in all its dimensions. For Saharan housewives, the sense of feeling well emerged in relationship to local expectations for creating order in social, emotional, economic and spiritual life. To achieve the desired sense of order, the body needed the energy to perform household chores and entertain visitors, the capacity to achieve ritual purity and pray attentively, and the constraint to manage emotions and maintain harmony in the household. According to the practical logic of Saharan culture, disruptions to the creation of interiority, unity, balance, or purity in ritual or in everyday life had the potential to compromise well-being and increase susceptibility to health problems.

The customs Saharans performed during known contexts of danger aimed to protect the participants from harm but sometimes other factors increased or decreased feelings of vulnerability. In addition to explicit signs of illness or emotional distress, implicit changes to the social and natural environment also triggered a desire for added protection. For example, the bride from Tinii described in Chapter 5 wore an amulet over her wedding costume to increase her sense of security in the form of interiority when she left her home and village on her wedding day. Similarly, Naima's household worried about complications with her pregnancy and the birth, in part, because her divorce and her move to Zaouia hindered her ability to create unity and balance in her social life. The success of Naima's previous 2 pregnancies suggests that the source of concern was not the transitional state of pregnancy but rather the particular conditions of this pregnancy.

In contrast, contexts which reflected the appropriate alignment of aesthetic patterns could create a sense of security and protection from danger. As illustrated in Chapter 8, Fatim-Zahra's calm and even skeptical reaction to her infant son's exposure to mard shim suggested that she felt little sense of vulnerability to this feared childhood illness. By orienting individual bodies and selves in a structured cultural environment, the aesthetic patterns of everyday life created an embodied sensibility for anticipating the outcome of a given situation as either good or bad.

Participation in group interaction at the levels of the household and the community played an important role in establishing common embodied sensibilities toward the order of everyday life, but an individual's past experience also influenced Saharan expectations related to health dangers. This element of Saharan evaluations of vulnerability overlaps with Nichter's category of "trait-based vulnerability" (2003:15). My analysis of this factor, however, situates the individual's past experience in terms of the aesthetic composition of the context in question. For example, Halima's sense of security when she gave birth to her 5th child stemmed in part from the aesthetic of unity that she established with her in-law's household through the healthy births of 4 other children. In contrast, Fatim-Zahra's previous miscarriages amplified her sense of isolation from her husband's family and compelled her household to maximize the use of protective measures for the birth of her first child (described in Chapter 3).

While Fatim-Zahra chose home birth as a good strategy for reducing her vulnerability, Fatiha, who was also a first time mother, chose to breach the protective aesthetic of interiority established in a home birth and pleaded for a hospital birth when her labor pains intensified. Positive interactions with a nurse at the provincial hospital in the past led her to view hospital birth as safe. Her expectations were not a response to health promotion messages about the safety of medically attended birth but rather to her belief that she could trust the nurse more than her mother-in-law, who had been acting as her midwife. Fatiha's opinion of the hospital changed later because of the staff's lack of sympathy, but in the urgency of the moment she sought a social connection that seemed protective.

Fatiha was one of 3 young mothers in the study whose experience with childbirth involved an emergency trip to the hospital resulting from a sudden sense that home birth was unsafe. This switch in strategy suggests that the protective measures that midwives and caretakers employed to ensure a good birth outcome at home were insufficient to quell feelings of vulnerability in all cases. Most of the study participants preferred to contain labor and delivery in the household with the protection of herbal infusions, incense, and trusted assistants. They were also, however, well aware of the dangers encountered during home births. Collective memory of the recent past when complications during birth led to maternal and infant death reminded everyone that household measures of protection were less than 100% effective. The poorly equipped provincial hospital had an imperfect record as well, but increasingly younger mothers saw medical professionals as a resource for preventing tragedy during childbirth.

Evidence of skepticism about household customs of protection also appeared in the data on breastfeeding practices. Saharan popular health culture offered 3 different strategies for protecting a new mother's milk during the first 40 days post-partum: performing protective rituals on the 3rd day post-partum, wearing a protective talisman, or sharing food with other lactating women. Lalla Kabira's story, however, suggested that those strategies offered no guarantee against lost lactation. In the first case she described, she admitted that she forgot to use a protective strategy. In the other cases, however, she was careful to avoid eating with other nursing mothers unless they split a symbolic loaf of bread first. Still, she lost her milk. Stories like Lalla Kabira's were common in my interviews. They conveyed an appreciation that it was impossible to control every threat to health, but that through reliance on faith and on family and friends, health could be restored.

The importance of faith, family, and friends in Saharan household practices was an indirect indication of the marginal socio-economic status of the majority of households participating in the study. Few families could rely on the market as a consistent resource for health care. Amina was the only mother in the study sample who could afford commercial infant formula when her lactation stopped, and that was only a temporary solution. Less expensive market resources for health care included herbalists and spiritual healers. Fatiha's household, for example, paid a fqih to diagnose and treat her post-partum breakdown. These kinds of consultations, however, were usually a last resort when other measures failed to work. Reliance on neighbors and friends with expertise in health matters was the preferred strategy for coping with health problems that exceeded the knowledge of women in the household. The maintenance of local networks of assistance aimed to ensure long-term social and economic security as family and friends performed favors and acquired debts in on-going relationships of balanced reciprocity. As Naima's story shows, the management of a positive reputation was an important requirement for participating in those networks. The need for long-term security could translate into the need to take short-term risks, such as Naima's avoidance of the immunization campaign.

Saharan Principles of Health Practice

The case studies provide a brief overview of the multitude of contingencies Saharan housewives had to consider when deciding how to prevent illness and promote health in everyday life. The focus on preventive and protective dimensions of the household production of health illuminates the ambiguity inherent in the practical application of health knowledge. Unlike illness narratives, which merge experience and health knowledge in an ordered and meaningful explanation of a past event, the meaning of preventive and protective strategies hinges on events in the unknowable future. For that reason, a veil of uncertainty promoted the tentative way in which Saharan women—especially the devout Muslims—put preventive health knowledge into action.[1] As described in the previous case studies, protective strategies involved more than a straightforward reaction to cultural beliefs in the danger of illness agents such as the Eye or in the effectiveness of symbols such as open hand amulets.

Culture shaped the local understanding of danger, vulnerability, and security in far more complex ways that involved embodied sensibilities of health and implicit modes of being-in-the-world.

I have argued that Michael Jackson's (1998: 79) phenomenological view of vulnerability offers a useful framework for conceptualizing the dynamic contexts in which Saharan housewives transformed health knowledge into courses of action. His emphasis on the intersubjective and embodied nature of vulnerability reflects a common theme in cultural phenomenology, which argues that culture shapes experience and subjectivity (see Gieser 2008 and Throop and Murphy 2002 for a more extensive review of this perspective). As explained in Chapter 5, Jackson discusses vulnerability in terms of the dialectical relationship between the particular and the universal in human experience. The dialectic is intersubjective in its juxtaposition of particular embodied subjects and social dynamics with general knowledge and culturally constructed objects (1998: 1–9). In the Saharan case studies I described, the embodied subjects included housewives experiencing pregnancy, childbirth, and breastfeeding as well as the caregivers in their social group who contributed to health decision-making. For Saharan housewives, the intersubjective experience of vulnerability was embodied not only in the sense that the body provided the fundamental source of health-related experience, but also in the sense that Saharan culture conditioned bodily experience in particular ways. Cultural dispositions or sensibilities generated common patterns in the way housewives responded to culturally constructed objects (both harmful and protective), general medical knowledge, and particular social dynamics. Although the 4-parts of the dialectic combined in multiple ways in the pluralistic health context of Saharan Morocco, the recurring themes of interiority, unity, balance, and purity suggest that Saharans shared common cultural ways of experiencing vulnerability and security.

In contrast to Jackson's emphasis on the loss of power or control as a universal condition that triggers the experience of vulnerability, I have framed Saharan vulnerability as an experience of disruption. This perspective emerged from situating my analysis of household health practices in the full context of Saharan culture rather than in the narrow context of health dangers. The holistic assessment of health behavior reflected the kinds of contextual information household healers took into consideration when evaluating a person's vulnerability and devising strategies of protection. The concept of disruption in my analysis rests on the assumption that culture constructs a particular intersubjective order for human experience. This order appears in the cultural arrangement of space, the rhythm of activities, the dynamics of social interaction, and the modes of relationship between humans and the material and spiritual worlds. Illness and feelings of vulnerability are among the wide range of forces that disturb the learned sense of order that culture provides. The concept of disruption also applies to forces that hinder efforts to create order in everyday life. That is to say, individuals participate in the construction and maintenance of cultural order, and they know (consciously or tacitly) when their efforts fall short of the goal.

These ideas about culture and experience derived from a synthesis of perspectives related to cultural phenomenology. In particular, the concepts of habitus (Bourdieu 1977, 1990) and the aesthetics of everyday life (Desjarlais 1992) provided heuristics for explaining the connection between the structures of everyday practices, embodied experience, and health behavior. Additionally, their emphasis on cultural conditioning offered a way to bridge Mary Douglas' (1966, 1983, 1994) insights about the cultural construction of danger and risk with Jackson's phenomenological theory of intersubjectivity. Douglas' idea that culture emphasizes particular events, circumstances, experiences, and environments as dangerous highlights the centrality of the cultural context, which Jackson downplays in his conceptualization of vulnerability. Douglas' theory, however, overlooks the variable relationship between general cultural patterns in the construction of danger and individual experience. Although neither Bourdieu nor Desjarlais examined vulnerability or risk in their studies of embodied subjectivity, their insights on the cultural underpinnings of practice and experience have shaped my reconfiguration of Jackson's perspective with respect to Douglas' contributions to the study of risk and culture.

Bourdieu's (1977, 1990) theory of practice established a foundation for my dynamic theory of vulnerability by disentangling individual action from broader social norms. The concept of habitus includes the idea that real life—as opposed to abstract codes of conduct—is full of contingencies. When the taxonomies and protocols of abstract, general knowledge fail to match the observed conditions of a particular situation in real life, individuals rely on internalized principles to negotiate a culturally suitable course of action. Unfortunately, the nature of those internalized principles of habitus is vague in Bourdieu's writing on the logic of practice. Nonetheless, his insights about the implicit structures that guide human behavior in all its variable forms serve as a vital element in understanding the relationship between culture, subjectivity, and behavior.

Desjarlais' (1992) ethnography on shamanistic healing in Nepal transforms Bourdieu's ideas about habitus into a more concrete construct by proposing that the implicit structures of subjective experience are aesthetic in nature. Whereas Bourdieu emphasized symbolic patterns in social and economic activity, Desjarlais focused more on cultural styles of being and feeling. This shift reflects a historic change in ethnographic methods and writing between the

1960s when Bourdieu examined village life in Algeria and the 1980s when Desjarlais studied illness experience in Nepal. Increasing attention to individual perspectives—both of the anthropologist and the research participants—has generated more nuanced theories of how culture shapes subjectivity. Experience-near ethnography has the capacity to generate rich detail about the lives of individuals or households, but the narrow focus sacrifices an appreciation of broader patterns and variations in the relationship between the individual and the social group as a whole.

My analysis of variations in Saharan health practices combined the strengths of Bourdieu and Desjarlais in their perspectives on culture, embodiment, subjectivity, and practice to explain the themes in my data. Desjarlais' study of common structures of feeling, being, and doing in Nepal provided me with a framework for organizing and describing the implicit structures of Saharan household practices. At the same time, Bourdieu's theory of practice offered an explanation for how and why individual practices diverged from collective representations of health knowledge and customs. The recognition of individual agency in the enactment of those variable practices sets Desjarlais' perspective apart from Bourdieu. Desjarlais' research demonstrated a fundamental connection between embodied sensibilities, individual experience, and health behavior through his close attention to the styles of behavior among Nepali villagers. They monitored their emotions and actions in attempt to maintain a particular mode of being. Moreover, their embodied awareness of the implicit cultural order alerted them when something was wrong (e.g., signs of illness or distress) and provided tacit guidelines for how to address the problem.

I noticed the same kinds of subtle cues at work in Saharan culture. Saharan housewives enacted health strategies that aimed to produce a particular quality of life. The cultural logic of their health practices derived from the fundamental structures that organized everyday life in the space of the body, the household, and the community. The aesthetics of interiority, unity, balance, and purity organized Saharan domestic work, social interaction, spiritual practice, and emotional expression in time and space. Through participation in everyday social, economic and ritual life, Saharan housewives internalized the set of aesthetic patterns as an implicit cultural index for understanding experience in the world. Similar to Bourdieu's concept of habitus, the theory of everyday aesthetics asserts a connection between the patterns of group life and individual experience. This link includes the symbolic associations people use to make sense of what they have done as well as gut-feelings that motivate them to act in particular ways in the first place. Preventive and protective behavior stems not simply from general knowledge about risk or even recognition of the presence of danger in a context, but also from feeling susceptible to danger in culturally salient ways. This perspective places greater emphasis on the cultural dimensions of what Jackson (1998: 32) called the body subject in his theory of intersubjectivity. For Saharans, feelings of openness, isolation, imbalance, and defilement signaled a shift from the implicit, cultural order of everyday life.

Whether the shift in the aesthetic order occurred at the level of the individual body, the household, or community, housewives acted as healers in their attempts to repair the rupture and prevent further disorder. Their capacity to recognize the implicit conditions of vulnerability developed from the central role women played in activities that composed the cultural structure of everyday life: cooking, cleaning, visiting, praying, caring for children, lending to and borrowing from the neighbors, and monitoring movement into and out of the house.

Senior housewives played the most prominent role in the household production of health. Their accumulated knowledge about at-tib at-taqliidii (traditional medicine) as well as their shrewd understanding of the micro-politics of Saharan social life generated a keen sense for managing a range of health dangers. This wisdom was particularly important for evaluating the level of vulnerability among the household members because Saharan social life entailed constant fluctuations in relationships of trust and distrust based on suspicions of envy. As gate-keepers and representatives of the household, senior housewives interacted with the community more than the younger women. The mothers-in-law and grandmothers managed relations with the neighbors and extended family members. They negotiated marital arrangements for their children and they supervised the upbringing of their grandchildren. In almost all the participating households, the senior housewife (except when she was elderly or disabled) directed the activities related to prevention, diagnosis, and healing. In this role, she had power over the activities of her daughters and daughters-in-law. Younger women in the household served as a labor force and as health care assistants for the senior women and in so doing learned the Saharan arts of protection and healing.

Mechanisms of Embodying Cultural Knowledge

While it was easy to observe how senior housewives transferred explicit discursive knowledge about health care to the next generation, it is less clear how young women acquired the implicit embodied knowledge their elders used to assess vulnerability in a given context. Bourdieu argued that the internalization of the principles of habitus happens passively and unconsciously, but more recent scholarship on embodiment and subjectivity has challenged this perspective. Starrett's (1995) textual research on Islamic ritual prayer in colonial and contemporary Egypt argues that social groups "consciously ascribe meaning to—or learn to perceive meaning in—bodily disposition" (1995:954). He shows how Egyptian school texts equate Islamic ritual ablution and values of cleanliness with secular ideologies related to health promotion and responsible citizenship (1995:961). He contrasts these findings with Bourdieu's concept of bodily hexis (1977:82), which describes the unconscious internalization of cultural structures specific to the body to create durable dispositions. The examples of explicit discourse about ritual ablution and other aspects of ritual prayer demonstrate Egyptian reflexivity about the value of purity for the spiritual body as well as the body politic.[2]

Mahmood's (2005) research on Islamic ritual practice, also in Egypt, makes an even stronger argument against Bourdieu's contention that the embodiment of habitus occurs unconsciously. Mahmood conducted ethnographic research among Muslim women involved in a popular piety movement in Cairo. The women attended seminars and discussion groups at local mosques to improve their devotion to Islamic ritual practice and to cultivate virtuous dispositions in their everyday life. Mahmood draws on Aristotle's conceptualization of habitus (from *Nicomachean Ethics*) to explain the piety movement's attempt to use intentional external practice to produce a particular internal state. She describes how the women advocated the repeated practice of ritual prayer and virtuous acts, all with the appropriate attitude (a combination of sincerity, humility, and respect) to encourage the embodiment of the desired form of piety (2005:120–123). The popularity of the lessons among women of diverse backgrounds and social classes indicates that the disposition to engage in Islamic practices, either formal or informal, did not arise spontaneously from living in an Islamic society. Rather the women had to learn to have the appropriate attitudes and desire to live a pious life.

The pedagogical dimension of embodiment also serves as a central theme in Gieser's (2008) examination of the role of emotion and empathy in apprenticeship learning. Gieser's theory of embodiment builds on Ingold's (2000) phenomenological perspective on the transmission of cultural knowledge. He emphasizes learning practical skills rather than abstract systems of norms, values, classifications, and so on based in language. Gieser argues that individuals learn practical skills from other members of their social group through the imitation of bodily movement and the appreciation of intention, including emotion (2008:300–301). He views imitation in the transmission of cultural knowledge as "a complex intersubjective process comprising minds, bodies and (social and natural) environments" (2008:303).

Similar to Mahmood's findings among women in Egypt, Gieser views this kind of learning as something that develops through repeated practice. His emphasis, however, is on how the empathetic intertwining of emotions between student and teacher leads to the generation of particular modes of attention (2008:307). Gieser recognizes a dimension of learning that both Starrett and Mahmood overlook. Even in contexts that involve the explicit teaching of practical knowledge there is an implicit dimension to mastering the skill. He uses the concept of empathy to describe the implicit process of appreciating the perspective of the other (Gieser 2008:308). That process is necessary in practical learning because of the non-discursive and internal dimensions of practical knowledge. The successful transmission of those implicit, embodied dimensions of practice depends on the degree to which the teacher and student share a common foundation of experience. The concept of intersubjectivity connects the kind of formal learning discussed by Mahmood and Gieser with the informal internalization of cultural structures discussed by Bourdieu.

Both mechanisms of practical learning contributed to the embodiment of Saharan sensibilities related to vulnerability and security. The explicit pedagogy took place during the enactment of local customs and rituals during life cycle transitions. The participants in and observers of those formal practices learned to associate individuals in transitional states—brides, new mothers, and children—with vulnerability. At the same time, they learned to view certain symbolic objects (e.g., amulets, charms), ritual practices (e.g., circumambulation, burning incense), and social support as forms of protection against harm. In Mahmood's terms, repeated participation in these activities cultivated culturally appropriate feelings of vulnerability and security, even when those feelings failed to arise spontaneously during life cycle rituals.

The explicit mechanisms of embodying Saharan modes of feeling vulnerable or protected, however, must be considered in relationship to the implicit dimensions of experience. Practical learning also happened informally in the process of participating in everyday domestic life. The connection I make between Saharan sensibilities of vulnerability and security and the aesthetics of interiority, unity, balance, and purity echoes Anthony Giddens's (1990, 1991) theory of the self in the modern world. He argues that the predictable, routine order of modern life creates a sense of ontological security as children go through the process of socialization. In contrast a break or disruption in the routine triggers feelings of anxiety (1990:98). Giddens's perspective adds a psychological dimension to Bourdieu's concept of habitus by focusing on the emotional states of individuals. Cultural structures not only organize social and economic practice, but also establish an internalized measure of the conditions that create feelings of security and anxiety, which I see as potentially connected to vulnerability.

The application of all these theoretical perspectives to the study of Saharan health practices contributes to a theory of knowledge-in-action in which the implicit dimensions of experiencing vulnerability and security mediate the more explicit cultural constructions of danger in popular health knowledge and ritual protocols. The process of learning when and how to enact strategies of protection involves both implicit and explicit forms of practical knowledge. My lack of familiarity with the implicit aspects of Saharan culture put me at a disadvantage in my attempts to protect myself from harm, even though I had learned the explicit constructions of danger through my interviews with housewives. It was only through careful observations of Mama's disposition during our interactions with other women, both in our household and during visits to other households, that I began develop a Saharan sensibility for recognizing contexts of danger. Young Saharan women who shared a more extensive cultural basis for empathy and intersubjectivity with senior housewives had a greater capacity than I did to learn the implicit dimensions of practice this way.

It is important, however, to remember that Saharan responses to dangerous contexts varied considerably. Housewives disagreed with each other in assessing the level of danger in a given context or the course of action needed to protect the individuals involved. These disagreements occurred even in the hierarchical relationship between mother-in-law and daughter-in-law, as described in the case of Fatiha's hospital birth. Gieser's model of apprenticeship learning assumes a harmonious synergy between the teacher and student as they pursue the challenge of conveying implicit embodied knowledge. The transmission of health knowledge in Saharan households and communities, in contrast, encountered discord at least as often as there was agreement. Some of the discord resulted from variations in individual health experience. Women who suffered miscarriages or whose children died in infancy, despite following prescribed customs of protection, assessed vulnerability differently from women who had uneventful pregnancies and healthy children.

Another source of disagreement involved the type of protection needed for the vulnerable person. Grandmothers advocated using charms and symbolic rituals to protect their grandchildren, while the mothers preferred immunizations and a balanced diet.[3] These disagreements reveal that the process of embodying preventive health knowledge involves something more than learning a skill akin to baking bread or weaving a rug. The techniques housewives learned in the process of reproducing the local customs of domestic life did contribute to embodied knowledge of vulnerability and security, but in an indirect way. Participation in daily routines of cooking, cleaning, socializing, and praying established a taken-for-granted order for the body, household, and community comparable to Giddens' notion of ontological security. For most households participating in my study, feelings of vulnerability were an anomaly to the daily routine. Hence, the embodiment of this kind of knowledge was less straightforward.

Learning the skill of distinguishing the conditions of vulnerability from conditions of security required household healers to employ a holistic synthesis of cultural knowledge. They had to combine cognitive knowledge about the forms and conditions of danger with a common sense evaluation of dynamic real life contexts. Bourdieu's (1900:81–82) comparison of the logic of practice to a game of soccer offers a helpful analogy in explaining how actors apply cultural knowledge in dynamic contexts. Unlike the practice of baking bread or weaving a traditional rug where the outcome is predictable, playing a game of soccer entails a good deal more uncertainty. To succeed players rely on their cognitive knowledge of the rules of the game and spontaneous feelings about how to act—and react—in a given play during the game. As Bourdieu explains it, skilled players develop a "feel" for the game and capacity to anticipate what will happen next: the player "passes the ball not to the spot where his team-mate is but to the spot he will reach—before his opponent—a moment later" (Bourdieu 1990:81). That capacity to predict how others will act and how events will unfold in the imminent future derives from the internalization of common patterns of play learned from past experience. As fans of world soccer know, the patterns of play vary considerably between teams in South America, Europe, and Africa.

The same theory of practice applies when one moves from the soccer field to the dynamics of everyday domestic life in Saharan Morocco. Through experience with the organization of space, the rhythm of activity, and the styles of social interaction for different kinds of events (e.g., hosting honored guests vs. hanging out with the family), housewives learn how to anticipate what will happen next. Within this framework, feelings of vulnerability signal an anticipation of pending harm in the form of illness or some other misfortune. This sense of anticipation derives from more than general knowledge about the potential agents of illness (e.g., microbes, spirits, cold, magic, and the Eye). It also requires a sense of illness agents as players in the high stakes game of everyday life. What are the circumstances in which they attack? When can a counterattack diminish their power to cause harm? The way a housewife responded to these questions varied according to the extent of her knowledge of popular health culture and her past experience with health dangers, as a victim, healer, or observer.

Over time, Saharan housewives became more discerning about how much protection they needed regardless of the customary precautions of traditional maternal-child health practices. Embodied knowledge of how past experience compared to the context of the current situation established a tacit index for interpreting the relative degree of danger or safety at a given moment. The basic aesthetic structures of Saharan domestic life that I described in Chapter 4 represent the principal dimensions of that index. Overlap and contradictions among those structures as they combine in various ways adds ambiguity to the process of interpreting just how much danger a situation entails. As such, the skills needed for managing vulnerability and protection in the household involved discernment, improvisation, and creativity rather than rote adherence to a traditional protocol. For that reason, I have characterized household strategies of protection as an art rather than a practice or skill. This assessment reflects the recognition of agency in contemporary theories of practice. Whereas Bourdieu portrayed his soccer players as unconscious of the underlying principles that shaped the way they played, theorists in the field of cultural phenomenology (Desjarlais 1992, Geiser 2008, Mahmood 2005) have argued that embodied knowledge entails an element of tacit awareness. Actors recognize disruptions in the taken-for-granted cultural order and take measures to repair it.

Cultural Aesthetics and Historic Change

A significant source of disruption in the Saharan cultural order in recent years has come from the process of rapid social and economic change. This context has presented both benefits and challenges to the study of health promotion and disease prevention in Saharan culture. On one hand, changing patterns made Saharan housewives more reflective about cultural assumptions and habits from the past (MacPhee 2004). On the other hand, however, culture change made it difficult to identify the core aesthetic structures. Between the time when I left the field in 1997 and returned in 2005, the aesthetic of interiority had become far less prominent. Even during my fieldwork in the mid-1990s (the focus of the data I present here), the foundation of Saharan culture was shifting. Development initiatives and outreach campaigns in health and education introduced several new elements to the patterns of household health practice. Some of these elements took the form of new fields of play (such as hospitals), new players (specialist physicians, traveling nurses, peace corps volunteers), and new ways of learning the game (school-based education, television, books). Although biomedicine had been a part of medical pluralism in the southeastern Sahara since the colonial era, public health initiatives at the end of the 20th century expanded its presence in the daily life of low-income households. The modernizing changes, in turn, began to generate new aesthetic principles and new sensibilities in the younger generation. My observation of the new aesthetic of openness when I visited Errachidia in 2005 is an example of how modernization is transforming the structure of everyday life. The openness of space in urban planning and architectural facades also appeared in women's clothing styles. These patterns contrasted sharply with the aesthetic of interiority that I observed during my previous fieldwork.

Another change related to the aesthetics of social interaction was a dominant theme during my conversations with women in 1996 and 1997. Some of the tensions I observed between mothers-in-law and daughters-in-law emerged from rudimentary forms of Western individualism learned from television, the children of migrant laborers, and the development of new social inequalities based on educational achievement and cash wealth acquired from wage labor. Public health messages supported the aspirations of a few young wives and mothers to make decisions independently of their mothers-in-law. Those decisions included the use of the contraceptive pill, prenatal care, hospital birth, and pharmaceutical medicines for their children. The mothers-in-law in the study resisted the growing influence of biomedical care, not because they distrusted scientific knowledge but because it fell outside their expertise and it undermined their power. Disagreements about health care were often signs of broader disharmony in the household. In the most extreme cases, the daughters-in-law lobbied their husbands to move out of his father's household and start a new nuclear household with his wife and children. The new value of individualism contradicted the well-established values of unity and balance, on which elder women depended for their security in old age. The resulting sense of vulnerability was so unsettling for some mothers-in-law that they were unsure of how to protect themselves and they turned to their neighbors for emotional support.

Ferzacca (2001) and Simon (2009), both of whom conducted ethnographic research in Indonesia, noticed similar responses to modernization's creation of cultural pluralism. Ferzacca observed a tension between traditional Islamic modes of being and modern lifestyles. Public discourse on chronic diseases such as diabetes and cancer associated modern lifestyles with being out of control. In response to this problem, Javanese Muslims viewed the Ramadan fast as an opportunity to establish a sense of embodied order and to counteract the disruptions that modern consumption habits inflicted on their bodies (2001:64). Similarly, Simon found that West Sumatran Muslims viewed ritual prayer as a strategy to lessen the anxiety they felt in response to the demands of modern life. Yet, several participants in his study felt incapable of meeting the religious obligation to pray despite the worries that troubled their minds.

Simon attributes the paradox to contradictions between Islamic values of social integration and ethnic (Minangkabau) values of individual autonomy,
which reflected the structure of the modern economy. His discussion of the
conflict in West Sumatran subjectivities refers to the notion in cultural anthropology that humans dislike the ambiguity and contradictions that arise
from changing or overlapping cultures (Simon 2009:270). At the same time,
however, culture provides ways to resolve the anxiety it produces.[4]

My research on household health practices and my experience as a bride
taught me that the Saharan cultural system was full of contradictions. Despite
the cultural preference for constructions of interiority, Saharans also found
value in gestures of openness to guests, to potential marriage prospects and
business partnerships, and most importantly, to Allah. Despite a strong desire for balance in social life, households were hierarchical and competition
for status was a central (but discrete) part of social life. All of the defiling bodily substances and acts that are necessary to maintain health and the perpetu-
ation of life (i.e., sex, menstruation, birth) constantly thwarted attempts to
maintain purity. Similarly, the pull of individual interests and needs struggled
against the desire for social and spiritual unity. The current anxiety about the
influx of individualism in Saharan society is simply the most recent form of a
struggle between jism (flesh) and ruH (spirit) that has been a central theme in
Islamic theology for centuries (al-Badawi 2002; MacPhee 2003, 2004; Nasr
1997). The art of protection was one way in which Saharans managed these contradictions. As I learned in my attempts to protect myself from women who
envied my marriage to Yussef, the system was always in flux. A woman who was
a trusted ally of the household one week could become a threat the following
week. Coping with those fluctuations in the effort to maintain security and
avoid danger required familiarity with local patterns of practice and attention
to subtle shifts in the structures of relationships, behaviors, and environments.

Applications of Embodied
Vulnerability in a Risk Society

Although the types of danger and modes of vulnerability I have discussed
are particular to the social and historic context of Saharan Morocco between
1994 and 2005, the insights I gained from taking a knowledge-in-action approach
to research on health behavior have broader implications for the field of health
promotion and disease prevention. The ambiguities and complexities that Saharan housewives encountered when applying general knowledge to the context of real life is a common dilemma cross-culturally for both practitioners and

the general public. Even when the knowledge in question comes from scientific research about health risks, the translation from population patterns to individual bodies entails considerable uncertainty, especially with respect to disease prevention strategies. Sometimes flu vaccines fail to prevent flu infections and some people who smoke never develop lung cancer or emphysema. These kinds of discrepancies when situated in the real life context of multiple overlapping risks create a challenge for the field of health promotion and disease prevention. Attention to the embodied experience of vulnerability and social context may help to illuminate patterns in the range of behavioral responses to risks warnings and health promotion messages related to diverse public health problems.

The study of embodied experience and social context expands the study of health behavior from its roots in cognitive and social psychology to incorporate the perspectives of cultural phenomenology. In recent years, critical scholarship in medical anthropology and public health has recognized the need to situate studies of health behavior and risk perception in the confusing, imperfect contexts of people's actual lives (Coreil 2010; Lupton 1999; Nichter 2003, 2008; Yoder 1997). Increasingly health researchers have recognized that multiple overlapping factors influence health behavior and that the determinants of health outcomes are complex and multi-dimensional (Coreil 2010, Glanz, et al. 2002, Committee on Future Directions for Behavioral and Social Sciences Research at the NIH 2001). In response to this insight, ecological models of health and health behavior have become popular in public health scholarship. These models integrate multiple layers or spheres of factors that influence health behavior and health outcomes. Although each model emphasizes different dimensions of health determinants, social and cultural factors tend to appear in the form of interpersonal, institutional, community and societal factors. The concepts and perspectives of cultural phenomenology offer insight into how the macro-level factors integrate with micro-level factors such as individual experiences, feelings, interpretations, and practices.

As my research in Saharan Morocco has shown, the examination of implicit patterns in the experience of vulnerability and practices of protection provides a productive strategy for understanding the integration of the macro and micro dimensions of health behavior. My use of cultural phenomenology to assess patterns of health behavior in Saharan households yielded a perspective on vulnerability that emphasizes the influence of the social and cultural environment. This perspective reflects an emerging theme in medical anthropology that advocates for attention to vulnerability rather than risk in health research. For example, Leatherman's (2005) political-economic analysis of nutrition and health status in Peru argues that researchers must consider how global, regional, and local inequalities affect health status in poor communities. He incorporates both subjective and objective perspectives into his analysis of the creation of "a space of vulnerability" (using Chambers' (1989) concept): "social actors operate under multiple constraints and with limited options based on their personal reading of specific circumstances" (Leatherman 2005:52). Similarly, Ribera and Hausman-Muela (2011) argue that the constraints of vulnerability increase over time. Their ethnographic study of malaria in an impoverished farming community in Tanzania found that past episodes of illness shaped the context of current problems. The consideration of individual history was important "not only because the previous events and experiences condition the therapeutic path but also because hardship and problems tend to accumulate" (2011:104). The concept of vulnerability serves to describe circumstances in which adverse social, biological, environmental, and economic forces coincide.

These realist interpretations of vulnerability raise important questions about the degree to which Saharan women had the capacity to produce health and well-being in their households given their low socio-economic status. Although I discuss how socio-economic factors and the remote location of the province constrained access to resources (e.g., commercial infant formula), it was beyond the scope of my study to evaluate in an objective way the overall level of vulnerability in Saharan households or in the community. My focus on how culture shaped health behavior stopped short of evaluating how it shaped health outcomes, either from a biomedical or local perspective.

Nonetheless, my research did shed light on how global and national socio-economic and political structures influenced the strategies Saharan women used in the household production of health. The theoretical frameworks I used in my analysis revealed how broader issues of power and inequality played out in the local context. In some respects, Saharan women were pragmatic and pious in their comments about the constraints that poverty placed on their lives. The influence of Islamic values was evident in many of the responses to my interview questions including the way this middle-aged Berber mother-in-law answered my question about how she protected the health of her children:

> We eat good food and cook it well. My mother-in-law taught me that. I am careful with my housework. Everything has its place. We wash everything and sleep well. If you leave things, leave the mess, people become sick. I make sure that the children wash their hands before they eat. The rest is up to Allah (October 22, 1996).

Other women responded to the same question by saying that they ate "whatever Allah brought" and that "it is important to pray; Allah decides what happens." These comments reflected a culturally appropriate attitude of the acceptance of fate, but housewives were hardly passive in their roles as caregivers. Through watching television, interacting with foreigners (such as anthropologists and Peace Corps volunteers), and hearing stories from migrant workers, Saharans knew that they fell on the lower end of social inequalities in the world. They were critical about the quality and expense of health care offered at the provincial hospital and they appreciated the limits of the folk strategies they used to produce health. Although it was beyond their power to change the global and societal inequalities that affected their lives, housewives did have the capacity to maximize the few health resources available to them. One of the main strategies they used in that endeavor was to manage relationships with other people in the community. The attempts to create structures of unity and balances as well as interiority aimed simultaneously to establish bonds of mutual obligation (i.e., to share resources) with other households and to prevent any social inequalities that would provoke feelings of envy and cause harm.

When evaluating these strategies through the lens of vulnerability as a realist construct, it is important to keep the full context of everyday life in mind. While I agree with Leatherman that health researchers should consider how global, regional and local inequalities affect the health status of the poor, I find the objective interpretation of vulnerability to entail some of the same problems as the household production of health framework. In particular, the assertion that local cultural practices perpetuate vulnerability resembles the shortsighted characterization of culture as an obstacle to health. It is possible to argue that some Saharan household health strategies perpetuated their vulnerability to health problems. Women who shared their contraceptive pills with sisters-in-law and friends as an expression of unity put themselves at greater risk for unplanned pregnancy (MacPhee 1998). Similarly, women who avoided prenatal care in an effort to hide their pregnancy from envious neighbors and health care workers missed an opportunity to enhance the health of the fetus and avoid complications at the time of birth. This perspective, however, examines the practice out of context and overlooks the ways that these same practices contributed to broader strategies of producing well-being not only for the woman but also her household. The dual emphasis on socio-economic factors and biomedical constructs ends up reducing culture to the practices and beliefs people employ when they have no access to biomedical care. Although the realist examination of vulnerability in an ecological framework may enhance understanding of the overlapping determinants of a health problem, the ultimate burden of that assessment seems to fall on individuals who act in ways that researchers view as risky or unhealthy.

This tendency reflects a fundamental set of assumptions underlying what Giddens (1990) and Beck (1992) have called the risk society. The proliferation of

research and discourse on the determinants of risk has fueled a collective preoccupation with managing hazards through education and policies designed
to control behavior. Jeanine Coreil (2010:131) has observed that one of the
consequences of the risk society has been the creation of an "at risk role," which
holds people accountable when they engage in unhealthy behavior.[5] Ecological models contribute to the power of the risk society and the "at risk role" by
expanding the potential for identifying multiple, overlapping determinants of
disease and suggesting new strategies for prevention. Those strategies place an
unrealistic burden on individuals when the ecological studies examine health
risks in isolation from the overall context of dangers and constraints in people's lives. As my research in Morocco has shown, biomedical constructions
of health risks represent only one dimension of the dangers individuals strive
to manage in the everyday lives. Public health goals have a better chance of
success when they are situated within that context rather than against it. The
best way to achieve that synergy is to incorporate the subjective dimensions of
health and vulnerability into ecological studies of health problems.

The subjective interpretation of vulnerability complements objective interpretations in the effort to understand how individuals, households, and communities experience health threats. Contexts of inequality, discrimination, and
constrained resources represent conditions that potentially generate feelings
of susceptibility, weakness, and exposure to danger. Systematic studies of the
strategies people use to increase a sense of security in such contexts could yield
new insights on cultural patterns in health behaviors as well as culturally com-
patible interventions for health promotion. Anthropologists who have examined the subjective sense of vulnerability have gained a more nuanced
understanding of health behavior than past researchers who focused on risk perceptions and behavior. Launiala and Honkasalo (2010), for example, argue
that in Malawi feelings of vulnerability to witchcraft and AIDS took prece-
dence over concerns about malaria, in part because effective treatments for
the former two problems were harder to find. In contrast, Chapman's (2006)
attention to social risk in the study of malaria prevention shows how women
use multiple prevention strategies from different medical traditions simultaneously. By situating health risks in the overall contexts of people's lives anthropological research illuminates how individuals in poor communities manage
an overlap of social, emotional, supernatural and physical risks with few resources at their disposal.

The embodied, context-based theory of vulnerability I describe in this book
adds to this scholarship by providing a comprehensive model for examining the
cultural and personal factors that influence how and when individuals respond
to health risks. The cultural phenomenological approach that I use reflects

Nichter's (2003) behavior-in-context approach to studying vulnerability but places greater emphasis on describing the structure of the social and cultural contexts in which people act. The combined concepts of embodied subjectivity and the aesthetics of everyday life allowed me to gain a deeper understanding of the way Saharans interpreted those contexts with respect to local constructions of danger. My dual focus on embodied experience and cultural structures suggests that feelings of vulnerability and security vary along a continuum rather than as a dichotomy or typology.[6]

Nichter's use of the concept of harm reduction and Launiala and Honkasalo's idea of hierarchies of risk also suggest a continuum model of vulnerability, although neither describe it as such. Their effort to propose general concepts of vulnerability ends up losing sight of the specific social and cultural contexts that generated the behavior. The same critique applies to Jackson's (1998) intersubjective interpretation of vulnerability. General theories provide valuable contributions to comparative studies, but understanding health-related experience and behavior at the micro-level requires detailed knowledge of local cultural meanings and structures. Experience, thought, behavior, and context are intertwined dimensions of social life. As my description of Saharan health behavior has shown, experience and behavior shift from one context to the next. The more health researchers can understand how individuals assess contexts—much of which happens implicitly—the better we will understand health-related experience and behavior. My study establishes a first step in this direction, but far more research needs to take place in order to understand the processes and contexts in which individuals put health knowledge into action.

Recommendations for Future Research

As I mentioned at the beginning of the book, my main motivation for writing about the theme of vulnerability in my research on health practices in Morocco was its potential applications to the broader field of health promotion and disease prevention. Because my position as a cultural anthropologist lies largely outside this field, it is hard for me to predict the variety of ways that public health professionals might incorporate the concepts of embodiment and cultural sensibilities into their work. For anthropologists, however, there are a few research directions that would produce a deeper understanding of the cultural phenomenology of vulnerability with respect to health. My recommendations focus on the examination of the interaction of mind, body, and environment in different contexts.

First, there is a need to gain a better understanding of how well the connection between cultural aesthetics and the embodied experiences of vulnerability applies in other social and cultural contexts. The combination of ecological perspectives on health with cultural phenomenology provided a useful framework for organizing my data, but the limits of this perspective and my interpretation of vulnerability is unclear. The nature of medical pluralism in Saharan Morocco, especially with respect to the presence of personalistic illness etiologies helped me to see the structural connections between feelings of vulnerability, practices of protection, and the aesthetics of everyday life. Further research is needed in societies which employ scientific illness etiologies to examine how feelings of vulnerability mediate biomedical constructions of health dangers in different cultural contexts. It is also important to examine how feelings of vulnerability and practices of protection vary in culturally diverse societies. The internalization of the aesthetics of everyday life in establishing a sense of ontological security may vary according to generation, social class, and ethnic group. These types of investigation entail more complexity than I encountered in Morocco, but they will contribute valuable insights to the design of culturally sensitive health promotion interventions in urban and multicultural communities.

Another important dimension of the social and cultural context of vulnerability concerns the globalization of medical knowledge through migration, digital communication, and medical tourism. Ecological studies have the potential to generate a more nuanced appreciation of medical pluralism in both clinical and household contexts. My research in Saharan households challenged the assumption of a dichotomy between traditional and modern scientific medicine. Resistance to public health recommendations does not always signify adherence to traditional or folk medical advice. Saharan housewives ignored and modified popular knowledge about danger and protection as much as they resisted public health messages. These findings support the anthropological argument that individuals are active users of culture rather than passive vessels of it. The application of the concept of the aesthetics of everyday life to Saharan social life adds to Geertz's (1973) proposal that humans actively create meaning to suggest that they also actively create structure. What new perspectives does cultural phenomenology offer toward understanding the role of vulnerability in the dynamics of health development and culture change?

A second direction for expanding research on vulnerability raises questions about the meaning of environment in the phenomenological view of being-in-the-world. My research focused on how structures in the local social and cultural environment shaped embodied subjectivity, but paid little attention to geographic, material, or biological dimensions of the environment. The interaction of body, mind, and environment in the phenomenological view of being-in-the-world has multiple dimensions that may affect feelings of vulnerability and security. The household and community were the dominant forms of environment for most of the housewives who participated in my study, but other dimensions of environment influenced their lives. The desert climate, palm trees, domesticated animals, and participation in Arab-Muslim geopolitics all contributed to Saharan embodied subjectivity. Future research on the relationship between various levels and dimensions of environment and embodied subjectivity will generate a richer understanding of the implicit structures of vulnerability and security.

Lastly, there is a need for more research on the links between feelings of vulnerability, health behaviors, and health outcomes. A few studies in the past have drawn attention the increased health risks that result from cultural strategies enacted to cope with feelings of vulnerability. Leatherman's (2005) research in Peru, for example, describes situations in which individuals ignored symptoms because the demands of work and lack of resources proscribed sick leave. Alternatively, Nichter (2003:23) describes how Filipino sex workers used antibiotics as prophylactics against STD infections. He views this practice as harm reduction, a strategy of managing multiple vulnerabilities with few resources.[7]

These findings provide important insights for public health, but further research is needed on positive health outcomes in relationship to managing feelings of vulnerability. This research must move beyond the dichotomy between traditional and modern approaches to health care, which frames cultural beliefs and practices as obstacles to health. Now that the scientific community has begun to recognize the health benefits of social support, positive emotions, and spiritual practice, there is an opportunity to examine the effects of a wide range of cultural practices that people use to promote health and prevent illness. In the short term, the effects encompass feelings of security and the sense of well-being generated by protective practices—not limited to scientific interpretations of which behaviors are protective. In the long term, the effects encompass the range of actual health outcomes, both positive and negative, associated with cultural strategies for prevention and health promotion. Attention to embodied experience and cultural context in concert with objective measures of health in the study of health promotion and disease prevention opens new opportunities for developing initiatives and interventions that resonate with individuals and communities. The outcome of ecological studies of vulnerability (both subjective and objective) should not be the development of interventions that will control behavior more effectively, but rather to develop a better sense of the kinds of contexts and behaviors that increase people's sense of well-being and thereby increase the potential for better health outcomes.

Notes by Chapter

Chapter 1:
Introduction

1. The names that I use to represent the people discussed in the book are pseudonyms to preserve their anonymity.

Chapter 2:
Errachidia

1. "Mama" is a common Saharan nickname for Fatima. The term for mother in Moroccan Arabic is *uumi*. Saharan children living in extended family households, however, addressed their mothers by first name.

2. Aggressive immunization and family planning campaigns in the 1990s achieved a low fertility rate (3.38) and infant mortality rate (48.9/1000) in the economic region (Centre-Sud) that encompasses Errachidia as well as Meknes, a large city in central Morocco. According to a 1992 survey these were the lowest rates in the country. The mix of urban and rural areas in the economic regions measured, however, makes it difficult to discern how Errachidia compared to the aggregate data (Direction de la Statistique 1994).

3. The political climate in Errachidia Province changed considerably after King Mohammad VI replaced his father, Hassan II, in 1998. When I returned to the region in 2005, Saharans were excited to show me how recent development projects had modernized their lifestyle and provided new opportunities, including an increased freedom of speech.

4. Because villages in the Ziz Valley are so small, the anonymity of the women who participated in this study would not be protected if I used the real name of the village. I chose the common village name of *Zaouia* (sanctuary) to represent the religiosity of women in the village as well as my own view of the village as a sanctuary from the heat and dust of Errachidia.

5. The housewives I interviewed and observed in Errachidia and Zaouia were socially connected to each other with respect to residential proximity, family (natal and affinal), birth village, and participation in regular exchanges of gifts on formal and informal occasions.

6. Of the 22% of the participants in the study who had attended school at all, only 1/3 of those women continued past primary school. One of the factors contributing to my dif-

ficulty finding patrilocal households with educated daughters-in-law was that senior women preferred their sons to marry uneducated brides.

Chapter 3:
Maternal-Child Health in Perspective

1. The national infant mortality rate dropped from 124.4/1000 in 1967 to 57.3 in 1992 (Direction de la Statistique 1994:63).

2. I heard more details about symbolic magic once I gained the trust of women in our social network. The practice of tqaf involved the use of charms, plants, animal parts, and bodily substances (blood, hair, post-coital fluid) to control the actions of another person or cause misfortune. The most common reason that the housewives I knew discussed tqaf was to learn how to block or reverse its power. These methods included safeguarding bodily substances, burning incense, and wearing protective charms.

Chapter 4:
The Aesthetics of Saharan Domestic Life

1. In addition to the frequency with which housewives listed the hospital (*Sbiitar*) or the doctor (*l-tbiib*) as a treatment strategy for childhood illnesses, several mothers in the study told me about their experiences with taking their children to a health dispensary or to the hospital. My observations of clinical settings, however, were limited. I visited the local pediatrician's office only once when my 5-year-old nephew was ill. The parents and children in the large waiting room filled every available seat and the wait was over 2 hours.

2. Divorce was common among families in Errachidia and Zaouia. Some of the older participants in the study had divorced and remarried more than once. Saharans viewed marriage, especially one's first marriage, as a precarious bond. Disagreements arose within the household, usually among the women, or between the families who arranged the marriage. A local proverb advised young bridges to "dig the stakes of their tent" soon after marriage by having at least three children—lest the tent (i.e., the marriage) fly away (MacPhee 1998).

3. See MacPhee 2004 for further elaboration on the connection between the Salat ritual and embodied expectations about the timing of digestion.

4. See MacPhee 2003 for further elaboration on the importance of spiritual experience in the Saharan household production of health.

5. My emotional reaction to the possibility that Djo had leprosy overrode my academic knowledge that the disease was only minimally contagious. The rags on her hands reminded me of images I had seen as a child in films that depicted leper colonies as dangerously contagious.

Chapter 5:
Vulnerability and Security

1. Lack of time and money prevented Yussef and me from following this tradition for our own wedding, even though his family was Berber. I did have an opportunity, however, to dress in the Berber bridal costume during my field research. For entertainment on a quiet summer afternoon, my sisters-in-law dressed me in the bride's costume to show me what they had endured. I can attest that the complete costume is very heavy, stuffy, and difficult to maneuver.

2. Occasionally, I saw an Arab woman pull her lizar over her face when passing a group of men on the street or in the market. More commonly, Saharan women covered only their hair and their bodies from the neck to the ankles.

3. Ordinarily, young women wore their hair bound in a single twist fastened to the back of the head and covered with one or two scarves.

4. The Moroccan marriage contract required the payment of bridewealth to the bride's family when the couple became formally engaged, but usually the amount of cash exchanged was token in marriages arranged between kin or close friends. The exception was when the bride lived abroad with migrant parents and the marriage secured the groom a work visa in Europe.

Chapter 6:
Naima's Pregnancy

1. The rate of prenatal consultation for Errachidia Province alone is hard to discern because the statistics for births that year (1992) record only births in medical facilities (n=3061) (Direction de la Statistique 1994:227). When compared to the number of hospital births, the number of consultations in the first trimester (n=1911) and all other prenatal consultations (n=4897) yields a higher rate than Rabat, the capital of Morocco (Direction de la Statistique 1994:225). When one considers the estimate that the number of hospital births represents only about 25% of all births in the province, the rate of prenatal consultation seems more realistic.

2. The formality of respect and social distance between mother-in-law and daughter-in-law diminished over time. While most of the young daughters-in-law in the study were too shy to discuss topics related to reproduction in the company of their mother-in-law, older women who had several children spoke openly about sex, often in a joking tone, regardless of their mother-in-law's presence. The only young participant who spoke openly about sex and pregnancy with her mother-in-law present was a high school graduate who was also the niece of her mother-in-law.

Chapter 7:
The Birth of Fatiha's Son

1. A 1992 survey estimated that the average rural fertility rate was 5.5, compared to 2.5 in urban Morocco (Population Council 1994).

2. The notion that labor and delivery drains the mother's body of its humoral heat (from pregnancy) is found also in societies outside Morocco. Onder (2007) and Manderson (2003) observed similar uses of warm or hot medicines and treatments in popular Turkish and Malaysian versions of humoral medicine.

3. It is unlikely that Haja Abicha's teenage daughter on her own made the judgment to let us into the household's private quarters. Saharan housewives usually looked out a window or shouted "*shkun?*" (who) to discern who came to visit before opening the door. Given this household's preoccupation with Halima's sick son, it is likely that they invited us inside because they were interested in our family connections at the provincial hospital and my knowledge of biomedicine.

Chapter 8:
Lalla Kabira's Stolen Breastmilk

1. As mentioned in Chapter 3, Saharans associated hedgehogs with illnesses caused by a jinn.

2. The delay also gave the mother a chance to wash her breasts before nursing the infant. This ritual used clarified butter or olive oil mixed with crushed herbs. Khaira, one of the knowledgeable Berber grandmothers in the sample, said that washing the breast prevented it from turning the baby's mouth black. Her comment suggested that the washing ritual was a type of purification, which protected the infant from the defiling humoral byproducts of labor and delivery.

Chapter 9:
Embodied Knowledge in Action

1. One of the central components of the Islamic worldview in Saharan Morocco is the notion that the future is unknowable to humans. This mindset demonstrates respect for divine will and the power of Allah to determine future events. Although some Western scholars in the past viewed this mindset as fatalistic, I found that Saharan women made attempts to influence various outcomes in everyday life. They tried to prevent illness and other forms of misfortune but at the same time realized that there were no guarantees that their strategies would work.

2. Starrett's (1995) point about Egyptian reflexivity with respect to Islamic practice does not necessarily contradict Bourdieu's point about bodily hexis. The existence of discourse about ablution and prayer is a reflection of the principles of hexis and contributes to its re-

inforcement. The absence of ethnographic research in conjunction with Starrett's text analysis makes it impossible to judge how Egyptian school children incorporated the discourse into their own lives—which for most would not occur until many years later.

3. As described in Chapter 4, local interpretations of a balanced diet included the use of spices and the variation of meals from one day to the next. Housewives mixed and matched the staples of vegetables, meat, and starches (bread, rice, or pasta) in their culinary repertoire.

4. Simon's perspective falls in line with the insights of Weber (1958) and Geertz (1973) in pointing out that cultural systems often revolve around an attempt to manage their own internal contradictions (Simon 2009:301). See Ortner (2005) for a more extensive discussion of Geertz's and Weber's theories of how culture shapes subjectivity.

5. Coreil argues that the "at risk role" is replacing Talcott Parson's (1951) concept of the "sick role." In the 1950s, the interpretation of sickness as a chance misfortune exempted the patient from responsibility for his or her condition. The concept of risk, however, changed that attitude. Now, "people who engage in unhealthy behavior are held accountable for the consequences" (Coreil 2010:131).

6. My interpretation of Saharan feelings of vulnerability and security as a continuum was inspired by studies of the social self in Japan in Nancy Rosenberger's edited volume, *The Japanese Self* (1992). Bachnik (1992), in particular, described the concept of *kejime* in terms of an embodied sense or index through which people in Japan discern the degrees of formality or informality in a given social and cultural context. They, then, tailor their behavior according to that spontaneous interpretation.

7. The concept of harm reduction appears in wealthier communities as well. The ubiquitous reminders about risk in affluent countries create the sense that health risks are unavoidable. Marketers manipulate this mindset by selling products that have less risk (Nichter 2003:25–27).

GLOSSARY OF ARABIC AND BERBER TERMS

arusa	bride
agusa	old woman, mother-in-law
at-tib at-taqliidi	traditional medicine
barani	someone from outside the community
bint-l-famila	daughter of the family, respectful girl or woman
bismillah	in the name of God; also l-bismillah: a talisman
dua-l-blad	country or folk medicine
fqih, fuqaha	spiritual healer, Quranic scholar
hashak	far be it from you; an expression of deference
haaduuz	(Berber) line dance performed at Berber weddings
Harmal	African Rue, plant medicine used during childbirth to repel spirits
isnan	(Berber) male representatives of the groom's family in the Berber wedding ritual
jellaba	traditional hooded robe worn as outerwear
jinn, jnun	invisible spirit that can cause illness
khaf	afraid
khaltii	my maternal aunt, also term of respect and affection for elder women friends
kiif-kiif	same-same
krsh	stomach; also slang for womb during pregnancy

ksar, ksour	(qsar) walled village found in Saharan Morocco
kuhl	antimony used as liner under the eyes
l-bard	cold, in temperature and in humoral quality
l-blad	countryside, homeland
l-ein	the Eye, evil eye
l-eshab	herbalist or spice dealer
l-eshuub	herbal medicine
l-luHam	cravings during pregnancy
lalla	title of a high status, sharifa woman
lizar	sheet worn as a cloak to preserve modesty
maHluul	unbound, open
mard shim	sickness of smelling, the most feared form of diarrheal illness in children
mariid(a)	sick
muqaddam	government official at the village level
muwazzin	person who broadcasts the call to prayer
nafisa	name used for a new mother during the post-natal period
nfas	the post-natal period extending to 40 days after birth
nishan	straight, morally upstanding
qabila(t)	kin-based social group, tribe
qabla	midwife
rHala	nomad
tabarak Allah	may God bless you
taharuut	(Berber) black embroidered cloak worn over women's heads and upper body
Tahir(a)	ritual purity
tawHiid	unity
tbiib at-taqliidi	traditional doctor of humoral or symbolic medicine

tdigidig	prickly
sbuae	infant naming ritual on the 7th day after birth
siHr	sorcery
suq	traditional market
shabi	popular or common status (as opposed to elite)
sharif(a)	honored or titled person, descendent of the Prophet Muhammad or a local saint
Saharawi	from the desert, resident of Errachidia Province
Salat	the Islamic prayer ritual requiring 5 daily prayers
SiHa	health, strength, well-being
tqaf	magical curses
zman	the past, time past, the old days
zwiin(a)	beautiful, nice

References

Abu Lughod, Lila. 1993. *Writing Women's Worlds: Bedouin Stories.* University of California Press.

al-Badawi, Mostafa. 2002. *Man and the Universe: An Islamic Perspective.* Amman, Jordan: Wakeel Books.

al-Jawziyya, Ibn Q. 1998. *Medicine of the Prophet.* Cambridge, UK: The Islamic Texts Society.

Bachnik, Jane. 1992. Kejime: Defining a Shifting Self in Multiple Organizational Modes. In *Japanese Sense of Self,* edited by Nancy R. Rosenberger. New York: Cambridge University Press.

Bakhtiar, Laleh. 1999. *The Canon of Medicine: Avicenna.* Chicago, IL: Great Books of the Islamic World.

Bakker, Jogien. 1992. The Rise of Female Healers in the Middle Atlas, Morocco. *Social Science and Medicine* 35, no. 6:819–829.

Beck, Ulrich. 1992. *Risk Society: Towards a New Modernity.* London: Sage.

Bellakhdar, Jamal. 1989. Pharmacopoeia and Traditional Medicine in Morocco. *Curare* 12, no. 1:23–40.

Berman, Peter, C. Kendall, and K. Battacharyya. 1994. The Household Production of Health: Integrating Social Science Perspectives on Micro-level Health Determinants. *Social Science and Medicine* 38, no. 2:205–216.

Biehl, J., Good, B., and Kleinman, A. 2007. *Subjectivity: Ethnographic Investigations.* Berkeley: University of California Press.

Bourdieu, Pierre. 1977. *Outline of a Theory of Practice.* Cambridge, UK: Cambridge University Press.

Bourdieu, Pierre. 1990. *The Logic of Practice.* Stanford, California: Stanford University Press.

Chambers, R. 1989. Vulnerability, Coping and Policy. *IDS Bulletin* 20, 1–7.

Chapman, Rachel R. 2006. Chikotsa—Secrets, Silence, and Hiding: Social Risk and Reproductive Vulnerability in Central Mozambique. *Medical Anthropology Quarterly* 20, no. 4:487–515.

Committee on Future Directions for Behavioral and Social Sciences Research at NIH. 2001. *New Horizons in Health: An Integrative Perspective.* Edited by Burton H. Singer, Carol D. Ryff. Washington, DC: National Academy Press.

Coreil, Jeannine. 2010. *Social and Behavioral Foundations of Public Health.* Washington, DC: Sage.

Crapanzano, Vincent. 1973. *The Hamadsha: A Study in Moroccan Ethnopsychiatry.* Los Angeles: University of California Press.

Crapanzano, Vincent. 1980. *Tuhami: Portrait of a Moroccan.* Chicago: University of Chicago Press.

Csordas, Thomas. 1994a. *The Sacred Self: A cultural phenomenology of charismatic healing.* Berkeley, CA: University of California Press.

Csordas, Thomas. 1994b. Introduction: The Body as Representation and Being in the World. In *Embodiment and Experience: The Existential Ground of Culture and Self.* Cambridge: Cambridge University Press.

Desjarlais, Robert. 1992. *Body and Emotion: The Aesthetics of Illness and Healing in the Nepal Himalayas.* Philadelphia: University of Pennsylvania Press.

Desjarlais, Robert, and Jason Throop. 2011. Phenomenological Approaches in Anthropology. *Annual Review in Anthropology* 40, 87–102.

Direction de la Statistique. 1994. *Femmes et Condition Feminine au Maroc.* Rabat, Morocco: Direction de la Statistique.

Douglas, Mary. 1966. *Purity and Danger: An analysis of the concepts of pollution and taboo.* New York: Routledge.

Douglas, Mary. 1994. *Risk and Blame: Essays in Cultural Theory.* New York: Routledge.

Douglas, Mary, and Wildavsky, Aarron. 1983. *Risk and Culture.* University of California Press.

Dwyer, Kevin. *Moroccan Dialogues: Anthropology in Question.* Baltimore, MD: Johns Hopkins University Press.

Early, Evelyn. 1993. *Baladi Women of Cairo: Playing with an Egg and a Stone.* Boulder, CO: Lynne Reinner Publishers.

Ferzacca, Steve. 2000. Actually, I Don't Feel That Bad: Managing Diabetes and the Clinical Encounter. *Medical Anthropology Quarterly* 14, no. 1:28–50.

Ferzacca, Steve. 2001. *Healing the Modern in a Central Javanese City.* Durham, NC: Carolina Academic Press.

Finnerman, Ruthbeth. 1989. Tracing home-based health care change in an Andean Indian community. *Medical Anthropology Quarterly* 3, no. 2:162–174.

Geertz, Clifford. 1973. *The Interpretation of Culture.* Cambridge, MA: Harvard University Press.

Geny, Clement. 1979. Aspects de la Medecine Traditionnelle au Maroc. Ph.D. diss., Universite Louis Pasteur.

Giddens, Anthony. 1990. *The Consequences of Modernity*. Stanford, CA: Stanford University Press.

Giddens, Anthony. 1991. *Modernity and Self-Identity: Self and Society in the Late Modern Age*. Stanford, CA: Stanford University Press.

Gieser, Thorsten. 2008. Embodiment, Emotion and Empathy: A Phenomenological Approach to Apprenticeship Learning. *Anthropological Theory* 8, no. 3:299–318.

Glanz, Karen, Rimer, Barbara, and Lewis, Frances M. 2002. The Scope of Health Behavior and Health Education. In *Health Behavior and Health Education: Theory, Research and Practice*, edited by Karen Glanz, Barbara Rimer and Frances Marcus Lewis. San Francisco, CA: Jossey-Bass.

Good, Byron. 1994. *Medicine, Rationality, and Experience: An Anthropological Perspective*. London: Cambridge University Press.

Greenwood, Bernard. 1981. Cold or Spirits? Choice and Ambiguity in Morocco's Pluralistic Medical System. *Social Science and Medicine* 15B, 219–235.

Harrell, Richard S., and Sobelman, Harvey. 1966. *A Dictionary of Moroccan Arabic*. Washington, DC: Georgetown University Press.

Heidegger, Martin. 1962. *Being and Time*. San Francisco: Harper Collins.

Heidegger, Martin. 1975. Building, Dwelling, Thinking. In *Poetry, Language, Thought*. New York: Harper and Row.

Ingold, Tim. 2000. *The Perception of the Environment: Essays in Livelihood, Dwelling, and Skill*. New York: Routledge.

Inhorn, Marcia. 1994. *Quest for Conception: Gender, Infertility, and Egyptian Medical Traditions*. Philadelphia: University of Pennsylvania Press.

Jackson, Michael. 1996. Introduction: Phenomenology, Radical Empiricism, and Anthropological Critique. In *Things as They Are*, edited by Michael Jackson. Bloomington, IN: Indiana University Press.

Jackson, Michael. 1998. *Minima Ethnographica*. Chicago, IL: University of Chicago Press.

Johns Hopkins University Center for Communication Programs. 2000. *Communicating Safe Motherhood in Morocco: Family Planning/Maternal and Child Health Phase V Project, Final Report*. Baltimore: Johns Hopkins University.

Kapferer, Bruce. 1986. Performance and the Structuring of Meaning and Experience. In *The Anthropology of Experience*, edited by Victor W. Turner and Edward M. Bruner. Chicago, IL: University of Illinois.

Kleinman, Arthur. 1988. *The Illness Narratives: Suffering, Healing and the Human Condition*. New York: Basic Books.

Launiala, Annika, and Marja-Liisa Honkasalo. 2010. Malaria, Danger, and Risk Perceptions among the Yao in Rural Malawi. *Medical Anthropology Quarterly* 24, no. 3:399–420.

Leatherman, Thomas. 2005. A Space of Vulnerability in Poverty and Health: Political-Ecology and Biocultural Analysis. *Ethos* 33, no. 1:46–70.

Luhrmann, T. M. 2006. Subjectivity. *Anthropological Theory* 6, no. 3:345–361.

Lupton, Deborah. 1999. *Risk*. New York: Routledge.

MacPhee, Marybeth. 1998. *Vulnerability and the Contraceptive Pill: The Balance of Household Health and Marriage in Morocco.* Paper presented at the Annual Meeting of the American Anthropological Association, Philadelphia, PA.

MacPhee, Marybeth. 2003. Medicine for the Heart: The Embodiment of Faith in the Everyday Life of Moroccan Women. *Medical Anthropology* 22, 53–83.

MacPhee, Marybeth. 2004. The Weight of the Past in the Experience of Health: Time, Embodiment and Culture Change in Morocco. *Ethos* 32, no. 3:374–396.

MacPhee, Marybeth, Suzanne Heurtin-Roberts, and Christopher Foster. 2005. Traveling the Uncharted Path of Leadership in Federal Anthropology. *Practicing Anthropology* 27, no. 3:25–28.

Mahmood, Saba. 2005. *Politics of Piety: Islamic Revival and the Feminist Subject.* Princeton, NJ: Princeton University Press.

Manderson, Lenore. 2003. Roasting, Smoking, and Dieting in Response to Birth: Malay Confinement in Cross-Cultural Perspective. In *The Manner Born: Birth Rites in Cross-Cultural Perspective*, edited by Laura Dundes. Walnut Creek, CA: AltaMira Press.

Maroc Banque Central Populaire. *Monographie de la Region Economique Centre-Sud.* Casablanca: Direction des Etudes et de l'Information Economique, 1995.

Meneley, Anne. 2007. Fashions and Fundamentalisms in Fin-de-Siecle Yemen: Chador Barbie and Islamic Socks. *Cultural Anthropology* 22, no. 2:214–243.

Merleau-Ponty, Maurice. 1962. *Phenomenology of Perception.* New York: The Humanities Press.

Ministere de la Sante Publique. 1995. *Tous pour la Sante.* Casablanca: Editions Le Fennec.

Ministere de la Sante Publique. 2000. Sante de la Reproduction. In *Enquete Nationale sur la Sante de la Mere et de l'Enfant (ENSME) 1997.* Rabat: Ministere de la Sante.

Nasr, Seyyed H. 1991. Preface. In *Islamic Spirituality: Foundations*, edited by Seyyed Hossein Nasr. New York: Crossroad Publishing Company.

Nichter, Mark. 1981. Idioms of Distress: Alternatives in the Expression of Psychological Distress, a Case Study from South India. *Culture, Medicine, and Psychiatry* 5, no. 4:379–408.

Nichter, Mark. 2003. Harm Reduction: A Core Concern for Medical Anthropology. In *Risk, Culture, and Health Inequality*, edited by Barbara Herr Harthorn and Laury Oaks. Westport, CT: Praeger.

Nichter, Mark. 2008. *Global Health: Why Cultural Perceptions, Social Representations, and Biopolitics Matter.* Tucson, AZ: University of Arizona Press.

Nichter, Mark, and Carl Kendall. 1991. Beyond Child Survival: Anthropology and International Health in the 1990s. *Medical Anthropology Quarterly* 5, no. 3:195–203.

Obermeyer, Carla M. 1993. Culture, Maternal Health Care, and Women's Status: A Comparison of Morocco and Tunisia. *Studies in Family Planning* 24, no. 6:354–365.

Obermeyer, Carla M. 2000. Pluralism and Pragmatism: Knowledge and Practice of Birth in Morocco. *Medical Anthropology Quarterly* 14, no. 2:180–201.

Onder, Sylvia W. 2007. *We Have No Microbes Here: Healing Practices in a Turkish Black Sea Village.* Durham, NC: Carolina Academic Press.

Ortner, Sherry. 2005. Subjectivity and Cultural Critique. *Anthropological Theory* 5, no. 1:31–52.

Park, Thomas K. 1996. *Historical Dictionary of Morocco, New Edition.* Lanham, MD: The Scarecrow Press.

Parsons, Talcott. 1951. *The Social System.* Glencoe, IL: Free Press.

Population Council. 1994. Morocco 1992: Results from the Demographic and Health Survey. *Studies in Family Planning* 25, no. 1:59–63.

Rabinow, Paul. 1977. *Reflections on Fieldwork in Morocco.* Berkeley, CA: University of California Press.

Ribera, Joan M., and Susanna Haussman-Muela. 2011. The Straw that Breaks the Camel's Back: Redirecting Health-Seeking Behavior Studies on Malaria and Vulnerability. *Medical Anthropology Quarterly* 25, no. 1:103–121.

Scarry, Elaine. 1985. *The Body in Pain: The Making and Unmaking of the World.* New York: Oxford University Press.

Schumann, Debra, and W. H. Mosley. 1994. The Household Production of Health: Introduction. *Social Science and Medicine* 38, no. 4:201–204.

Schutz, Alfred. 1970. *On Phenomenology and Social Relations: Selected Writings.* Edited by Helmut R. Wagner. Chicago: University of Chicago Press.

Seligman, Rebecca. 2010. The Unmaking and Making of the Self: Embodied Suffering and Mind-Body Healing in Brazilian Candomble. *Ethos* 38, no. 3:297–320.

Simon, Gregory M. 2009. The Soul Freed of Cares? Islamic Prayer, Subjectivity, and the Contradictions of Moral Selfhood in Minangkabau, Indonesia. *American Ethnologist* 36, no. 2:258–275.

Starrett, Gregory. 1995. The Hexis of Interpretation: Islam and the Body in the Egyptian Popular School. *American Ethnologist* 22, no. 4:953–969.

Stokols, Daniel. 1992. Establishing and Maintaining Healthy Environments: Toward a Social Ecology of Health Promotion. *American Psychologist* 47, no. 1:6–22.

Stoller, Paul. 1989. *The Taste of Ethnographic Things: The Senses in Anthropology.* Philadelphia, PA: University of Pennsylvania Press.

Swartz, David. 1997. *Culture and Power: The Sociology of Pierre Bourdieu.* Chicago, IL: University of Chicago Press.

Throop, C. J., and Keith M. Murphy. 2002. Bourdieu and Phenomenology: A Critical Assessment. *Anthropological Theory* 2, no. 2:185–207.

United Nations Population Fund. Skilled Attendance at Birth. 2008 [2011]. Available from www.unfpa.org/public/mothers/pid/4383.

Weber, Max. 1958. *The Protestant Work Ethic and the Spirit of Capitalism.* New York: Scribners.

Wehr, Hans. 1980. *A Dictionary of Modern Written Arabic.* Edited by J. Milton Cowan. Third Reprinting ed. London: MacDonald and Evans, LTD.

Westermarck, Edward. 1968 [1926]. *Ritual and Belief in Morocco.* London: MacMillan.

Wikan, Unni. 1996. *Tomorrow, God Willing: Self-Made Destinies in Cairo.* Chicago, IL: University of Chicago Press.

World Health Organization, Department of Reproductive Health and Research. 2004. *Making Pregnancy Safer: The Critical Role of the Skilled Attendant.* Geneva: World Health Organization.

Yoder, P. S. 1997. Negotiating Relevance: Belief. Knowledge, and Practice in International Health Projects. *Medical Anthropology Quarterly* 11, no. 2:131–146.

Index

vulnerability, *continued*
  dialectical structures of security
    and, 95–96
    defilement and purification,
      103–4
    imbalance and equilibrium,
      101–2
    isolation and unity, 99–101
    openness and enclosure,
      96–99
  as disruption, 162–63
  elements of, 157–61
  embodied knowledge and, 167
  of ethnographer, 21
  future research on, 177–79
  intersubjectivity of, 85–86
  as mediator of objective health
    knowledge, 19, 168
  medical anthropological view of,
    173–74

  realist view of, 83, 173–75
  Saharan constructions of, 80–81,
    82–83
  Saharan feelings of, 84–85,
    158–59, 164–65, 167, 169
  security continuum and, 177
  states of being contributing to,
    81–82
  subjective sense of, 93, 176
  theories on, 85–86, 93, 162,
    173–74, 176–77
  transitional status and, 81,
    86–87, 98

weddings
  aesthetics of, 96–104
  Berber customs of, 86–93
  Saharan practices of protection
    at, 89–90, 92–93, 98